WE
FLEW
OVER
THE
BRIDGE

Children's Books
by Faith Ringgold

Tar Beach

*Aunt Harriet's
Underground Railway in the Sky*

Dinner at Aunt Connie's House

Bonjour Lonnie

My Dream of Martin Luther King

*Talking to Faith Ringgold
(with Linda Freeman and Nancy Roucher)*

Invisible Princess

Counting to Tar Beach

Cassie's Colorful Day

Cassie's Word Quilt

*If a Bus Could Talk:
The Story of Rosa Parks*

Oh Holy Night

WE
FLEW
OVER
THE
BRIDGE

The Memoirs of
Faith Ringgold

Duke University Press   Durham & London   2005

Printed in the United States of America on acid-free paper ∞
Originally published in 1995 by Bulfinch Press.

*Duke University Press gratefully acknowledges
the support of the Mary Duke Biddle Foundation,
which provided funds toward the production of this book.*

Library of Congress Cataloging-in-Publication Data

Ringgold, Faith
We flew over the bridge : the memoirs of Faith Ringgold /
Faith Ringgold. — Pbk. ed.
p. cm.
Includes bibliographical references and index.
ISBN 0-8223-3564-6 (pbk. : alk. paper)
1. Ringgold, Faith. 2. African American women
artists—Biography. I. Title.
N6537.R55A2 2005
709'. 2—dc22   2004028226

Faith Ringgold is Professor Emerita of Visual Arts
at the University of California, San Diego.
She is the author of several children's books,
including *Tar Beach*, *Aunt Harriet's Underground
Railroad in the Sky*, *Dinner at Aunt Connie's House*,
and *My Dream of Martin Luther King*.

*This book is dedicated to my father, Andrew Louis
Jones Sr., who bought me my first easel and has always
made me feel special. If he could see me now…*

CONTENTS

PREFACE

I have always wanted to tell my story, or, more to the point, my side of the story. As the youngest of three children, I grew up in a family of wonderful storytellers. My older brother Andrew, my sister Barbara, my father, my mother, aunts and uncles, as well as cousins and family friends, had endless tales to tell based on their own experience. Being "the baby" in my family, my experiences were not much to tell—thank God—so I kept quiet and listened.

My life as an artist began as a child during the many hours I spent bedridden with asthma, picturing my small world and the people in it. By the time I became a teenager I started using my art to tell my story. When images alone were not enough, I added words to my pictures and later quilted them. *We Flew over the Bridge* was my first attempt (in 1980) to write a book, and it took all of fifteen years to get it published in 1995.

My first version of *We Flew over the Bridge*, then titled *Being My Own Woman*, was begun in the late seventies when I returned from a trip to West Africa. I completed it in 1980 and submitted it to an agent, who rejected it. It was then that I hit upon the strategy of self-publication through masked performance pieces and readings of my story quilts at college lecture dates and exhibitions. I created the story quilt, *Tar Beach*, in 1988. Andrea Cascardi, a children's book editor at Random House, suggested that *Tar Beach* would make a good children's book, and since then I have written and illustrated a total of eleven children's books. During slavery, it was said that some slaves were able to fly to freedom. *Tar Beach* is about a little girl named Cassie, and writing and illustrating the story constituted my own metaphorical flight to freedom, although at the time I wrote it, I hardly knew I was writing a children's story, much less flying to freedom. Writing and illustrating children's books kind of sneaked up on me in a delightful way. What a joy not to struggle against interminable odds, to have the freedom to write and illustrate eleven books for children, all with the greatest of ease. My stories and illustrations are a tribute to the endless beauty and creativity of children.

I am so grateful to all the wonderful editors and art directors I have worked with since 1991, for the greatest experience of my life after a veritable lifetime invested in the struggle to become an artist. Children are the greatest, most consistently innovative artists of all. Their parents and teachers, together with the added joy of having completed the building of my beautiful home and studio in New Jersey, have made my happiness as an artist complete.

ACKNOWLEDGMENTS

First, I'd like to thank my mother, Willi Posey, who was our family photographer and historian-storyteller. She left me a million stories and almost as many photographs documenting the details of my life. And second, I want to thank Hilary Breed for suggesting that Marie Brown, my literary agent, send Brian Hotchkiss, a senior editor at Bulfinch Press, the 1980 manuscript titled "Being My Own Woman." After four years at Bulfinch Press, Brian moved on to other things, and Karen Dane, my present editor at Bulfinch Press, and I are doing just fine, though I certainly miss Brian. And many thanks to my good friend Moira Roth, who did the laborious and brilliant editing job of helping me transform "Being My Own Woman" to "We Flew over the Bridge." Although we live on separate coasts, we began work in Paris in person in January of 1994, then had extensive contact during the year on the various drafts — phone conversations, Federal Express packages — and finished a year later faxing back and forth between Berkeley, California, and Englewood, New Jersey. Whew! And we're still friends. Moira and I both want to thank her assistants, Kristine Kim and Anne Fischer; and we especially want to acknowledge Janet Everett's invaluable and extensive help. And a very special thanks to Annika Marie, who meticulously entered the final edits to the manuscript. And to my assistant, Vanessa P. Williams, who labored endlessly over the photograph selections to get them just right. And to my husband, Burdette Ringgold, who put up with massive disorder in our house and my twenty-four-hour work schedule. What I really want to say is thank God it's over.

INTRODUCTION

Tangiers and Paris, Englewood, New Jersey, and Harlem, New York, San Francisco and La Jolla, California, have been sites for my many meetings with Faith Ringgold over the last fifteen years. We met first as artist and critic. Since then we have become close friends, staying frequently in each other's houses; eating and traveling together; confiding and sharing personal stories; discussing our mothers and the process of aging. From our different perspectives — that of a black American-born artist and a white European-born art historian/critic — we have planned actions and compared notes, analyzed and argued over the history of art and politics in this country.

During the time I have known Ringgold I have watched dramatic changes and shifts in her art, life, and status in the art world. The first time I saw a sizable body of her work was in 1983, when we spent several days viewing it together in her rented storage bins on 132nd Street and Broadway. There for the first time I saw her now-legendary powerful 1967 paintings, *The Flag is Bleeding* and *U.S. Postage Stamp Commemorating the Advent of Black Power,* and what she described as her "art trunks," in which her soft paintings and sculptures were neatly rolled up — waiting to be taken on the road, so to speak. In 1983 she was a nationally known artist who, shrewdly and ingeniously but somewhat precariously, supported herself through exhibitions, performances, and lectures around the country on college campuses. She had not exhibited in New York City for many years and it was only a year later, in 1984, when, in the context of her first major retrospective in New York, she boldly showed *Who's Afraid of Aunt Jemima?* — the first of the story quilts for which she is now internationally known. This event was followed by more mainstream success. Her work, especially the story quilts, has been purchased by many major museums and collections, and is exhibited all over the world, in Japan and Egypt as well as in Europe. In contemporary American art generally, as well as in African-American and feminist circles, Ringgold is now a major figure recognized and sought out by critics, historians, and audiences alike.

A few years ago, I wrote an article entitled "A Trojan Horse" in which I praised Ringgold as a "terrific and successful troublemaker during the 1960s," contrasting this time to her later, more covert actions as a troublemaker. Ringgold has always taken great delight in this description of her smuggling subversive material into the citadel of the art world in seemingly benign forms. But, whether one thinks of Ringgold as the young firebrand of the 1960s or the distinguished world-famous older artist of the 1990s, there are constants — her boldness and originality as an artist and human being; her fiery independence, remarkable pragmatic savvy, and strategizing abilities; and her steadfast passionate political and feminist goals. She is also inveterately inventive — in her subjects, approaches, and materials. And increasingly, she has turned to writing: first the texts of her story quilts, then children's books, and now this autobiography.

In assuming the roles of writer and editor, Ringgold and I added another layer to our relationship. The last year has been an intense year of exchanges while she wrote and I edited *We Flew over the Bridge.* In February 1994, we spent a heady week in a small hotel on the Place du Panthéon in Paris while we participated in a conference at the Palais du Luxembourg ("A Visual Arts Encounter: African Americans in Europe") and worked late each night on drafts of the first two chapters of the book. More important, we spent time exploring the dynamics and parameters of the editing process. After that, we communicated between East and West Coast by mail, fax, and telephone. Drafts went back and forth: sometimes sporadically, almost languidly, over weeks; at other times frantically over the space of a few hours. Pages covered with handwritten notes and questions, explanations and arguments, poured in on our respective fax machines. We invented "East Command" and "West Command" headquarters and sent imperious orders back and forth in high-spirited faxed notes. In July 1994, Ringgold and her husband, Burdette, went to dinner at the White House, and I waited with impatience for her report on this event. One lovely morning, a drawing of me flying to the post office appeared. Occasionally, we disagreed over ideas and attitudes in terse exchanges and abrupt faxed memos. There were long early-morning telephone conversations, and even longer late-night talks in which we discussed content, style, pacing, and the emotional and political implications of the text — as we moved through her life and art.

This experience with Ringgold has been extraordinary for me. On one level, I found it endlessly demanding, fascinating, and full of surprises; and on another level, intensely difficult, sometimes deeply troubling. It seems to me that at the heart of successful editing is trust and respect on both sides. But there is also an element of risk — one has to take risks in editing and that is unnerving. Frequently I would ask myself, particularly late at night, was I too intrusive, too demanding or editing from an ignorant vantage point? Was I displaying a Eurocentric attitude in my suggestions? Was I insensitive to the issues of motherhood as I have no children of my own? (In retrospect, one of the funniest editing moments came when I squeamishly and absentmindedly edited out much of the description of pain in a childbirth scene, only to realize what I had done, and shamefacedly restore it.) Sometimes, too, I became enthralled with Ringgold's thoughts and memories and blithely and eagerly read page after page, forgetting that I was supposed to be reading slowly with a diligent critical eye.

I would like to thank Faith Ringgold deeply for inviting me to be the book's editor. It has made me think anew about the nature and importance of autobiographical narratives and of their history, particularly in this country, and of Ringgold's contribution to all this. The experience of reading and editing *We Flew over the Bridge* has moved and inspired me. Clearly, I am only one of the first among thousands of readers whose lives will be positively imprinted by this book, and who will respond strongly — emotionally, intellectually, politically, and psychologically — to the brilliant, tough, and insightful voice of Faith Ringgold, a voice that speaks with equal eloquence on the printed page and on the painted canvas.

Moira Roth
Trefethen Professor of Art History, Mills College
February 5, 1995, Berkeley, California

PART I
HARLEM BORN AND BRED

Chapter 1: From the Cradle to the Classroom in the 1930s

Barbara, Andrew, and me, 1931

I was born on October 8, 1930, in New York City's Harlem Hospital. My mother, Willie Edell Jones, told me that no sooner had she arrived at the hospital than she was rushed to the delivery room. The nurse, a stern black woman, tried to tie Mother's hands with a cord. Mother protested, saying she would rather die than be shackled, and promised to be good. But the new life inside her was compelling her to push forward before the doctor was ready. So, despite her promise, Mother pushed even harder. The doctor was still scrubbing up when the hair on my head began to show. The nurse became furious and nervously slapped Mother's face, and crossed Mother's legs together. "Hold back!" she yelled. "The doctor's not ready yet." Once he was, Mother gave one grunt and the doctor's huge hands guided me effortlessly into the world. I came out screaming.

At the time of my birth, Mother was still mourning the death of Ralph, her sixteen-month-old baby, who had died of pneumonia. She was already three months pregnant with me at the time of Ralph's death. Was I to be a replacement for him? Had Mother prayed for a boy instead of me? When I asked her, Mother assured me that she had always expected a girl because her children had been born that way: first a boy, then a girl, then a boy, and now, a girl — me. I accepted that.

Before leaving the delivery room I had to be named, because some babies had gotten mixed up in the hospital. Mother didn't have a name for me, and it was not like her to be caught so unprepared. The nurse must have sensed that her indecision was the result of more than the normal trauma of giving birth. She suggested, "Name her Faith," almost as if she knew faith was what my mother really needed now. Mother agreed.

There were five of us in our family. My father's name was Andrew Louis Jones Sr. My mother called him "Big Andrew," and she called my brother "Little Andrew." Andrew was six years old when I was born, and my sister Barbara was three. Barbara shared my mother's middle name (Edell) and I got Mother's first name (Willie) — but I never knew this until I was twenty and getting married. Then I saw it on my birth certificate: "Faith Willie Jones." All through school I had been known as Faith Elizabeth Jones. (Mother had intended to change my middle name from Willie to Elizabeth but she never did so officially.)

Our family was usually extended to include more than just the five of us; there was always an aunt, cousin, or close friend living in our four-room apartment on West 146th Street. They might have just come up from Jacksonville, Florida, my mother's home-

Barbara, Mother, Ralph, and Andrew, circa 1929

town, and needed a temporary place to stay while looking for a job and a home of their own. Or, they might have hit a stretch of bad luck in New York. Twice Daddy's nephews came to New York from Tampa, Florida, but only for a short visit. However, Baby Doll Hurd, Daddy's mother, stayed with us. Grandma Baby Doll woke us up each morning at the crack of dawn to go to the store for fresh milk, butter, and eggs. She then made a huge down-home breakfast that was delicious. I was surprised to learn she was divorced and remarried to a man who owned a plantation. Daddy's father had been a minister and, as far as I know, he never came North. It was a fine experience growing up in an extended family. When mother was tired, or didn't want us to go somewhere or do something, there was always another adult to help her.

My father spent very little time at home. I saw him in the morning having breakfast before going off to work; it was still dark when he left home. He came home in the evening just in time for dinner, frequently with a friend. Most nights, soon after he arrived, the downstairs bell would ring. "Is Andrew home?" a voice would yell up the stairs. "Dad-blab-bitt, you son of a gun," my father would invariably respond, and then he would call out to Mother, "Look who's here, Bill?" (Daddy called Mother "Bill" — short for Willie.) Mother, drying her hands on a starched and ruffled apron, would then come out of the kitchen to greet Daddy's friend. Mother was very good looking, so the visitor usually gushed,

My parents, Willie and Andrew, circa 1920

grinned, and stammered, "Pleased to meet you, ma'am." If he was Mother's friend too, he would hug her and tell her she was "a sight for sore eyes," and warn Daddy that he was "gonna steal" her. Then he'd inevitably ask Mother, "How's this boy treating you?" and Mother, smiling, would say something that wasn't meant for a child's ears.

By this time Andrew, Barbara, and I were lined up to meet the guest. Even if we knew the person, we still had to pay our respects and hear that we were "growing like weeds," and that the last time we'd been only "knee high to a tadpole." Andrew, as the oldest and the only boy, got to shake hands with our guest. My parents would tell him to "stand up there, boy," and Andrew would stand tall like a little man. Daddy would beam with pride. The guest would remark that Andrew was the "spitting image" of Daddy, and Barbara would be told that she had become "quite a young lady." At this point Daddy would remind everyone that Barbara was "The Princess," a name my uncle Cardoza gave her in response to my sister's rather superior image of herself. Then they would turn their attention to me, "The Baby." (My father never called me anything else, even after I had obviously outgrown the title.) He would pick me up and tell people that I was "one of a kind." "Yeah, we tore up the pattern after that one." Everybody would laugh.

During these introductions, Mother stood guard over us to make sure that we were well behaved, and, terrified of tuberculosis, she watched to see that we didn't get "kissed-in-the-mouth." Tuberculosis, the scourge of the 1930s, was a disease of epidemic proportions for which there was no known cure. Anyone who got TB was banished to Welfare Island, a place people only whispered about.

During the week our meals were simple, consisting of a boiled vegetable with meat and either rice, potato and cornbread, or hot biscuits. In summer, we drank lemonade or Kool-Aid, and in winter there was Ovaltine for the kids, and coffee or tea for the adults. If we were out of tea bags, we'd all have "Cambridge Tea," which was a cup of hot water, evaporated milk (which you could buy for three cents a can), and sugar. One more person for dinner was never a problem, especially since Mother was in the habit of cooking a big pot of food. When we had someone else living with us, this made almost every night seem like a party, with all the adults talking and several pots of food on the stove.

The unexpected guest was always welcomed to dinner. We children had usually eaten, so Mother just had to set out an extra plate. My father, a big talker, would ramble on and on. At some point he'd say, "For crying out loud, how the heck did you find me?" Then the friend would relay a detailed account involving many people they both knew. I was fascinated by these stories.

Conversation was the high point of every meal in our house. Daddy's voice could always be heard above all the others. "I'll bet you a fat man" was a favorite expression of his — then he'd stand up, dig deep in his pockets for money while the guest begged off. I could never figure out what they were betting about — perhaps on Joe Louis; or Daddy's favorite baseball team, the Giants; or one of Daddy's beloved trivia questions (Is a tomato a vegetable or a fruit, and why?). Talking, teasing, and testing were real passions for him, along with drinking and playing cards. Shortly after dinner, Daddy and his friend would go out and Mother would settle down for a quiet evening at home. There were nights when she went out, too, and we had a baby-sitter, but that was rare. By the time Daddy got home, we would all be asleep.

Every night at seven o'clock we were put to bed, no matter if other kids were just going out to play. We had been to school and the park, our homework had been checked, and we'd had dinner and our bath. Once we were settled in our beds, Mother was often visited by friends who knew that she was now free to talk over coffee and cornbread. We would lie awake listening to the adults as they spoke of family gossip, dreams, daily news, reminisced, and speculated about the future. I was always amazed that adults knew about so many people, places, and things.

Sometimes the three of us kids would have our own nighttime conversations. Barbara and I would curl up at the foot of our beds and listen to Andrew, who would lie in the doorway of his room. He told outlandish stories in whispers so that Mother could not hear us. We could always tell when she did because we saw her approaching through the lace curtains on the French doors that separated our bedrooms from the living room. Andrew would scare us with tales of the boogeyman who was surely going to get us. We didn't have television to entertain us; instead, it was books, movies, radio, people, and everyday experiences that sharpened our imaginations. Andrew was an expert storyteller. We would laugh till we cried or shuddered with fear, our heads buried in our pillows, and our hands covering our mouths.

Mother was strict with us. If we misbehaved we were sent to bed early, sometimes without dinner. A bath always followed a spanking. I rarely got one of those, but Andrew and Barbara got their full share. Indeed, Barbara might get two spankings in one day. When I was growing up, I never heard anyone mention giving children love. We got attention, care, a comfortable and good home, clothes and food, and all of Mother's time and energy. What more could "love" bring? My mother gave us the kind of love that was lived, rather than verbalized. She never actually said the words "I love you," but we all knew she did.

I don't remember when Mother and Daddy actually officially separated (perhaps when I was two or three), since Daddy was apt to be at our house at any time after the separation. Mother would send a message for him to come by when she needed money or something was wrong. Daddy would show up after work, just as he had when he'd been living at home. If Andrew had misbehaved, Daddy would take him to his room and they would talk. Afterward they would put on the boxing gloves that Daddy had bought for Andrew and they would go a few rounds. Although Daddy was a gentle man, he was committed to giving Andrew "boxing lessons," which were a kind of beating. Daddy would have been hurt, however, if someone had suggested he was beating the hell out of his son. He would have said, "I don't believe in beating children. Andrew and I are just boxing. He's a man; he can take it." And Andrew did.

My father looked rather like Joe Louis. He was a big handsome man with powerful arm muscles. Barbara and I used to swing on his arms, and he'd hold us up with our feet off the ground to show us how strong he was. I used to think my father could beat Joe Louis, but then I found out there were a lot of kids who also thought that about their fathers. Little Andrew, on the other hand, was a skinny boy. When Daddy roughed him up he would laugh good-naturedly. Even though those punches Daddy gave him had to hurt, Andrew had been taught that a man doesn't run from a fight: Daddy was clear about that.

Any hint that one of us had told a lie was enough to cause my father a lot of grief. He never spanked us, but instead chastised us. We were used to getting long talks about honesty, another thing he was dead serious about. Lying and stealing were wrong. Daddy's father, Grandpa Jones, was a preacher who lived in Tampa, Florida. We never saw him, but he must have been good in the pulpit because Daddy himself was such an effective speaker and actor. When he chastised us, he would sit and pause, lean over and place his elbows on his knees, with his head in his hands. Sometimes we had done nothing, but more often it was that Andrew had failed to do his homework, or that Barbara had refused to eat her dinner or had thrown her milk down the drain. The way Daddy delivered his message was very effective, and I'll never forget it.

Around the age of two, I had my first asthmatic attack while Mother was in Atlantic City for the weekend. She had left us with Mrs. Brown, a close family friend and neighbor. Having asthma was a frightening experience — gasping for breath for hours, and my chest feeling like a house was on top of it. I remember often feeling so sick that I wanted to die. Now I know that indeed I must have been near death on more than one occasion. Yet I remember Mother telling me that no one had ever died from asthma, and, since the doctor never said anything different, I believed her. How much that lie affected my survival I will never know, but I am sure it did no harm.

After my first asthma attack, Mother was very careful with me. I had to eat a special diet, which meant no fried food or pork, no whole milk or store-bought ice cream, no white bread, cake, potato chips, or anything that today we would call junk food. My vegetables had to be steamed and I could eat meat only if it was baked, boiled, or broiled. What's more, the whole family had to eat according to my diet as it would have been too expensive to cook two pots of food. Thus we grew up eating rather little soul food. Except for fish every Saturday, Mother never fried anything. Nobody else we knew then had ever heard of broiled porgies.

On the days when I was recuperating from an asthma attack, Mother would prop me up on pillows in my bed. She would do her housework, cook and clean, wash and iron while I would read, write, and draw and color in my books. I can't remember a time when I was not doing some form of art. Having asthma was perfect for making art. I could sit in my room without exerting myself and draw and make things with bits of cloth my mother would give me. I got a chance to do all the things I really liked to do and I can't recall a time I missed anything of consequence, including important exams at school. Like magic, I was always well enough just in time.

I never did go to kindergarten and I hardly remember the first grade. The doctor felt that going to school might expose me to possible infections from the other children, which might only complicate my already delicate asthmatic condition. So, for me, school really started in the second grade.

Despite the asthma, I had a happy childhood. Going to the hospital for my frequent stays of five days or so was fun. The nurses and doctors at the Presbyterian Medical Center always made a big fuss over me. They would take me on tours of the hospital to look at the operating rooms and I remember being the subject of lectures held in spacious rooms for groups of doctors. Of course, I never understood a word that was said, but it was all about me.

Mother was an energetic person, so if I was well, we often went out. While Andrew and Barbara were in school, Mother and I went to museums and the park, or shopped at Bloomingdale's and Klein's on 14th Street. (Klein's is now out of business and Bloomingdale's is a trendy remake of its former self.) Every so often we went downtown to the Paramount Theater and the Roxy Theater on Broadway, or to the Apollo Theater on 125th Street in Harlem, to see a stage show.

I saw all of the stars. Mother paid fifty cents for her admission, but I got in free. Each time we got a packed show with several big-name stars, two bands, a comic, a dance act and one or more singers, a feature movie, and a newsreel. We had to meet Barbara and Andrew after school, so we couldn't ever stay for the movie, but I will never forget the stage shows. I saw Jimmy Rushing, Cab Calloway, Chick Webb, Count Basie, Louis Armstrong, Duke Ellington, Benny Goodman, Gene Krupa, Glenn Miller, and Lionel Hampton. Singers with the bands included Frank Sinatra, Billy Eckstein, Billie Holiday, Ethel Waters, Ella Fitzgerald, Lena Horne, and Fats Waller. Bill Robinson and Peg Leg Bates and the Ink Spots were also favorites.

I always had a story to tell Andrew and Barbara about the show I had just seen. I would also bring them candy from Woolworth's, which Mother had grudgingly let me buy, although I was not allowed to eat it. The candy was a peace offering to them, so they wouldn't be angry with me for having so much fun while they were in school.

Daddy took me out, too. By order of the family court, he could spend time with us on his day off, weekends, and holidays, as long as it did not interfere with our daily schedule or school. Since I wasn't in school, I got a chance to go out with him more often than Andrew or Barbara. Mother objected to the places we used to go, but there was nothing she could do. The court was on Daddy's side about this. We went to see his lady friends and then we would stop off at the bar on Seventh Avenue around the corner from our house.

Reading the signs in the bar was my earliest reading lesson. Daddy would sit me up

Mother and me, circa 1933

on the bar, and have me entertain his drinking buddies by reading all the signs and the labels on the bottles. I mistook "Bar and Grill" for "Bar and Girl." Daddy loved things like that. He would pick me up and laugh and laugh, and repeat what I said to anyone who came into the bar. And then he would explain to me with great care that a bar had to have food in it by law, that a grill was a stove, thus "Bar and Grill." Many bars didn't allow women, and those that did often had a sign in the window saying "Ladies Invited." I always thought that meant it was all right for me to be there. When I told my father this, he roared with laughter. "No, baby," he said, "that sign is for ladies to come in and sit at the tables. You're with your daddy."

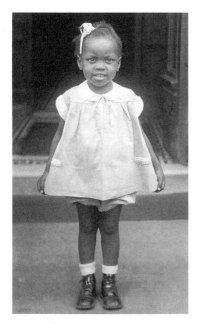

Barbara, circa 1928 (far left); Andrew, circa 1928 (near left)

He always gave me pennies (as many as I could hold) to buy penny candy at the candy store up the street before bringing me home from our trip to the bar. I bought all our favorites — gumdrops (you got five big pieces for one cent); Mary Jane's, a peanut-filled taffy; Torpedoes, a chewy bar-shaped lollipop; and, our absolute favorite, Hooten, a dark chocolate square that could be purchased with or without peanuts. I hid these candies in the dresser drawer by my bed for Andrew and Barbara to eat after dinner. They always diverted my attention and later I would find they had eaten their candy long before dinner. Andrew ate his in a few mouthfuls, with bulging cheeks and his hand conspicuously placed over his mouth, laughing and teasing all the time. Andrew was my idol. Whatever he did may not have been right, but it could never be wrong.

I idolized Barbara, too; after all, she was my big sister and I wanted to be like her. She was cute, dainty, smart, and always the class president and teacher's pet; and she had a book bag full of school books and a lot of studying to do. All of these she handled like "The Princess" that she was. Barbara had many friends, but they were too big for me to play with. Mother made Andrew and Barbara stay with me despite our age differences. She knew we would protect each other, so, for as long as she could, she insisted that we play and stay together. When we were kids Barbara would constantly remind me that she was a princess and that I was her lowest slave. When we became adults she would call me up and order her dinner to be delivered and I'd send it to her by Michele and Barbara just as she commanded. It never felt demeaning; rather, it was a duty. Barbara had us all trained that way.

Every summer, as soon as school closed, we all went off to Atlantic City on the Greyhound bus. Mrs. Brown and her two daughters, Catherine and Bernice, went along too. Catherine was close to my age, and Bernice was close to Barbara's. Mother's friend, Florence Patterson, and her son, Junior, lived in Atlantic City. Junior was Andrew's age and Mother, Mrs. Brown, and Florence were all the best of friends. We were perfectly suited: we had our friends and Mother had hers. From time to time during the summer, Lottie Belle and Agnes and other friends of Mother's and Mrs. Brown's would come and stay for a day or two. All these women had husbands or boyfriends

Mother in Atlantic City, late 1930s

who would come along. The men were always lots of fun and as talkative and entertaining as the women; and they gave us spending money, too. Mother was a different person in the summertime. She got a chance to enjoy herself and relax — something she couldn't or wouldn't do during the rest of the year.

The high point of the summer was our trip to the Steel Pier, a huge amusement center that extended out a mile or more into the ocean on the boardwalk in Atlantic City. The Steel Pier had everything: joy rides, movies, 3-D movies, water shows, ice skating, stage shows, a circus, and side shows.

The culminating event of the summer was the Miss America Day Parade on the boardwalk. Mother was the family photographer, so she took pictures of all the beauties on the floats. We all tried to be enthusiastic about Miss New York, but what really spoke to us was that none of the participants was black. Most people accepted this, but not my mother and her friends. They knew that the Miss America Pageant would not be truly representative until they put a "little black gal" up there on one of those floats. But I never saw a black woman on one of those floats in all the summers we spent in Atlantic City. (In 1983 Vanessa Williams became our first black Miss America.) The next day after the parade, we returned home to Harlem to see the kids on the block and go back to school.

Andrew and me on the boardwalk in Atlantic City, circa 1935

No matter whatever else I have become over the years, I am Harlem born and bred and proud of it. Harlem of today is very different from the way it was in the 1930s. So, if you didn't know that Harlem, don't try to imagine what life was like for us. Let me tell you.

We lived at 222 West 146th Street between Seventh and Eighth Avenues (the streets have since been renamed Adam Clayton Powell Drive and Frederick Douglass Boulevard, respectively). We had a comfortable four-room apartment, facing the street, on the fourth floor of a walk-up. My mother was a housewife and kept us and our home as clean as a pin. My father was a truck driver for the Sanitation Department, and his pay of $36.20 per week was a good wage in those days. Most people made only half as much, and many had no jobs at all.

The stock market crash of 1929, which devastated the rich and sent them flying off their roofs, had just the opposite effect on poor black people. It drew us closer together, and most people were very serious about their jobs. There was no public money to be tapped, no grants or stipends. It was not until the late thirties that the New Deal made welfare and unemployment insurance available to those who qualified. Many poor families were too proud to apply for it, fearing the stigma attached to asking for a handout. This was just a bad period and everyone said that things would be better soon when they "hit that number" or their "ship came in." The future was viewed as something to look forward to with hope. Besides, the regular tasks of each day kept us busy. Our clothes had to be washed by hand, scrubbed on a washboard, and white things boiled on the stove, and then starched and ironed. There was no time to reflect on the quality of life, nor was there an Oprah Winfrey show to make us aware that we should.

Being poor was acceptable. Everybody was poor except rich white people, and we never saw any of them except in the movies. There was no television to flaunt before our eyes the good life of the "Joneses" next door. Our teachers were mostly Irish Catholic, and many of our classmates were Jewish refugees who had recently come to America to escape Hitler. Their parents worked with our parents, so we knew firsthand that white people could be poor.

In our household Mother managed the money. There was never any waste and she always managed to make ends meet. She rarely gave us money just to spend. Movie money for Saturday morning came from Daddy or from Aunt Bessie, Uncle Hilliard, or a family friend. Mother kept quiet about the details of our family budget. I used to hear her in the morning before we were out of bed, scrubbing her clothes on the washboard, and saying, "If God spares me, I'll take Faith to the Medical Center to get her allergy shot; then we'll go down and pick up Big Andrew's check from the family court; stop by Klein's and catch that sale on boys' coats; pick out one for Little Andrew; and see if I can find a nice dress for Barbara to wear when the teacher takes her class to see Shirley Temple next week."

Some of my best childhood memories were of mealtimes. I wasn't a fat child, but I never missed a chance to eat. Mother did not allow us to snack or eat out. We had three square meals a day, and after dinner the kitchen was closed for the night. (None of us kids dared to open the refrigerator without permission.) We had simple meals. On Sunday, when other people had fried chicken, we had leg of mutton or fricassee chicken. In the morning they ate Wheaties, "the breakfast of champions," and we had oatmeal. Like other families, we, too, ate pancakes; especially on Sunday morning, although we never had bacon and sausage to go with them. I couldn't eat pork, and anyway Mother considered bacon and sausage something we could do without. Instead she would buy a calli ham (the least expensive cut) and boil it — I could have that. Or, for breakfast she would get the butcher to slice the calli ham into thin steaks and we'd have them with hominy grits or Cream of Farina and butter.

Although I missed having the food and things other people had, there was no pressure to conform as there is today. Others might eat bacon and fried chicken, but we had trips to Atlantic City. People were doing the best they could with what they had, and in my day kids had to accept their parents' decisions in such matters.

Sunday nights drew the family together around the big radio with its built-in, cloth-covered speakers. I always thought that the stars of our favorite radio programs — The Shadow, Amos and Andy, Jack Benny and Rochester — were inside the radio. We would sit with our ears pressed to the speaker and our imaginations running wild. Mother saved dessert on Sunday evenings so that we could eat it while listening to *The Shadow* or some of the other Sunday radio serials. I remember wonderful smells coming from the kitchen and the sound of dishes being taken out of the cabinet. Soon Mother would call us and we would see our ice-cream glasses piled high with tapioca, or Jell-O topped with whipped evaporated milk, or her special lemon ice-cream recipe. With it we would have Mother's homemade pound cake, sweet potato pie, or her delicious, crisp, deep-dish apple pie, piping hot from the oven.

In my experience, being poor had nothing to do with the way people looked. To look poor was an indication of a lack of pride and upbringing, not of money. Most women could sew and kept their families well dressed on small incomes. Boys could get by with one suit for church, a couple of pairs of pants and a white shirt and tie for school. School clothes were for school, not for play. We were all checked for cleanliness and neatness at school. If your nails and ears were unclean, that could be embarrassing. Our teachers frequently asked the class to recite the big slogan above the blackboard, "Cleanliness Is Next to Godliness." And, of course, we all knew who was and who was not clean.

On Sundays people dressed up, and almost everybody went to church; if they didn't, they stayed home until church was out. We had clothes that were worn only on Sundays, special occasions, or holidays. On Easter Sunday we were completely outfitted in new clothes that Mother had sewn for Barbara and me. She rarely got anything new for herself, but she was a wiz at alterations. A new collar, belt, ruffle, or buttons, or a colorful flower or bow here and there, and you would have never guessed that she was still wearing the same outfit she had worn for years.

There was simply no need to spend money as we do today. Transportation didn't cost much and we walked almost everywhere since the bus and subway systems weren't as extensive as they are today. Hardly anyone had elevators or any need for them since our buildings were no more than four stories high.

Since nobody had a telephone until the forties, we kids were often sent on errands to deliver messages to friends and relatives. It seems we were always on one errand or another — to the store to get a pound of sugar (which cost a nickel and was scooped loose from a huge burlap bag), or to Mrs. Brown's house to deliver a message or do her a favor. People had to stay in touch through personal communication on a daily basis. There were, of course, people who managed to keep to themselves, but they really had to work at it.

Once there was a fire in our apartment building and everybody had to evacuate immediately. To the surprise of the entire block, we discovered that a teenage boy had been living in our building, whom nobody had ever seen. His father brought him down in a wheelchair and, as I recall, the boy appeared to be deformed and made queer noises and peculiar faces. People whispered that he was sick in the head and that his parents had been hiding him for all these years. After the fire was extinguished we returned to our apartments. Although the fire broke the secret, nobody spoke about it openly. Later we used to hear those same queer noises coming from the "sick" boy's apartment. Finally, one day he started coming down to the street in his wheelchair to get some air and sun.

Me in my pram, circa 1931

Some people did talk to the boy, or tried to, but most people pretended not to see him. At that time there was a great stigma attached to having a relative who was mentally ill or retarded. Few people knew the difference, or were able to deal with such a seemingly irreversible situation.

In the twenties, families in Harlem could go out and not lock their doors. By today's standards Harlem in the thirties was still safe, although the depression created hard times. People who didn't have anything soon thought up ways to take things from others. Nevertheless, people looked out for each other during my childhood. If a stranger entered a block, his presence did not go unnoticed. He would be asked whom he came to see and then directed to the correct house and apartment number. If the person

16

wasn't at home, someone always knew where that person had gone and for how long. We called such people nosy, but they were the ones who kept the neighborhood watch. If something happened, you could be sure they saw it.

When I was a baby, Mother used to leave me in my buggy to get some sun while she ran upstairs to do something. I remember Miss Flossy talking to me. She was a colorful lady who came by our house at the same time each morning on her way to work. Mother told me that it was Miss Flossy who retrieved my bottle when I would hurl it out of my buggy. Miss Flossy never forgot our daily encounters, and the older I got, the more she remembered them. "Girl, you be laying up there in that buggy looking for me like you was expecting me to pass by. You sure had a lot of sense for a baby."

Mother in the 1930s

On hot summer evenings, we would go up to the tar-covered roof of the building, which was known as "Tar Beach." We would take blankets, a jug of lemonade, some sandwiches, and a watermelon. While the adults would play cards or talk, we kids got a chance to stay up late, snack, and look at the stars until we fell asleep. In the daytime it was cooler on the fire escapes, and we would pad them with blankets, and sip lemonade while we caught the sun. This was our "terrace." When we looked around, we saw the whole neighborhood perched on their fire escapes.

Raising children in the thirties was far simpler than it is today. Everybody agreed that parents were in charge of their own children and were accountable for their actions. As a result, being a child came with a certain security, but not too much freedom. It was understood that parents knew best. You didn't really have to listen to your peers, because it was your parents you were trying to please, not them. A perfect excuse for not doing something the other kids were doing was to announce that "My mother [father] doesn't allow me to do this." Nobody questioned parental authority — although some tried to get around it, because it is natural for children to test authority.

Although we were told to stay together whenever we went out to play, Andrew inevitably found a way to get away from Barbara and me in order to play with his friends. We were given strict orders by Andrew to find him when it was time to go home. Most of the time we played right in front of our house so Mother could keep an eye on us and call us in when it was time. The street was an ideal playground since there were few parked cars and very little traffic. The one or two parked cars provided us with "seats" in the form of the running boards. This was where we had our "girl talk." We played hopscotch and jump rope, both Double Dutch and Single File. Double Dutch was the best because each girl got a chance to jump as long as she could without entangling the rope around her feet (that was called "a miss"). A person who missed had to turn the rope for the others to jump. We sang when we jumped rope and Mother could hear us from the window as we chorused,

> 1 2 3 4 5 6 7 8
> Mother's in the kitchen
> Father's at the gate
> Better get in the house
> Or you'll be late. . . .

When we stopped jumping to rest on the running board of the parked car, Mother would invariably put her head out the window and yell, "Andrew, Barbara, and Faith, come upstairs." When we tried to act as if we didn't hear her, the whole block would echo, "Your mother's calling you."

Barbara and I played "house," cooked and served tea and cookies. (We were role-playing being mothers and wives.) Mother mixed the cookie batter to bake the cookies on our for-real electric stove and we would invite Andrew to have tea. He would eat up all the cookies and drink from the teapot instead of from the much tinier teacup we had poured for him. He, too, was role-playing, training to be a man, although not necessarily a husband or father. Still we were delighted to have him present despite his behavior. After all, he was a boy, and we knew even then that "boys will be boys will be men."

Andrew and I were both good skaters, and in the winter he would take me ice skating on a pond in Colonial Park. I pretended that I was Sonja Henie, the famous ice-skating movie star of the 1930s and 1940s, with Andrew as my handsome skating partner. Andrew liked to pretend to himself that he was a hockey player — since he almost always skated with a cut-off broomstick held across his chest. All the boys skated like that, even when roller skating. Can you imagine what people would think today if they saw a group of young boys skating down the street holding cut-off broomsticks across their chests?

Inspired by the movies, the boys on our block played noisy games of cops and robbers, and cowboys and Indians. Unlike the movies, the robbers and the Indians always won on our block. It was not uncommon to see a boy playing "robbers" or "Indians" alone. He would shoot himself, run over and catch the bullet in his chest, and keel over dead. The boys also played marbles and "loadies." Loadies were bottle caps that were "loaded" with orange skins or wax to make them slide when shot across the ground. These games were played by the boys in the gutter on their knees. Mother had forbidden Andrew to play in the gutter, and she always knew, just by looking at his dirty hands and knees, if he'd disobeyed her. It was popular, too, for boys to make their own skateboards and scooters, constructing them from nailing skates and pieces of wood together. Whole groups of boys would ride through our block on their scooters, which were all painted in the same color with their names printed on them. When they all got together to ride, everybody in the neighborhood could hear them.

In the summer Mother dressed Andrew in short pants and in knickers in the winter. Finally one year she reluctantly let him wear long pants. Mother didn't want him to look like those boys who wore zoot suits. At the time zoot suits were in fashion with their long jackets and wide-legged pants, pegged at the ankles; musicians wore them and so did boys who hung out on street corners. Every day Andrew sewed his pants with big stitches at the ankles to make them appear pegged, but before he came into the house, he'd take out the stitches.

In the 1930s gangs were beginning to make news in Harlem. Daddy was told that Andrew was a gang member, but that didn't worry him since he associated gangs with the harmless slapstick *Our Gang* movies of the 1920s. But Mother saw something coming that had no precedent in the past. She recognized that life as we knew it in Harlem was changing.

In my house and all other houses at the time, sex was a subject not to be discussed openly. On those nights when we listened to my mother exchanging tidbits of gossip with guests in our living room, any part that had to do with s-e-x was whispered. That was what attracted my attention to these conversations in the first place, because Mother otherwise spoke with a full voice. When she was telling a story about s-e-x, however, her voice would fade out and then come back with ". . . And, girl, ain't that something?"

Even the movies we saw revealed no more than my mother was willing to discuss. Stories of unrequited love were the only kind we saw, and the kind I secretly dreamed about. I dreamed that my husband would love me so much that he would not touch me. Maybe one night by accident he would forget his promise, and I remember thinking that I would forgive him because I would have been asleep at the time. We all wanted to be pure, and it was very clear from all that I had ever seen or heard that s-e-x was dirty, dirty, dirty. Even when we got married and had children it would be a sacrifice. We would never enjoy "it."

When I was about nine or ten I had a boyfriend whom I saw only when I was with my brother and sister. Lionel was the same age as I was and he had a large family of brothers. On Saturdays he and his brothers went to the movies with me, Barbara, and Andrew. It was understood that he and I would not be alone at any time, so there was no discussion about what we would do if we were. The first time we kissed was at a party. We were playing spin-the-bottle. All the kids were in a circle and the bottle I spun stopped in front of Lionel. I nearly died. At that moment I decided I hated him. By the time he actually kissed me, I knew I did. He was wet-lipped and breathing heavily and held me far too tightly. Our romance ended abruptly with my first childhood kiss.

Where I grew up, childhood was over by the time children were in their late teens. If the family could afford a college education, a child might stay home and receive family support while going to school. If not, it was expected that a boy would get a job, and a girl would get married and start a family. Young people left home or remained, but either way they were expected to become adults and assume full responsibility for themselves and often for others as well. It would have been unthinkable to put a beloved mother or father into a nursing home. Time out for "finding" oneself was reserved for wealthy white kids who could go to India or Europe. Most of us in the thirties were lucky if we could get to Philly and back.

Art was the one thing I had always loved to do. Yet, because I had never heard of a black artist, male or female, when I was a child, I did not think of art as a possible profession. In retrospect, I think I must have taken art for granted at this time — as something to do rather than be. I knew that I wanted to communicate ideas and thereby make a contribution to society; and to do that would require a college education. This had been drilled into my head by my mother and Uncle Cardoza from the day I was born. Although I craved an education, I never really liked going to school. I loved the learning, but I did not like the teachers. Most of them were excellent but very racist. I am sorry to say I have lived my whole life in Harlem and went to school there, but I never had a black teacher in grade school, high school, or even in college.

What I hated about school was the socialization. Children of all creeds and colors can be so cruel to each other. I never got used to the uncertainty about who might be my friend, hold my hand at lineup, be my partner in games, or pick me to be on the team. I complained once to my mother that the black children in my Sunday school class never seemed to like me. The next Sunday Mother came to Sunday school class to tell the children that I was a nice girl, and that I had often missed class because I had asthma. She brought some fruit-flavored lollipops and asked my peers to be friendly and play with me. That Sunday, when my mother left the room, I just wanted to crawl under the floor and stay there until time washed away the looks of quiet contempt. The only person who was nice to me after that episode was the Sunday school teacher. Teachers always told me that I was "very lucky to have such a fine mother."

I never liked following the leader but the alternative — that of becoming a leader myself — never really appealed to me. I had my own ideas and I often gravitated toward the person the others had decided to reject. I might add that I was just as often that person myself.

My earliest memory of grade school is the first grade at Public School 90, located in the heart of Harlem. "That girl, the one in the red dress, stand up. What's your name?" That was the way my teachers got to know us. When I gave my name as Faith Jones, the kids in the class snickered. "Do you have Hope and Charity at home? Do you go to the Mission? Have you seen 'Father'?" the teacher asked me. She was intimating that I was a devotee of Father Divine, who had a practice of naming his female followers Faith, Hope, and Charity. The next day my mother was in school to explain to the teacher that my name had nothing to do with my religion. She proclaimed that I came from a good Christian home and had attended church and Sunday school regularly at the Abyssinian Baptist Church, where the Reverend Adam Clayton Powell Jr. was the minister. The next class I was asked the same string of questions from the new teacher and, again, Mother would be back in school. This went on until I was experienced enough to talk to the teacher myself without appearing insolent. If there was any complaint that I was disrespectful to a teacher, for whatever reason, my mother would reprimand me in front of the entire class. That was the practice then — parents gave teachers full support. If there was a problem, the parent handled it.

I remember another episode in first grade when the teacher was going over some spelling words, and I was eager to make a contribution. I informed the class that it was important to have good spelling habits because my brother had told me that if an author wrote a book and misspelled a word, he would be jailed for life. The kids in the class believed it and I was an instant hit. The teacher called me to her desk and had me repeat my story to her and later to a number of other teachers. No one said anything to me, but I knew I was being ridiculed.

In second grade Mother had me transferred from P.S. 90 to P.S. 186, the school on Sugar Hill that Andrew and Barbara attended. It was a distance from our house and out of our school district. (Mother managed to arrange this as a lot of black people did in those days: she used the address of a friend who lived in the school district where she wanted her children to go.) Public School 186 was on 145th Street between Broadway and Amsterdam Avenue. Every day we walked the seven blocks (six of them up a steep hill) from our house. I was already accustomed to walking this route since I had done it with Mother when she picked up Andrew and Barbara from school. Now it was different because I was carrying real schoolbooks in my book bag, not just nursery rhymes.

Public School 186 was a better school than P.S. 90. P.S. 90 had been a segregated school with an all-black student body and all-white faculty located in the heart of Harlem. P.S. 186 was a racially mixed school (with all-white teachers) located on Sugar Hill. Attending P.S. 186 were the black kids from Sugar Hill, Jewish kids (many were refugees from Nazi Germany), and the Puerto Rican kids whose families were moving into the side streets between Amsterdam and Broadway. The fact was that if a black child wanted to get a really good education in a New York City public school in the thirties, he/she had a much better chance of doing so in a school with white children than in a totally black school. The curriculum, educational resources, equipment, plant, and services would be better in the schools with predominantly white students. This institutional racism later was to inspire the Harlem Parents Committee in the sixties to an open confrontation with the Board of Education. The parents demanded the decentralization of public schools so that the schools in black neighborhoods could have black district superintendents, principals, teachers, community personnel, curricula, and programs that were sensitive to the needs of black children. Today, black children in Harlem finally have black teachers as well as white.

At P.S. 186 I became the class artist. As soon as my teachers found out that I could draw, they had me drawing on the blackboard, or creating one of those huge murals on heavy oak tag with big brushes and tempera paint. In the second grade I was asked to copy a scene in which George Washington's soldiers fed watermelons to some raggedy black boys. Each boy's head was centered in the middle of a slice of watermelon. All you could see of the boys were their eyes shining out of their black faces and their topsy-braided hair style. I

Barbara, Marie (my tap-dancing teacher), and me, circa 1937

told my mother about the subject of my proposed mural and the next day Mother was in school telling the teacher that black people had fought in the American Revolution and all other American wars — and that everybody likes watermelon. After all, there were some little white boys in the same picture. Why weren't they eating watermelon? Mother negotiated a change in composition so that I painted both white and black little boys eating watermelon.

Prejudice was all-pervasive, a permanent limitation on the lives of black people in the thirties. There seemed to be nothing that could really be done about the fact that we were in no way considered equal to white people. The issue of our inequality had yet to be raised and, to make matters worse, prejudice was blindly accepted as beyond anyone's control. From time to time, some kid would blurt out, "You ain' no better than me," but that was hard to prove in the thirties. All our teachers were white except for one or two black teachers, who were loved and admired by all the children. My teachers were men and women who "took no stuff." They thought nothing of our feelings and stereotyped all blacks as shiftless, lazy, and happy-go-lucky. We were taught the most degrading things about our history: slavery was presented as if it were our fault — a kind of deserved penalty for being born black. Some teachers taught us that black people enjoyed slavery so much that, after the Civil War ended, they wanted to remain with their former masters rather than go free.

I thought my teachers had more than a natural curiosity about the private lives of their black students — as if their own lives needed confirmation that they could only get by comparison with ours. Yet racist as they were, they did teach us. Nothing was watered down or made easier to compensate for our so-called racial disadvantages; in fact, just the opposite was true. Knowing this, our parents raised us to understand that we had to be twice as good to go half as far.

There was one rather glorious exception to these racist teachers — Dr. Bernath, the new principal in my last term at P.S. 186. He selected two black students, Catherine English and myself, to be his personal monitors. This was my first chance to be close to a teacher. On occasion we went to fetch his lunch from a fancy French restaurant on Broadway, a short distance from the school. I was thrilled, and Catherine and I fantasized that we were going to have dinner there. When we graduated, Dr. Bernath let us select two books each from his personal library in his office, and then signed them. Years later, my infant daughters obliterated his signature with scribbles. They could never understand what that signature meant to me, nor could I expect them to.

Catherine was my best friend. She lived on Sugar Hill in a brownstone her family owned and she, too, had an older brother and sister. Her mother was a housewife, and her father worked in a paper factory. They were like a "Dick and Jane" family to me, but colored. I wanted Catherine to come to my house to visit, but her mother would not allow it. By the late thirties things were rapidly changing in Harlem. Street gangs were beginning to form and they were staking out territories. Boys made homemade "zip guns" and they were just about as dangerous as the real thing. Parents had to be careful where they let their children wander. Because of this, Catherine's mother would not allow her to visit me. I kept nagging at Mother to move from the Valley up to Sugar Hill where the high-class black people lived.

Finally, we moved to Sugar Hill in June of 1940. On October 8, 1940, I was ten years old and began counting the days until I was thirteen. I longed to be a teenager, go out on dates, and wear a basic black dress, nylon stockings, and high heels. Weary of being "the baby," I was eager to grow up and begin to make my own decisions.

CHAPTER 2: GROWING UP ON SUGAR HILL IN THE 1940S

Me at Edgecombe Avenue apartment, 1946

In the summer of 1940 we moved from Central Harlem (the Valley) to number 363 Edgecombe Avenue, between 150th and 155th Streets. A beautiful tree-lined street on Sugar Hill, Edgecombe Avenue was strictly residential. It stretched ten blocks, from 145th to 155th streets, and faced Colonial Park (now called Jackie Robinson Park). The park side was lined with benches shaded by stately oak trees, and 150th Street was the only cross street. But all of us kids found shortcuts through the park to the Valley below and to St. Nicholas Avenue through the backyards and back doors of apartment buildings.

Our apartment was in a row of small buildings facing Colonial Park. In the summer the foliage from its huge oak trees hid the old wooden benches filled with people catching the breeze on the park side. From our fourth-floor window we could see the entire park, Central Harlem, and had a spectacular view of downtown Manhattan clear to the Empire State Building.

With the depression years at an end, we now had something more than bread and butter to think about: the war in Europe. The forties hurled America into a patriotic renaissance. Freedom and democracy were what everybody talked about. When Pearl Harbor was bombed in 1941, men all over the country rushed down to the military enlistment centers to volunteer for active duty. Patriotic war movies and songs were on the top of the charts. All of the armed services were segregated but still black men wanted to fight. In their mind Hitler was the personification of "the man" they battled daily at home. My father, with tears in his eyes, told us of his attempt to join the army and his rejection because of his age (he was then thirty-eight). I won the "I Am an American" essay contest at school for writing on "What It Means to Be an American." The winner for this citywide competition was appointed deputy mayor to Fiorello La Guardia (then mayor) of New York for a day. Everyone bought war bonds and contributed care packages for the refugees in war-torn Europe.

During the war many black families got "on their feet" by working in defense plants. My mother, like so many women all over the country, went to work for the first time outside the home. She worked in a defense plant sewing Eisenhower jackets for the army; she also sewed at home, designing and making clothes for friends and relatives for extra cash. She no longer had to depend on Daddy for support. Her newfound financial independence gave her peace of mind and, at the same time, this was to be the start of her career in fashion design. In 1942 Mother got a divorce from Daddy and shocked the family by changing her name to Willi Posey, her maiden name. Moving to Sugar Hill began a new way of life for all of us.

Sugar Hill got its name from the "sweet" lifestyle of its black middle class and the fabulous black entertainers who lived there. They included Duke Ellington, Willie Mays, Marian Anderson, Jimmie Lunceford, Sarah Vaughn, Dinah Washington, and Harry Belafonte — just to name a few. Many of these celebrities lived right on Edgecombe Avenue in number 409, the big fourteen-story luxury building at the corner of 155th Street. Everybody knew 409 Edgecombe — the house with the doorman, maids, service entrances, and terraced penthouse apartments. The lobby was huge and beautifully appointed with period furniture. This was a house where Negroes knew how to be swanky and had the cars and fine clothes to prove it. Since the Harlem Renaissance period of the 1920s, the "New Negro" intelligentsia had been centered around 409. Birdie (my present husband) grew up in that building. He remembers all the black luminaries and the numbers of the apartments in which they lived: Thurgood Marshall in 11B; Walter White in 13B; W. E. B. Du Bois in 13A; Roy Wilkins in 7G; Aaron Douglass in 4I; and Dr. Chin, one of our most prominent women doctors, in 1E. The boys and girls I grew up with were deeply inspired by these people. They were a part of the "Negro history" we discussed so often.

But still the most exciting figure on Edgecombe was Joe Louis, the heavyweight champion of the world. When Joe came to New York (he normally lived in Detroit) for a fight, he stayed with Mrs. Armstead, a much-loved fifth-grade schoolteacher who lived at 381 Edgecombe. Birdie remembers the night the Champ had a fight at Yankee Stadium and the whole street was blocked off clear to the Viaduct. Edgecombe was crawling with police brass as Joe and his wife, Marva, got into their limousine to go to the stadium. Joe wore his legendary dark brown fedora, with the brim broken down on one side, and his loose-fitting Hollywood wrap camel-hair coat. Marva, swathed in mink from head to toe, and Joe appeared casual to the crowd although they looked like a million dollars. Mounted police held back the fans as motorcycle police lined up to speed the Champ to the fight. After he won, as he always did, all of Harlem turned out to cheer the Champ's victory. Those who lived on Edgecombe Avenue, like Birdie, got a close-up view of their illustrious visitor, and a chance to rub shoulders with the great champion and shake his hand.

When we moved to Edgecombe Avenue, Andrew continued to hang out in the Valley, either on the corner of 146th Street and Eighth Avenue or in Clark's Billiard Parlor on 145th Street and Bradhurst. He had only moved with us in order to have a place to sleep. All his free time was spent in the Valley. Andrew's gang name was Baron Dupree. Mother didn't know anything about the Comanchees, or that Andrew was now a member of their gang. She still called him "Little Andrew," oblivious to the fact that he was no longer little at all. Andrew was known as a "sharp-looking cat, a cool dude." In slang terms he was no "lame." Nobody messed with him, or us, in the Valley or on the Hill. Andrew was "bad."

Andrew was a good boy at home, however, and in school he had been an A student until he quit in his senior year at DeWitt Clinton High School. Quitting school was very common among black boys and girls who felt it was useless even to try to qualify for success in the outside world. By now Mother had finally lost control over Andrew. He always got what he wanted and he was soft-spoken and handsome. When he looked at us with those big soulful brown eyes, it was clear why all the women in our family could never tell Andrew, "No!" Girls liked him, even his former girlfriends. When I walked down the street with him, the women we passed flirted with him. "Oh Baron . . . ," they'd say in that whinny voice women have when they are playing up to a man. I heard one say, "You working, baby? You too good-looking to work." I guess he agreed with that because he didn't work very often. Sometimes Andrew worked as a shipping clerk in the garment district to make enough money to buy flashy clothes like the ones musicians wore. He even bought them at Phil Kronfeld's and Leighton's on Broadway in the West 40s where the musicians bought theirs. Curiously, Mother never demanded that Andrew contribute to the household. I resented this and felt that, if he was not going to school, he should work

Sister Barbara on graduation day from junior high school, 1939

and pay Mother for food and lodging, or move out. He stayed and I lost respect for him.

At the same time Barbara was still the reigning "Princess." In 1943 she was sixteen years old and already a freshman at New York University. Kids used to follow me home to get a look at the smart little girl whom everybody talked about, but few people knew. In the 1940s it was rare for a black kid to go to college, especially one so young and cute.

I graduated from elementary school in June of 1942. The war was on in Europe and we had frequent air raid drills to prepare us for an unexpected attack. Because of this we were not allowed to invite our parents to our graduation ceremony and, thus, graduation was like any other day. We had a quiet assembly, said good-bye to our teachers and friends, and I left the school that I had come to love. I went on to Edward W. Stitt Junior High School 164, located on Edgecombe Avenue and 164th Street.

I continued my friendship with Catherine English in junior high school. Now that I was living on the Hill around the corner from her, we saw each other all the time. She used to bring an extra sandwich for me to eat at lunchtime — I usually ate my lunch from my desk, pinch-by-pinch, long before the twelve o'clock bell rang. I also had a bad habit of coming to school unprepared, but Catherine always had extra pens, pencils, erasers, and loose-leaf paper to loan me. I usually left mine on the kitchen table where my mother had packed them. I admired Catherine's maturity. I'd be willing to bet that she never wet the bed or her pants when she was a baby. She already dressed like a grown-up at thirteen. She had a basic black dress and wore nylon stockings and "heels."

I turned thirteen in 1943. That was the year I had my first big birthday party. All of my earlier birthday parties had been family parties attended by just the three of us kids. I enjoyed those parties with my older brother and sister, but this party marked the beginning of my teenage social life on Edgecombe Avenue. It was my first opportunity to entertain all the new friends I had met since moving there.

I told several kids who could be counted upon to carry news that I expected every-one to bring me a gift. If they wanted to have time to dance I told them to come early because Ma Jones (the name the kids had for Mother) planned to end the party promptly at 9 P.M. She already had a reputation for enforcing early departures. The news was out and some kids started arriving around 5 P.M.

First some girls came in twos and threes, followed later by the boys. Later when Mother opened the door, she found a hallway full of boys, each one carrying a gift for me. Mother stood aside as they filed by her chorusing, "Hi, Ma Jones." Those who were not new to our house gave Mother a bear hug and a kiss on the cheek. The "coolest" boys were the last to arrive, some so "cool" that I had never even met them before. All brought presents: my message had been well delivered. I could tell that many of their presents were afterthoughts — brown paper bags from the corner drugstore containing five nickel candy bars. I loved these. The other gifts, though more expensive and at the time greatly appreciated, I no longer remember.

Kids had a good time at my house. They seemed to love listening to my mother's "roots" lectures on "When I Was a Girl. . . ." She was very attractive and young boys liked being around her. Often they would come to see Barbara or me and end up spending all their time talking to her. "Ma Jones is down," they used to say about her, meaning they felt comfortable around her. With Mother, they knew they were not expected to be anything but who they were — young boys. Girls their own age often made them feel and act like "little boys." But not Mother.

Post Office was one of our favorite party games. We played it when the adults were in the kitchen cleaning up, and we could use the coat room as a kissing place without being detected. To play Post Office all you needed was a dark room, some kids who wanted to kiss each other, and a "postman" to deliver or call out the names of those to be kissed. A letter was one kiss, an airmail was two kisses, and a special delivery was three kisses. The postman would pick someone to start and place him or her in the coat room. Next he would ask what mail the starter wanted to be delivered and to whom. The postman would then call out: "One airmail special delivery for Connie." We would fall all over the floor giggling, while Connie got up shyly to walk into the kissing room to receive her "mail." Next Connie told the postman what mail she wanted delivered.

Sonny Rollins was at my thirteenth birthday party. He was one of those who gave me a twenty-five-cent bag of candy bars. He lived a few houses up the street from me. I had heard that Sonny thought I was cute and that he liked me, so I wasn't surprised when he called me in for Post Office. Sonny had a large nose, and in the dark it seemed even larger and got in the way of our kiss. Sonny was good-natured and only fourteen years old at the

Me and Earl, 1946

time. We had a great time laughing before we finished our kiss, and Sonny bashfully went out to a roomful of teasers. I called in Earl Wallace. I knew Earl liked me because he had told me so. He let everybody know he did by calling me back to the Post Office when it was his turn. I was embarrassed but felt flattered by the attention.

Earl Wallace lived in the next apartment house to mine and would eventually become my first husband. He was the first friend Barbara and I had on Edgecombe Avenue. Although he had been born in America, he went to Jamaica (where his mother and father were from) as an infant and was raised by his grandparents until he was seven years old. At this time his mother, separated from his father, took a job as a seamstress in a dress factory. She could now afford to bring Earl back to America where she was determined to continue his strict Jamaican upbringing, alone. Bob Wallace, Earl's father, was a brilliant man who made a hobby of learning to speak Swahili and Xhosa (a South African language spoken with a click sound). My daughter Barbara told me that when she was at the University of London, Grandpa Wallace would write letters to her in Swahili as well as Spanish, Italian, and Portuguese. He also wrote to Michele, my other daughter, in French. Bob Wallace would have loved to pursue a career in horticulture, but was able to do this only voluntarily in the community gardens in Brooklyn. After immigrating to America he worked at odd jobs to provide the bare necessities, but only ones near libraries so he could read during lunchtime. Michele describes her grandfather and her father as intellectuals who valued ideas above monetary gain. In fact, Bob Wallace graduated from Monroe College in Jamaica, but chose not to go to Oxford to study medicine after winning a Rhodes scholarship.

Although Earl was a brilliant student, he wanted to hang out and play in the street just like all the other boys on the block. Despite Earl's rebellious spirit, he was a nice boy who loved music, took piano lessons, and gave award-winning recitals of classical music. My mother liked him and Barbara and Andrew did, too. He quickly became one of my best friends.

Music was important to the boys on Edgecombe Avenue. With all of the famous musicians we had as neighbors, that was not surprising. Our house was the scene of weekend jazz concerts played on an old RCA Victor console that had belonged to my uncle Cardoza. He had intended for us to play only the classical recordings he had given us, but Earl and several boys on the block added jazz to our record collection. We now had music from Duke Ellington to Enrico Caruso, Louis Jordan to Marian Anderson. Sonny Rollins often brought over his saxophone, and once or twice I sang while he played.

Sonny was always serious about his saxophone. He could be heard practicing his horn above the street sounds and the boys' screams as they played stickball in the street below his window. He had a strong sense of purpose. I don't know anyone who has become successful who didn't feel this way. To do something special in life, as Sonny had in mind, was undertaken only with a great deal of trepidation as well as determination. Sonny was one of those who did not give up. People would laugh at him when he played "off notes" as a kid just learning the saxophone. My mother would say, "Sonny, please, you're disturbing my neighbors," when Sonny would bring over his horn on the weekends. But Sonny knew he would become one of the great jazz saxophonists of his time.

When I graduated from junior high school, I was fourteen, but still not "old enough" (according to my mother) to wear nylon stockings. I decided to fake illness and stay home rather than be the only girl to wear socks to graduation. When Barbara graduated, Mother had made her wear a large hair ribbon to match her light blue taffeta graduation dress. With the giant bow atop her head she looked like a baby, but Mother refused to let her take it off. When Barbara led her class out at the end of the ceremony, everybody began buzzing about her red eyes and tear-stained face. To spare myself Barbara's predicament, I got a sudden asthma attack about an hour before it was time to get dressed.

For the graduation ceremony I never attended, Mother had bought me a white lace suit, white sandals, and white socks. Later that summer I wore the sandals without socks, and colored my legs with leg makeup to pretend I was wearing stockings. But what would I wear to high school in the fall when the other girls were wearing their nylons? To cope with this situation I went on a hunger strike, staying in bed all the time, and losing a lot of weight. One day I heard Mrs. Curry, our next-door neighbor, chatting with Mother in the hall. "You know, Willi, Faith is a big girl now," she said. "So why not let her wear stockings? Don't you think she's ready to grow up a little?" Mother consented reluctantly. I don't think it was my mother's intention to make us different from the other kids, but she did. For example, even our gym suits were blue-green and designed by Mother instead of the regulation green worn by the other girls.

I went to George Washington High School in Washington Heights, just north of Harlem. The faculty at George Washington High School had a reputation for coming down hard on black kids. High school was the last bitter mile for many black kids in the forties, so if they dropped out, as many did, it wasn't unexpected. I was not a good student in high school and it was there I learned to cut classes. I worked in the "cutting" office, so it was easy to cover myself and I was often absent. Asthma was still my excuse, but there were times when I was home because I was unprepared for an exam or a written assignment.

I cannot remember the name of a single teacher I had in high school. There was one white teacher I definitely remember, but not by name. He had called me into his classroom for excessive absence and looked more than usually red-faced and sweaty that day, but I didn't notice it until he stopped talking and told me to turn around. The fashion then was to wear very tight skirts and sexy sweaters — "the sweater-girl" look — and I was in style. I thought there must be something on my skirt, maybe a thread, until I felt something lightly touching my derriere. I looked over my shoulder and into his quivering flushed face. "What are you doing?" I asked indignantly. His hand froze. Pleadingly, he attempted a come-hither smile, the kind I associated with deviant old men who exposed themselves to young girls in doorways. "You ought to be ashamed of yourself," I blurted out without thinking. But I was immediately terrified because I knew I could get in trouble for this. I said nothing more, but gathered my books in my arms and proceeded straight to the door. "Get on out of here," I heard him snarl as I left his office, "and don't let me have to speak to you again about your absence."

In my senior year I transferred to Morris High School in the Bronx. I had failed two courses in my junior year at George Washington and needed them to graduate, so I made them up and graduated from Morris High School in June of 1948. I was now seventeen. Despite the fact that I did not graduate from high school with honors, my social life in the forties was a hit.

A year earlier, when I was sixteen, I had started going steady with Earl. He was eighteen, my first real boyfriend, and by now also my best friend. We had long talks about philosophy, politics, sex, morality, Negro history, science fiction, the fate of the universe, and everything else. We were very much alike in that we both questioned the true meaning of everything. We spent a lot of time together, as much as Mother would permit. She didn't know that we were going steady. Earl's mother and I had a good relationship too, although I am sure she would have preferred him to date a Jamaican girl.

My mother had no concern about Earl's Jamaican heritage, she just disapproved of my going steady. Although she was afraid of pregnancy, now that I was sixteen she consented to let me go out with boys. At that time a lot of nice girls got pregnant and "had" to get married — there was no such thing as birth control. I often heard my mother talking about some girl who had gotten "caught" and needed to see a doctor who took care of unwanted pregnancies. Many of these women were married but could not afford to have any more children. Getting pregnant outside of marriage was shameful. Whether or not you had an abortion, it was still a disgrace. We were all supposed to be virgins, and only the men could admit to liking sex.

Me at graduation from high school, 1948

Earl and I were careful. For a long time our sex life consisted of light to heavy petting, with Earl assuring me that we would not "go all the way" until we were married. Eventually he changed his mind and began pressuring me to sleep with him and I finally agreed. I don't even remember where we were when this happened, but like a flash in the dark, it was over before it began. He was just too anxious.

Sex wasn't dirty to me, but it wasn't anything special. I faked liking it, and Earl enjoyed it just like they said he would. He was affectionate and loving — always kissing, holding, and touching whenever we could steal a few moments alone. He was a silent but passionate lover. When I would ask him, "Do you love me?" he would always answer, "Yes," and then I would demand to know how much. He always assured me, "More than anything else in the world." He never changed his words or his lovemaking style even after we got married. I was twenty-six, had two children, and was divorced from Earl before I met a man who could make love; I married him when I was thirty-one.

Earl felt compelled to tell me about the first time he got high. It was a big event in his life and he was very excited about it. "Pot makes you feel cool," he told me, "like you don't need to communicate; and you hear sounds other people can't hear, and laugh about things that aren't happening." I tried it once and was turned off. Besides, my father drank enough in his lifetime for both of us and I found that being sober was my "cool." But Earl was always looking to get stoned. I thought I could change him, stop him from getting high. We "colored girls" were always trying to change our men, and always finding out too late that the changes that had to be made were by us and usually involved leaving.

I got drunk once and had a hangover that I shall never forget. Someone mixed Calvert's whisky with Pepsi Cola and I mistook it for my drink. Earl and I were at one of those invitational dances given by a social club called the Swanksmen. Earl tried to sober me up with black coffee and when we got to my house, he ran upstairs ahead of me. Mother was already in the hall to make sure we didn't stand there smooching at the door for the neighbors to see. Holding my corsage in his hand, Earl approached my mother and said, "Press this flower for Faith so she can remember tonight. She was the prettiest girl at the dance. The only girl prettier than her is you." He continued to jive-talk Mother until I got past her and into my room to "die."

After I graduated from high school in June of 1948, I went on to City College on Convent Avenue, just ten blocks from my house. As a child I'd had vivid memories of hordes of young white male students pouring out of the 145th Street subway and up the hill to City College. I had always dreamed of going up the hill to this college I had never seen.

In my freshman year at City College, I selected art as my major only to discover that women were not allowed to declare a major in the School of Liberal Arts. So I registered in the School of Education, majoring in art and minoring in education. This was the only way I could get a degree in art at City College, and I was determined to go to that school. Tuition was only a few dollars a semester in the forties, and if you couldn't keep up, you were thrown out. There were no remedial programs for those who had difficulty doing the work.

Many of my classmates had come from the High School of Music and Art, where they had majored in art. Though I was a good student and my art teachers had always recognized me as gifted, this alternative high school was never suggested to me as an option. All through high school I made art at home and drew constantly in all my note-books in class. I suspect I would have done better in high school had I gone to a school like Music and Art where I could have taken art along with my academic subjects.

At City College competition was keen and I loved every minute of it, once I learned to compete. For example, in my freshman year I took a course in two-dimensional design and the instructor gave us an assignment to design a playing card. My playing card was a jack of diamonds created in tones of red, yellow, blue, and purple using tempera paint and brush. The other students made two or three examples of different designs using a variety of commercial art techniques. But I knew nothing about such materials and techniques; I had never even cut a mat or used an airbrush to create a design. It was all easy for me to learn and I began to use all my spare time to make art and try out new materials and techniques.

I also took drawing and oil painting in my freshman year. Professor Robert Gwathmey taught me oil painting. The first day in his class I was frightened by his deep southern drawl and I headed straight for the door. "No," he called out to me, "don't leave. I want to talk to you." He told me that he knew what I was thinking and why I wanted to leave. "I'm a nice guy," he pleaded, "give me a chance." I wasn't accustomed to meeting nice men with southern drawls. The only ones I had seen were on television explaining how they didn't believe in "no equal rights for Negras." Gwathmey turned out to be one of the three best teachers I had at City College. The other two were Professor Hurd, who taught art education, and Professor Goldberg, who taught painting.

Many of my teachers tried to discourage me from being an artist. Their efforts only served to inspire me to prove them wrong. For example I got a D in drawing from a teacher. I don't remember his name but I do remember that he painted portraits of rich people on horseback. He laughed at a drawing I did for a test he gave. "What's this?" he asked me derisively, pointing to the mountains in my composition. "Mountains," I explained. "You'd better write it on your drawing or no one will know," he said coldly. In my embarrassment I hurriedly wrote "mountains" on the paper and turned it in. His teaching assistants stood by listening with broad smiles on their faces. I guess it was funny, but not to me. Later I asked him why he gave me such a bad grade and he told me that he did not think I could draw. "Does that mean you don't believe I have talent enough to be an artist?" "Well," he said, "I don't see any." A year later, during class one day, this same man took me aside and apologized for having told me once that I couldn't draw. It was a lesson about what teachers should never do — and I learned it the hard way.

Recently I returned to City College to deliver a commencement address and receive an honorary doctorate in fine art. All of my professors, of course, were gone by then and I didn't think the graduates would find my depressing stories about their school inspiring. So, I decided not to tell them how much hell I had caught as an art student at City College forty years earlier. Instead, I gave them some advice: "The harder you work, the more talented you will become because your talent can only be defined by you."

At City College in the forties, most of the black students hung out at the "black" table in the cafeteria. I never liked hanging out because I spent my free time in the art studios, but sometimes I would stop by and relax while eating. It was not unusual to find a "hip" white kid sitting there, too. The feeling among the white students and professors, however, was that students who sat at the "black" table were segregating themselves. We were expected to prove that we were ready to integrate with whites. Nobody had begun to place the burden for racism on whites, and urge the necessity of change in their behavior. Faced as we were by unsurmountable racism, it was still our fault if we were not yet accepted as equals. Some black people believed that, too. If "bootstraps" could talk, the great stories told of black striving would never end but not the successes.

Once I had made the commitment I never for one moment doubted my ability to become an artist. I soon became competitive with the best of the art students at City College, including the only other black art student, Al Hollingsworth. Al was recognized as a prodigy before I arrived. Now all eyes were on me and I intended to have my aspirations as a painter taken seriously.

Despite my rather serious art student demeanor, I liked to do a lot of primping and wear pretty clothes. My daily ritual consisted of making up my face, and combing, straightening, and curling my hair. When I was going out, I often changed my clothes four or five times before I was satisfied with my outfit. I learned to sew my own clothes, so I could wear my skirts and dresses as tight fitting as I chose. I enjoyed looking sexy and showing off my figure and legs. I went out on dates with Earl and other boys as often as my mother would permit, which was not often enough. I used to wait almost until the last moment to ask Mother if I could go to a dance or party. If I waited too long she would say no, because I had not given her enough time to make a decision.

On October 8, 1950, I turned twenty years old. No longer a teenager, I was still not quite a woman. I felt restless, and dissatisfied with my life. I wanted to be with Earl all the time. I wanted to be his wife, and I thought if we could get married everything would be all right. We had been engaged since Christmas of 1949, when Earl had saved up his money to buy me a small custom-made diamond ring. It was beautiful but Mother returned it, stating that I was too young even to think of marriage, and that I had to finish college first. Earl secretly gave the ring back to me and the engagement was still on. I wanted to get married soon. Earl agreed.

PART II

MEN, MARRIAGE, AND MOTHERHOOD

CHAPTER 3: MEN AND MARRIAGE IN THE 1950S AND 1960S: SOMETHING OLD, NOTHING NEW, SOMETIMES BLISSFUL, OFTEN BLUE

My sister Barbara's wedding with me and attendant, 1950

In my twenties I had a good time acting out my independence, and getting started on a bedrock of mistakes, some of which would take the rest of my life to live down.

My sister, Barbara, and I both got married in 1950, Barbara in June and I in November. It is Barbara's wedding I like to remember, however, and not mine. She had the perfect wedding the whole family had been waiting for. The ceremony took place at the Abyssinian Baptist Church with eight bridesmaids and ushers, a flower girl, and a ring bearer; and the reception was held at Bowman's Rainbow Room on 155th Street and Edgecombe Avenue. She had a good-looking and attentive bridegroom, and enough gifts to stock a small gift shop. Mother designed and made Barbara's trousseau, gown, and all the bridesmaids' gowns. By now Mother, a fashion designer, had made weddings her specialty.

Abyssinian was a beautiful neo-Gothic church with high stained-glass windows, a marble pulpit, and a magnificently steep vaulted ceiling. Under Mother's supervision, I not only beaded the train of Barbara's wedding gown, but also made hundreds of paper flowers to decorate the church's choir loft and balcony. From a distance the handmade flowers appeared real since they resembled the fresh cut flowers on the pulpit and along the aisle where Barbara was to make her entrance.

My sister Barbara's bridal shower, June 1950

Just before the wedding began, Daddy slipped away from the wedding party to take a drink from his hip flask. Andrew found him and brought him back without too much delay, but Mother was furious and the rest of us in the bridal party were visibly shaken. I proceeded down the aisle after Barbara and Daddy, carrying my flowers over my shoulder like a club. It was only when I was almost at the pulpit that I realized this and shifted my flowers to the customary cradling position. Fortunately for me, all eyes were on Barbara, who made a beautiful bride.

Aunt Bessie and Aunt Edith took on the catering for the reception. They were master cooks in the southern tradition: great food and enough to feed an army. Barbara's wedding cake was a masterpiece with eight tiers. It had been baked by Mr. Wilson on Amsterdam Avenue, who delivered it personally with great style — attired in a baker's white coat and pants, with a high white baker's hat perched on his head.

Mother had planned Barbara's wedding to a fault; she even had the baker make eight other cakes iced in the colors of the rainbow to match the bridesmaids' dresses. These cakes, cut in squares, were gift-wrapped for the guests to take home. Mother had provided an assortment of soft drinks for the children and nondrinkers and a huge barrel of beer for the rest. There was plenty to drink, but no hard liquor. Even though Mother didn't drink beer, she believed that beer was not alcohol and should be properly served with ice and sugar to sweeten the bitter taste.

The musicians who played at Barbara's reception were the best: Sonny Rollins on tenor sax, Jackie Maclean on alto, Arthur Taylor on drums, and Kenny Drew on piano. All of them lived in the neighborhood and were friends more than stars. They played our favorite music: "April in Paris," "I'm in the Mood for Love," "Moonlight Becomes You," and some fast tunes like "Flying Home," "'A' Train," and "Tuxedo Junction." We danced till the last lingering notes of "Home Sweet Home."

After they returned from their honeymoon, Barbara and her new husband, Jo Jo, moved in with Mother and me. The apartment was crowded, since Andrew still stayed with us off and on. Although Andrew was married, he and his wife and child lived apart more than they did together. Jo Jo was a nice person on the surface and pleasant enough to live with. Now that he was living with us, however, Mother and I had to stay fully dressed at all times. Barbara, of course, could walk around in her underslip and be cool and comfortable on hot days. The television that mother bought for me as a graduation present became more Jo Jo's than mine. He had to see hockey and wrestling matches, the fights or war movies. I tried to assert myself

Daddy, Andrew, and Aunt Bessie in background, 1950

but I was put off quickly by Mother's menacing stare. Jo Jo was the man of the house now and Barbara was still "The Princess."

It was time for me to leave home. In 1950 that meant getting married, since no respectable young woman of twenty left home on her own. I was in my junior year at college and the two years until graduation were an eternity. It seemed as if Earl and I had been meant for each other, he a musician and I an artist. We were two struggling artists who could, if need be, live off love.

Earl and I were married on November 1, 1950, meeting early that morning at City Hall. Earl came with Arthur Wilson and I came alone. We planned to be married by a justice of the peace but I was under twenty-one, so we had to be married in a church — that was the law. We found a minister at the First Methodist Church who married us in a few minutes. I was scared speechless: the words stuck in my throat and I could barely whisper, "I, Faith, take . . . promise to love and honor . . . " In the back of my mind I thought that if it didn't work, I could get a divorce.

After the ceremony I rushed uptown to my class at City College. Later Earl met me, as was his custom, to walk home with me. We decided not to tell my mother about our marriage until I could move in with him. Earl's mother was preparing to leave soon for Guam to join her new husband, a sergeant in the Air Force. We knew that after she was gone only Earl and his cousin Frank would be living in the apartment. Within a couple of weeks his mother left and I moved in with Earl. Mother took the news of our wedding very hard. She suggested that we could get an annulment, but I rejected the idea, even though I had my doubts about the marriage.

I had expected to be swept off my feet on my wedding night. Accordingly, I took my bath, creamed and powdered myself, dabbed behind my ears and knees with Worth's Je Reviens, put on my new and very revealing nightgown, and waited.

Earl spent that night grooming himself for his job hunt the next day. After his bath and oil rubdown, he polished his shoes, pressed a razor-sharp crease in his pants, and ironed a white pocket handkerchief. He combed his hair, put on a stocking cap to keep it in place while he slept, and got into bed. I was already asleep. If there was an erotic wedding night episode, I missed it.

Our wedding night was not an accurate reflection of the nights to come, although many times I wished it had been. Earl was always ready for love — in the kitchen or the parlor, sad or happy, sober or high, whether he was tired or rested, with good news or bad, in the money or broke, regardless of whether we were getting along or not. My way of dealing with this was just to keep moving and swear I came before him. Soon enough he would be sitting on the side of the bed smoking a cigarette in silence. For a long time sex was more of a problem than an enjoyment. I had been told things would taper off and he would get used to me. But when? I hardly had time to want sex before Earl wanted it again. Thank God I was only faking orgasms — otherwise neither one of us would have seen the light of day.

I had a lot to learn about living with Earl. Cooking was my most immediate concern, since Mother had rarely given me an opportunity to cook at home. Barbara was not only a dietician, but also a very good cook. I was still learning how to boil water. One morning I decided to make Earl some pancakes. I could not remember whether pancakes were fried with a lot of oil, like fried chicken, or just a little oil, like eggs. Earl came into the kitchen and asked what I was cooking. "Oh, just pancakes," I said, averting my eyes from the mess smoking in the pan. Earl responded, "Don't give me any. It'll make me sick, and I won't be able to play tonight." Reaching for a box of cornflakes and two bowls he said, "You better not eat that either." He turned off the stove and offered me a bowl.

I asked Frank, Earl's cousin, for some of my mother-in-law's famous West Indian dishes. I could not hope to approach her virtuosity in the kitchen, but at least I could use some of the same ingredients such as brown rice, red beans, coconut, kidneys, oregano, and thyme. These foods were all new to me, as was Frank's West Indian accent. In time I learned to comprehend the language and some of the cooking. Earl was accustomed to taking care of himself so it was easy to keep the apartment clean and neat. He did the heavy cleaning in the apartment — the floors, windows, and all the laundry — and I did the rest.

Our first Thanksgiving together was memorable, especially when I got an attack of asthma. Earl was familiar with my pattern and had been with me many times when Mother rushed me to the Presbyterian Medical Center for a two- or three-day stay. This time Earl and I went alone and the doctor advised him to leave me at the hospital. Earl went to the admitting room, but he was back in a flash. "It costs fifteen dollars and fifty cents a day to have a bed on the ward here, and that's not including the medication you need. You can't stay here, we can't afford it," Earl told me regretfully.

It was quite clear we could not afford a fifteen-dollar-a-day hospital bill. Our living expenses were ten dollars a week and this covered five dollars for food and five dollars for rent. Fifteen dollars was a musician's scale for a gig and Earl made fifteen to thirty dollars a week, depending upon whether he had one or two gigs on a weekend. If we had extra money, it went to buy my art books and supplies or his music books and records. Our families had already helped us to pay the rent and buy food, and we couldn't ask them for more. So, I took a prescription from the doctor, bundled up, and Earl and I went home. Since that day I have never had an attack severe enough to warrant admission to the hospital.

No sooner had Earl given me my medicine and propped me up on a heap of pillows, than the door opened and a young woman named Hazel came bursting into the room. "You're sick, poor baby. You should not be left alone," she proclaimed. (I had discovered that musicians never were alone.) "Everybody come back here. Let's keep Faith company," Hazel declared. Hazel, a jazz musician groupie, was a very pretty nineteen-year-old girl who was soon to become a prostitute. Usually I admired her style and her ability to survive against odds that would have toppled most of us. That day, however, I could have hurled her and all the others out the nearest window. I was having difficulty just breathing and lying still in bed. They all came back, as Hazel had requested, and began the ritual of passing joints. Each person took a deep drag of smoke from the same joint, holding it until they exhaled slowly, making a hissing sound like a teapot at its boiling point. Of course, I had seen them do this many times, but I always had the option to leave the room. Today all I could do was make some rather unintelligible wheezing sounds, which Hazel interpreted as proof that I was indeed too ill to be alone.

After the joints, they set out plate glass with furrowed rows of white powder on it. The cut-off straws were passed around — a straw and a row for each person. Earl was first. Just watching him sniff that white powder up his nose shortened my breathing even more. Fortunately for me, there was no more smoke.

Finally, the smirking half-smile, the wry humor and mock laughter, scratching and nodding off of the heroin high took them over. The asthma medication also took, so I was able to lie back on my mound of pillows and fall asleep. When I awoke it was Thanksgiving Day and they had all departed.

After this episode, I began to put pressure on Earl to stop people from getting high in our house. But he was now dependent upon them for his own drugs, and he continued to let them come. I left instead.

In 1951, I moved to a black student house on the campus at City College where students could share a room for seven dollars a week. I had a nice roommate named Margaret, who was a librarian from New England. We found a lot to talk about, and sometimes went out to parties, or to dinner with her family or mine.

That semester I registered for evening classes and looked for a job in the day. Jobs were nearly impossible to find in the fifties, except in a factory, and unless I lied, I couldn't even get that. College students were considered poor risks and overqualified. I tried to get a typing job but could not get past the personal interview because of my race. On the phone they were willing to accept me as gal Friday, but when I showed up for the interview, they were shocked to see that I was not white. The job that I had been assured would be mine on the phone was now suddenly "taken." I became more determined than ever to complete my education and teach art. It seemed the only employment that would allow me to escape from dead-end jobs. Earl gave me money to pay my rent and came to see me regularly at the student house. I also spent some time with him on weekends. I loved him very much but still felt our marriage could not work. He pleaded with me to give him a chance, assuring me that he loved me and would change.

During this period of our separation I became pregnant. Earl and I both loved children. When we were teenagers dating, we had frequently taken children of neighbors with us on picnics and other excursions; when we married, however, we never talked of having any children of our own.

I was still having my menstrual cycle and I had no morning sickness or any of the other symptoms associated with pregnancy. I ignored the possibility of being pregnant, even though I found it increasingly difficult to fit into my clothes. Mother said that when she was pregnant with each of us she admitted to her condition only when it could no longer be denied. Other women were told first before my father. In the 1950s pregnancy was still something women only whispered about. My mother had known all along that I was pregnant, but had waited until I started to show before making my maternity clothes. When I saw what she was doing, I went to the doctor. "How many months?" I asked anxiously. "Three or four," the doctor replied.

It was on my initial visit to the maternity clinic at the Sloan Hospital for Women that I joined the natural childbirth classes. Earl and I had read a book about natural childbirth by an English doctor named Read when we first got married. It was just intellectual curiosity that led us to this subject, but now it obviously had practical implications. We wanted our child to be born naturally without forceps, drugs, or anesthesia. Natural childbirth was a new concept and not many people knew anything about it, so the classes were very small and experimental. I volunteered my services as an illustrator for the manual of exercises and charts of breathing instructions which our teacher was putting together. Earl went with me to some of the classes, although he had no intention of being in the delivery room (even if it had been permitted, which it was not).

Immediately after the Christmas holidays in December of 1951 I was admitted to the hospital. The doctor wanted to control my diet, reduce my weight, and get rid of the water I was holding. According to available information, my baby was due in a week or so but, with my history of asthma, they couldn't be too careful.

The other women on the maternity ward were a multiethnic group and appeared to be in their thirties and forties, whereas I had just turned twenty-one. None of the women had been in my natural childbirth classes and many of them had experienced serious problems giving birth. Some had endured cesarean sections and were suffering the aftereffects of gastritis; others had complications with diabetes, high blood pressure, kidney disease, anemia, and other blood ailments. The ones who were healthy and had normal births were plagued for days after delivery with the sickening effects of the drugs and anesthesia they had taken. Not having anything better to do while I awaited the birth of my baby, I began to give them what I considered much-needed counselling on "painless" natural childbirth. I focused mainly on the technique of breathing with the contractions. Some of the women had already delivered their babies, which would explain the "look-at-this-fool" expression they had. The others tolerated me, counted the days, and clearly hoped rather spitefully that they would be there when I went into labor "naturally."

I couldn't stop talking about natural childbirth. The sight of some babies' heads elongated by forceps during a drug-sluggish delivery was appalling to me. I had seen the doctor massage these babies' heads daily in order to reshape them. I wondered why the women didn't understand that it would be to their benefit to work with the birth process.

At about noon on January 3, 1952, I began to feel cramps in my stomach, and my water broke. "Have I begun labor? How soon will it be all over?" I bombarded the nurse and the doctor with questions. I was anxious to see my baby, I explained. "It won't be long now," they assured me. There was some muffled laughter and hidden signals from some of the women in the beds nearby. Everybody talked about the screaming and cursing that went on in the corridors outside the delivery rooms. Why should I be any different? How could they know that my doctor had assured me that the width of my pelvis would make childbirth a breeze?

I walked out in the corridor to the public telephones to call my mother to tell her the good news. "Mother," I said, "you'll soon be a grandmother again." (Andrew had a gorgeous little six-year-old girl named Cheryl.) My mother was silent on the other end. I could hear her nervously holding her breath. "Are you there?" I asked.

"Uhhh huhhh," she uttered finally.

"Listen," I said confidently, "I'll probably be going up to the labor room soon, so if you don't hear from me for a while, you'll know I'm up there having my baby." A whole gust of air hit my eardrum. She's terrified, I thought. "Talk to me. I'm fine. What are you worried about? . . . Do you hear me?" I demanded.

"Mmmmm hmmmm," she answered, forcing the sounds through her closed lips.

She's throat-talking, I thought — that means I'm in trouble and only she knows how much. Just then I got the first real indication of what she was worried about. "Hold on, Mother, I'm having a contraction and I have to do my breathing exercises," I said matter-of-factly. I began to blow my stomach up with air slowly so that at the height of the contraction my stomach felt full of air. It worked. This is easy, I said to myself — no worse than ordinary menstrual cramps. Picking up the telephone receiver, I reassured my mother, "This baby stuff is nothing. Don't you worry."

"Ummmm hmmmm," responded my worried mother in a high-pitched, anxious voice.

"Wait a minute before you hang up, I see Dr. de Martini, my old asthma doctor. He must be looking for me," I said, waving my hand to attract his attention. "Doctor, I'm having a few contractions, not bad ones, but I just thought I would tell you. The asthma is fine. However, I really want to know when am I going upstairs to have my baby?"

The doctor put his hand on my belly, paused, and said, "You're not ready yet. You'll know when you are."

"How will I know?" I blurted out, holding the receiver so my mother could hear the doctor's answer.

"They will be closer together for one thing," said the doctor.

"I'm talking to my mother on the phone here. That's all right, isn't it?" I asked him, now slightly anxious.

"Oh sure, that won't hurt anything. I'll see you later upstairs," the doctor reassured me. He walked away with a hint of a smile moving across his face.

"What's funny, doctor?" I said, but he didn't respond. "Doctors, they never tell you anything," I commented to my mother.

Just then another contraction hit me. It started in my back and then rather quickly began to creep around the sides of my belly. "What the heck is this?" I whispered to myself. "Hold on, Mother, I'm having another contraction," I said. This time I did my breathing more quickly, catching up with the contraction so that my stomach had a balloon of air in it by the time the pain reached its crescendo in the center of my belly. Slowly I let the air out and sat back on the telephone bench. "That's a little different," I said, trying not to let my mother know how different. She was silent. "I think I had better go now and lie down," I told her, as I felt the start of another contraction creeping around the sides of my belly.

"Mmmmm hmmmmm," Mother said.

They were coming more frequently now. As one subsided in the center of my belly, another contraction was already forming in my back. Now I had to concentrate all my efforts on breathing and relaxing in between contractions. I went back to the ward and crawled up in my bed, and lay there. Some of the women gathered around me, and one went to get the nurse. I heard her say, "I think she's ready now, nurse. She's quiet." The nurse told me that my mother and husband had just called. "They are both standing by for the big event. We're going to take you upstairs now to the labor room," the nurse told me. I responded in a whisper, "All right." By now I had a rock-crushing vise in my back and a veritable torture chamber in my belly. The contractions were coming steady and

My daughter Michele, 1952

hard. The easy delivery I was promised was fourteen hours away. Thank God, I didn't know it.

The labor rooms were small, equipped only with narrow beds and barred windows. I had a nurse sitting in a chair by my bed at all times. From time to time my natural childbirth teacher came to monitor my progress, and to ask me how I felt. I ignored the question. She said she was very proud of me. Why spoil it? Outside the labor rooms there were women walking the floor and screaming uncontrollably. They cursed their husbands and vowed never to let the "son of a bitch" touch them again. Others yelled "Mama mia," "Jesus Christ," "God," or "Goddamn." After a while I didn't hear them anymore. For the next fourteen hours, my body was racked with pain. I lay on my narrow bed and in between contractions I did my breathing exercises and saw God.

The doctor who delivered my baby was a stern-faced woman. Earlier on I had seen her in the maternity clinic, but she was not my doctor. She was middle-aged with steel gray hair and cold blue eyes that looked through you. She had a low-pitched voice and she swaggered when she walked. I admired her confident manner, although earlier on, in the clinic, I had been critical of her. She was tall, lean, angular, with a no-frills face unsoftened by makeup or accommodating feminine smiles.

Now this doctor bent over me, telling me to bear down. Her whole arm was swallowed up between my legs. She was the first to offer an explanation as to what was holding up the elephant I was trying to deliver. "The trouble is your baby's head is turned around to the side. I'm trying to reposition it so that it will be above the cervix. The next time you have a contraction, bear down hard like you are trying to have a bowel movement and I will turn the baby's head at the same time." Weakly, I obeyed her.

Finally my baby was beginning to come. I could feel a big load, as if I was super-constipated. My tiny room was crowded with nurses and doctors who gathered up my sheets and pulled me, bed and all, into the adjacent room. In a second I was off the bed and onto the delivery table. A parade of doctors followed the procession and stood several rows deep around my now-permanently-opened legs. My natural childbirth teacher was there and heard me as I shamelessly begged for gas. "Something, anything, to put me to sleep." I was exhausted. The anesthesiologist put the mask on my face but gave me nothing.

The lady doctor was still with me, her arm back in my belly. "Now bear down again," she instructed me, "when you get your next contraction. Come on, Mother, your baby is about to be born." I took a breath of air and held it. When the next contraction came, I made a body-ripping, ear-splitting grunt that would have made a lion proud and brought Michele Faith Wallace into the world head first.

It was 2:53 A.M. in the morning on January 4, 1952. "Do you want to see your baby, Mother?" asked the lady doctor with the no-frills face.

"Is she healthy and normal?" I asked.

"Yes, Mother," the doctor replied, "and beautiful too."

Michele was seven pounds and six ounces when she was born. Five days later, when we left the hospital, she was eight pounds, and I had not seen her eyes open or her mouth shut once. "Your baby is hungry, Mother. Give her some pabulum and milk in between breast feedings when you get her home," the nurse advised me. "She has kept us all busy since her first hour of birth, screaming mostly for food. However, she is a fine and healthy baby. It is easy to see that she will be smart and spoiled too. Good-bye," said the nurse. "We will see you back here before the year is out."

When I found out I was pregnant again, I welcomed the addition to our family even though I realized our marriage was not a secure one. I had always heard that an only child was apt to be selfish and lonely. At any rate, one child was not enough for me. I would have two children and no more. I didn't long to be a lone woman struggling with two kids, but if I had to, I would. On a teacher's salary I could support my children and myself. I had never intended to be a housewife with no career outside the home. Even when I was a little girl dreaming about being married, we were both going to be out in the world doing something — maybe I would be a glamorous movie star like Dorothy Dandridge or Lena Horne, but working was always a part of being a grown-up.

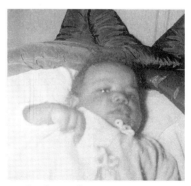

My water broke in the eighth month of my second pregnancy. Earl rushed me to the hospital. We thought that I would immediately go into labor but I didn't. I was admitted to the hospital and then several days passed with many false labor calls before the real thing started. This labor was different from my first. For one thing I was very apprehensive about the health of my

My daughter Barbara, 1953

baby. Everything had been done to insure that my baby would be born healthy, but premature births are unpredictable. I was in labor for four hours and was able to use my natural childbirth training more effectively this time around.

I promised God everything I could think of and on December 15, 1952, at 2 A.M. my prayers were answered — Barbara Faith was born and she was perfect! She weighed six pounds and eight ounces. Although she was tiny, she was the picture of health and, according to the nurses and doctors, Barbara was the most beautiful baby in the entire hospital. The same nurse that had predicted I would return within the year came to report that Barbara was bright, alert, good-natured, and, unlike Michele, rarely cried. I thanked her and assured her that I would never return.

Later, when the doctor came by, I asked him for a prescription for birth control. He was reluctant even to consider this since I was only twenty-two years old and I did not have my husband's permission. I told him that I birthed two babies in one year and that I did not need my husband to tell him that I would not have any more. He realized that I was serious and had me fitted for a diaphragm, which, along with condoms, was the only form of birth control at that time.

I had a studio now in the back room that Earl and I used to share when we were first married. In the evenings when the children were sleeping, I devoted as much time as I could to my art. One of the first paintings I did was of Barbara at about two months old. I was trying to find my own images and learn to paint them since they had not taught me how to do this in my art class.

Sometimes I joined the ongoing conversations in the living room with Earl and his friends. We discussed everything, from philosophy to current politics to what was going on in the street. No matter where the conversation started, however, it always ended up being about the fate of the Negro and the white man's prejudice.

A musician's lifestyle and earnings were uncertain, so we had to make adjustments to deal with the family finances. Earl frequently gave me money for food, only to borrow it back later to help a friend get his horn out of hock. Jazz musicians were a sight to see. They traded suit jackets to wear with mismatched trousers that were either too short or too big. Sometimes I wondered whether their habit of turning their backs to the audience was due to their shame concerning their appearance, rather than any hostility they felt toward the audience.

Now that we had two little girls, Earl was trying to assume some responsibility for being a father and husband. He spent time with the girls on weekends, taking them to the park; and at home he played music for them on the hi-fi so they would get used to hearing the music of Prokofiev, Borodin, Thelonius Monk, Oscar Peterson, and other classical and jazz favorites. More frequently the kids got live performances of Earl's repertoire of classical and modern jazz music, or of Sonny Rollins playing something on his horn. If the radio was turned to a station that played pop music, like "Tennessee Waltz," then the radio was considered "broken" or producing "static." Earl would turn the dial until it was on WQXR, the classical station, or WLIB to hear Symphony Sid, the jazz MC.

At first Earl and I were happy in our life together and our friends were supportive. No one had any money in the early fifties. We would all chip in for beer and chips and sometimes ribs and spaghetti from Sherman's Barbeque. The musicians and performing artists that I knew didn't seem to require the solitude needed by a visual artist. I understood this and always made sure that our house was ready for entertaining, and that the kids were out of the way in the evenings when our company would arrive.

Earl attracted a lot of musicians who came to ask him to transpose music for the various instruments in their bands. Although many of these musicians were brilliant in their medium, they didn't have Earl's technical skills. (Earl had been trained as a classical pianist, composer, and arranger.) Often they implied that he didn't have their improvisational skills or "soul." Maybe they felt that being a Jamaican he couldn't blow like a "cat" from "here." And maybe they were right. At any rate, he never made it as a jazz musician, but he sure helped a lot of them with their music. Among the cadre of jazz musicians who came to our house were Sonny Rollins, Arthur Taylor, Miles Davis, Jackie MacLean, Charlie Parker, and Kenny Drew.

The first angry black men I ever knew were the jazz musicians of the fifties. Their anger came from their daily struggle to be heard. The major radio stations played exclusively pop music performed by white bands with white singers. Black musicians and singers were only played on the so-called black stations (even they were white-owned) like WWRL and WLIB. But the black stations rarely played jazz. Nat King Cole was the exception. The only time I ever played hooky from school was to see Nat King Cole at the Paramount Theater in the 1940s. I was going to George Washington High School at the time. A bunch of us met in front of school one morning and headed downtown in droves, as if we were on a school field trip. When we got down to the Paramount Theater, the whole city's black high school population was there. I saw kids I hadn't seen since elementary school.

Barbara and Michele, circa 1955

Because of their lack of exposure, Charlie Parker, Bud Powell, Miles Davis, Sonny Rollins, and the other jazz greats had a tough time getting an opportunity to cut records and get gigs. However, the frustration of Earl and his musician friends was largely projected onto black people who did not support jazz. "One thing wrong with the Negro . . . " Earl would say bitterly, "he can't just sit back, shut up, and dig it. He's got to be loud, talking and partying all the time, showing off the latest dance step with his chick." The few blacks who went to hear modern jazz music were part of an exclusive circle of the jazz elite. They had a language and lifestyle that was uniquely different: the language was slang and the lifestyle was drugs. This was not true of all jazz musicians or jazz lovers, but it was true of a great many of them.

It was obvious to me that drugs could kill because so many of our friends had died. But slang was deadly in another kind of way; it stifled communication and no one knew what was being talked about. Being married to Earl, who used slang to the exclusion of traditional language, I learned to translate but not to imitate. He would begin each sentence with the word "like." "Like that 'cat's' an 'okee-doke' " (that guy is a nerd) and "Like those 'gray' boys got the 'bread' " (white boys have money). "Like, man, a 'paddy boy blows a yard' on some 'vines' to match his 'short' "(a white boy spends one hundred dollars on a suit to match his car). "Nigger 'cop' a 'short' he be have to live in it to get up that 'yard' down and keep them notes rollin' " (a black man who buys a car has to live in it to afford to put one hundred dollars down and keep up with the monthly payments). Probably the most bizarre usage was when Earl and his male friends addressed each other as "baby" all the time. When I'd hear them say "Hey, baby, what's happening?" I wanted to know, too. By the late sixties and seventies otherwise conventional people were using "like" and "baby" in everyday speech.

More and more Earl opted to speak this way so that often I was the only one in both my family and his who could understand him. One day Earl asked Barbara, my sister, "Have you got any 'bread'?" Barbara went scurrying into the kitchen to check the bread box only to find upon her return that Earl was thanking Jo Jo for the "bean" he had just loaned him. "A bean, what's a bean?" asked Barbara perplexed. "A dollar," said Jo Jo. "One dollar," exclaimed Barbara indignantly, "for bread?"

I had a project to redecorate our apartment. I made new slipcovers for the living room furniture with Mother's help, and draperies for all the windows. Our floors were scruffy and layered with years of old shellac and wax. When Arthur and Burdette Ringgold heard me mention to Earl that I wanted them scraped, they offered to do this for me for free. The two of them got together and scraped all five rooms in a single day.

Burdette Ringgold had been a frequent visitor to our house ever since Barbara was born. I paid little attention to him at first, but Earl liked him. I never saw Birdie outside our home unless I was walking up to 155th Street to catch the bus. Rather mysteriously, Birdie would come darting out of his building to accompany me to the bus stop whenever I walked by. Slowly I began to pay attention to him. He was not only nice, but always considerate and helpful. Whenever he saw me in a jam with the formula and the diapers or the housework, he offered to assist. I was beginning to depend on Birdie for his friendship and support.

I made several drawings of Birdie over the months. Everyone who came to our house had to sit for a drawing. Some people were impatient with sitting and disappointed with the results, but Birdie was a perfect model. He sat patiently and the results never offended him. What's more, he possessed a good sympathetic ear for listening. He knew all about Earl and the trouble I was having with his drug habit — although we never discussed it. There were times when Birdie would stay late into the night waiting up with me for Earl to come home. He sensed my fear that Earl would be coming home high or not at all.

Gradually, Earl began to slip back into his old pattern of getting high all the time.

Barbara and Michele holding their dolls, circa 1955

He'd come home in a stupor with a friend who had found him and walked with him for miles up Riverside Drive to keep his heart beating. I spent half of every day in tears. My life was so wound up in Earl's drug problem, it was all I could think about. There were no rehabilitation programs at this time, and the public was in denial about drug abuse. Earl's family felt that I could save him, despite the fact that I had tried everything and nothing had worked. Finally I decided to leave him. I had two small children to raise. They had no one but me to depend on and Earl, despite his drug problem, was a grown man.

I left Earl for the last time in February of 1954, taking Barbara and Michele back to my mother's home to live. Mother hired a family friend to take care of them in the day-time so that I could attend school full-time. In June of 1955 I graduated from City College and began teaching art in the fall in the New York City Public School system at Junior High School 136, located in Harlem.

My sister, Barbara, and Jo Jo were no longer living with my mother; they had gotten an annulment. It turned out that Jo Jo already had a wife all the time he was married to Barbara. When the wife discovered where they lived and presented herself at the door, Jo Jo disappeared. Barbara went back to work as a dietician and seemed to be enjoying her new single life in her own apartment.

I wanted a divorce from Earl, but the only ground for divorce in New York in the fifties was adultery. What chance did I have of catching Earl with his pants down in another woman's bedroom? None. I knew Flo Kennedy (the famous activist attorney) because her sister Faye and I had gone to school together. Flo pleaded my case for divorce on the grounds of misrepresentation. Earl was a drug addict and I hadn't known that until after I had married him.

The Roman Catholic judge on the bench that morning had a reputation for not granting freedom to women with minor children. He had already thrown out all of the cases that morning and mine was next. Flo eloquently presented my case to the judge and I was very proud to be represented by her. When I was asked to address the judge or Flo, I consistently forgot to address him as "Sir" and Flo as "Madam." The judge screamed at me and intimated that I lacked proper upbringing. At this point, my mother rose from her seat in the witness section and addressed the bench. In one motion the judge, Flo, and I turned to face Mother. "Judge, Your Honor, my daughter comes from a good Christian home and has had a very good upbringing. I don't know why she is not behaving well. She certainly has been taught otherwise." Mother could melt a glacier with her tongue and it worked.

The judge was initially shocked that Mother would dare to speak from the spectators without permission, but she got away with it. He softened and asked me compassionately: "Do you have a job? How do you intend to support your children?"

"Judge, Your Honor, sir . . . ," I responded. The spectators began to chuckle.

"Silence," demanded the judge, "or I'll clear this courtroom."

Everybody froze, including me. "I will be teaching school in the fall," I told him.

"Will you be working for the New York City Public School System?"

"Yes, sir," I said, nervously. He asked Flo to approach the bench and the rest of the proceedings are lost in my memory. But I was granted an annulment and it became final in 1956.

My annulment decree did not make any demands on Earl. He was free to pursue his music and deal with his life and addiction as best he could. Barbara, Michele, and I were now out of his life. I would not hold him financially responsible for their support — that was the decision I had made the day I left him. According to the family court at the time, a man who did not support his children could be a dangerous element in their lives — and, therefore, he had no legal right to see them. If he became rehabilitated from his drug habit, that might change the situation, but in the fifties drug addiction was a hopeless affliction. There was one place in Lexington, Kentucky, where drug addicts went to "dry out," but except for that place, no one ever spoke of a cure or a treatment for drugs.

In June of 1966 Earl's aunt called to tell me that Earl was dead from an overdose of heroin. The girls took the news of their father's death soberly. They hadn't really known him and I could not tell how they felt about his death. I had protected them from what I believed to be an unhealthy self-defeating relationship. After our annulment, he had lived in the apartment building next to ours, and even when we moved again, Earl never lived more than a few blocks away. Had he wanted to, he could have seen the girls as often as he chose to, with or without my permission. To this day, Barbara still blames me for her father not being more present in her life. It's probably easier for her that way. I felt a forced relationship with an indifferent nonsupporting father was worse than no relationship at all. My daughters feel guilty about the lack of connection to their father. I feel guilty, too. Yet I'm not sure how they would feel today if they had really known him for what he became. The man I fell in love with was young and hopeful. The man Earl became was a man with a "monkey on his back" and not much else. Children, by nature, are dependent and the process of childhood is to take (hopefully with gratitude) and to learn, to experience and to grow. Despite being an adult, Earl had nothing to give anymore and only the urge to take.

Mother and Birdie went to Earl's funeral. His new wife and his family and friends were there to mourn his death. Barbara, Michele, and I stayed home.

Men were my closest companions in my twenties. They helped me with my children, and were kind and understanding when I needed a friend. I had very little experience with men whom I did not know well. I never encouraged the possessive type of man, nor the smooth-talking, cool "cats" who recited poetry on the telephone. (That was very hip in the fifties — it meant you were cool but cultured, not just any old dude from the street, but a cat with class.) Any man who tried that act on me was asked to hold on while I got Michele or Barbara to pick up the extension and read something back from their book collection. Let him try to be cool beside *The Cat in the Hat*. I was in the market for a male companion, but not just anybody. I wanted someone who would not only like my daughters but would accept my mother, too. After all, I was very close to her. It was important to me to be with a man who wanted to be with me and my family.

I dated a few men in this period. One man I had known for a while but only from school. Now that I was separated, he asked for a date and I invited him over so that he could meet my family. He was a large tall man. (I never really liked large men, but he was nice enough and very gentle.) We started seeing each other but the relationship was short-lived as it became all too evident that he was a confirmed bachelor.

Most of the young men I knew were going to graduate school and still living in walk-up tenements in Harlem, Bedford-Stuyvesant, or the South Bronx with their mommas. During the sixties a lot of these men crossed over into the black middle class, never to be seen in the ghetto again. This type of guy belonged to a fraternity, and his graduate degree was in social work, education, medicine, or law. He was likely to reject his mother's Pentecostal religion for something more conservative, like the Episcopal church. This kind of man was always in the right place at the right time. Caution was his byword. If he did have a baby, he disapproved of the mother, and was passive about exercising his rights as the father.

In the sixties men like this were often part of the problem and not the solution. A modern-day Uncle Tom, he could not conceal his embarrassment about militant "niggers acting out on the street." He certainly didn't listen to Malcolm, and was not ashamed to tell his white colleagues that he was for "green" not black power. Mistakenly, I thought for a time that I had something in common with men like that.

By the early sixties, however, I found it more and more difficult to fantasize that such men were superior to me. They had superior status, yes, but I always knew that that was because they were men, and as such had more opportunities. Thank God, they found me too dark, too old, too ambitious, too political, or too well educated for them. The fact that I was an artist (an unconventional occupation, to say the least), a divorced woman, and the mother of two children did not help either.

Birdie was my confidant during this trying period. He was — as it turned out — the man I would marry. From the beginning Birdie was easy to be with, and over the years he has never lost that quality. Birdie is a man who was looking for his complement in a mate, not someone to hide behind him. It's not Birdie's nature to be overtly proud of his wife's accomplishments, but I don't believe he would have found me as attractive without them. Birdie's help with my children and my career as an artist has been motivated by his feeling that I was doing something significant, something unreachable in his own life.

The pre-sixties black men had very little opportunity to be someone and the women had even less. My situation was unusual and Birdie recognized and admired my solid family support system — something which he himself did not have. Birdie was part of a pre-sixties consciousness (among some black men) and was confident enough to subordinate his own achievements in favor of his wife's.

Birdie and Mother were good friends, and Barbara and Michele had adored him ever since they were babies. Birdie spent a great deal of time at our house. Frequently he would be there when I returned home with a date. Mother and he would be talking and having a late-night snack, and a lot of my dates wondered why he was always around. I explained to them that he was a good friend, almost like a member of the family, who had seen us through a lot of bad times. They didn't buy it, but I didn't care and considered it none of their business. I knew I was not going to do anything to discourage Birdie from visiting as often as he wanted to.

He was great with the girls. He took them everywhere — to the park and the circus; on picnics; rowing with them in Central Park and ice skating at Rockefeller Center and at the site of the old World's Fair grounds in Queens. If he knew of a movie that the girls might enjoy, like *The Wizard of Oz,* he took them himself or presented the tickets to me so that they would be sure to see it. He was exactly like a father to them. When they were sick with chicken pox or mumps or a cold, he made daily visits until they were well again. The girls took him for granted, expecting to see him on weekends and holidays, and he readily assumed that responsibility.

Birdie, Mother, and a friend of his with his mother-in-law, 1961

I began to take him for granted, too, assuming that I would see him regularly. He constantly proposed marriage to me and was always telling my mother that I was going to be his wife. I was not interested in him as a boyfriend or husband. He was just not my type. He was nice, and my family liked him, but I was looking for someone new. We were such good friends that it would be like marrying my best friend. Why would I want to do that?

Despite the rather heavily defined male/female roles we were all playing, black men and black women had much in common and sought one another's company. The men saw their manhood as being connected to the relationships they had with women. They needed us to confirm their identities, and we needed them in just the same way. The overbearing specter of racism, which hovered over all of us, made us more equal, more able to need one another. We were forced to be together because we were all that we had. No man ever thought he was having a good time socially if there were no women around. Men who were popular with other men were popular because they knew a lot of women. A woman without a man was an "old maid," but a man without a woman was much less. He was a man who had no real place in the world. Needless to say, things have changed over the years, and men as well as women have redefined their roles so that today none of this is necessarily true.

Although I was having fun, I was often made to feel that I was a failure because I was not with my husband. "Why did he leave you?" I was frequently asked. When I responded that I had left him because he was a drug addict, I felt shunned.

Earl's family was a problem, too. They openly resented me for leaving him and terminating our marriage. They also resented my decision to refuse him visitation rights. They knew that he was not liable for the children's support and that I would not interfere with his music or his life, if he did not interfere with mine. But they felt he was cheated out of the benefits of being around his daughters. I felt that Michele and Barbara had been cheated by having only one parent they could depend on. Raising my daughters without their father was one of the most difficult decisions I have ever had to make.

Living with Mother when Barbara and Michele were young was very good for all of us. We might never have left if Andrew had stayed away. He was now a part of the new drug culture of the fifties. He had been sent away once by order of the court to get a rest from his drug habit. When he returned he moved in with Mother. It was now time for the girls and me to move again. If I didn't want my children to be with their father because of drugs, then I certainly didn't want them to be with their uncle in the same condition. I left and Birdie helped me find an apartment and moved us into it. I began to take a serious fresh look at Birdie. He was so much a part of us by now that it was becoming difficult to imagine life without him.

One evening Birdie and I went out on the town — barhopping in Harlem. It was always great fun to go out with him because he knew everybody in the bars and on the street. "Hey, man, what's happening?" is all I heard when we hit the street. We were having a great time that night. We saw Redd Foxx at the Baby Grand on 125th Street, where he and Nipsey Russell played all the time. Later in the evening we stopped at a new bar that had just been opened by a friend of Birdie's. We were having a drink on him to celebrate the opening. "What's the lady drinking?" Birdie's bartender friend asked. "Oh, a Tom Collins," I said. Birdie was having the same, so I didn't understand why he was putting two fingers up like donkey's ears behind my head. (I could see him doing this in the bar mirror.) The bartender seemed to read him perfectly and went straight to work mixing two shots of gin in each Tom Collins. I must have had three of those before I began to realize how wonderful my companion was, and that the "donkey's ears" had something to do with it. We were in each other's arms before the night was over, making love for the first time. We had taken a long time to get there, but now the time was right.

Shortly after that night I finally said yes to one of Birdie's frequent proposals of marriage, but now Birdie wanted to avoid the issue. He thought we should live together first. I refused and stopped seeing him. I remembered the women we knew when we were growing up who had "front-room boarders." Often people thought they were really married to the men they were living with until the man died, and suddenly the real wife and his grown children appeared to claim the body and take it down South for a family burial. "Living together" was for women who didn't value the contract of marriage as I did. I would no sooner put money in the bank without a passbook than I would put time and energy into a man without the paper. What I wanted was a partner, a man who would not mind putting it in writing.

Finally, Birdie went to see the pastor of the Lutheran church that the children and I were attending. The pastor regularly made home visits to the members of the congregation. One Saturday he came with the news that Birdie wanted him to talk to me about getting married. I was impressed. My sister, Barbara, and my daughter Michele had secretly measured my ring finger so that Birdie could buy me an engagement ring.

"How long do you think we would have lasted if we had lived together instead of getting married?" I asked Birdie recently.

He responded, smiling wryly, "Not past the first year, if that."

"Why didn't you want to marry me?" I asked him.

"I didn't want the responsibility," he admitted.

"And then later you did?" I asked.

"No, I wanted you," Birdie replied.

On May 19, 1962, Birdie and I got married in a church wedding at Bethany Lutheran Church in the Bronx. Pastor Christ married us. I felt that old frog in my throat as I tried to recite: "I, Faith, promise to love, honor . . . " Birdie blasted out, "I, Burdette, promise to take Faith as my . . . " Where were these words which resounded from the rafters coming from? I saw Birdie standing next to me with tears in his eyes. "My God," I worried, "what does that mean?" I remembered that my father used to cry at weddings.

Often a man's mother has difficulty getting along with the woman her son marries. This is especially true if the man involved expects the two women to be rivals and, secretly or otherwise, enjoys seeing them fight over him. I don't know whether Birdie actually enjoyed the constant altercation between his mother and me, but he certainly did nothing to stop it. Interestingly, Earl had been very protective of me. He had never allowed his mother to make little digs about my hair, or my clothes, or whatever she thought would make me upset. I often heard Earl's mother speak about the "dumb Americans" and knew I was being contrasted to a "nice West Indian girl." But Earl was the first in his family to be born in America, and he had a stated preference for things American, especially women. Birdie, like me, was born in Harlem, and his family, like

Me and Birdie on our
wedding day, May 19, 1962

mine, migrated North from the South — his came from Alabama in the early 1900s. But there the similarity ends. The Blandons, Birdie's mother's family, would have been insulted if you called them black. The Blandon women, all light-skinned southern belles, married "black" men — except Birdie's mother, who married Birdie's father, a light-skinned man whose father was white. I always thought Birdie was very well adjusted to his "mixed blood," and unlike many other light-skinned black people, he never chooses to make it an issue.

For some time my life with Birdie became a burden. I tried to clear time for my painting, but it was impossible. The children's clothes were constantly piling up, and before I could wash the dishes from one meal, it was time to start the next. The house was never quite clean and Birdie objected to having someone come in to help me.

Birdie and me, 1961

I was also afraid of becoming too isolated. What I didn't know was that Birdie wanted just that. He was determined to be the man in his home and began by building a wall between himself and my mother. Mother tried to continue to help me in the ways she always had, but Birdie rebuked her at every turn. She became proud and hurt and stayed away. I felt caught in the middle. I needed and loved them both. What was I to do?

The worst thing about our marriage was that Birdie never took responsibility for being a companion during waking hours. He always came home just in time to go to bed. During the week Birdie worked at night and did not get home until two or three o'clock in the morning. The next day he would get up just in time to go to work — or to go out, if he was off from work. He knew he had me trapped in the house because of the girls, and because of my art. I figured out a plan which, although it didn't really work, made me feel less helpless in my situation.

On the weekends when he went out. I did my art work as usual. If he was not home by midnight, I got dressed and hid in the closet. Later, when he came home, I would be still in there bedded down for the night. After he searched the house for me and called my mother to find out where I was, he went to bed. Then I made my move out of the closet and into the living room where I'd make a lot of noise as if I had just come home from a real great party. Birdie would get out of bed and find me fully dressed with a big smile on my face. One night I almost got caught coming out of the closet, so I had to change my strategy. After this, when I saw Birdie come out of the garage late at night, I'd watch him until he crossed the street and walked into our apartment building — then I'd hide in the incinerator room. After he got into our apartment, I would put the key in the door and enter smiling, dressed like I had been out on the town. And some nights, just to let him know I hadn't come home alone, I'd yell a few good-byes at the empty elevator before it went down.

On the weekends Birdie went out with his buddies or to see his mother and step-father, just as he had always done before we got married. He often took Barbara and Michele out — ice skating and rollerskating, to the zoo and the park. I complained about his time away from home, but that time was really my time to escape. I used it for my art, and creating art became my salvation.

Earl and Burdette both could be characterized as gentle men who had a bark, but no bite. As boys, neither had ever belonged to a street gang, nor was either prone to having fights or disputes in the neighborhood or at school. They both could be rather passionate in arguments; neither of my husbands could be characterized as a passive man. However, I didn't expect that either would hit me, but both did.

The incident with Earl in 1952 was caused by my disagreeing with something he said. As I recall, Birdie, Raymond, and Toussaint were visiting us at the time of the argument. Before I knew it, Earl had slapped me across the face while I was ironing a shirt for him. I was so embarrassed and angry when Earl slapped me that I wanted to come back at him with the hot iron, but I thought better of it. He believed he had set-tled the argument and saved face in front of his friends. They were visibly shaken. "Earl, you didn't have to slap Faith — after all, she's a woman, man. You two talk this out," they counseled as they walked out, leaving us alone.

Earl went to sleep as was his habit when there was a problem that needed to be solved immediately. I stayed up plotting my next move. I had seen my father hit my mother once and remembered that she had gone right out the fire escape window to a neighbor's apartment to call the cops. I have never seen so many police before in all my life. They took Daddy to the police station and, by his own admission, "beat the hell out of him." He never hit her again.

While Earl was sleeping, I went to the police station and told the desk officer about the incident. He was very understanding. "Go home," he said. "When you get there, there will be an officer in a parked car outside your building. If you want him to go upstairs with you, go over to the car and request this." I did as he told me. There were three cops in the car, and two of them accompanied me upstairs. When Earl saw two huge cops (one black and one white) staring down at his nude — to the waist — body, he sprung up. He ran into the children's room, asking, "Has something happened to my baby?" and returned with Michele in his arms, looking perplexed but calmer. "Put your baby down, Mr. Wallace. Your wife reported that you hit her tonight and she is afraid you might try to do that again," the officer said. "Oh, no," Earl responded "I didn't even hurt her. It was just a slap." The officer retorted, "Your wife doesn't like being slapped and the next time you feel like hitting somebody, find a man. Because if we have to come here again we're going to work you over — let you see how it feels to be manhandled. Is that okay with you, Mrs. Wallace, or do you want us to take him in now?" Earl's eyes got as big as saucers. I assured the officers that, should there be a next time, I would report it. "I don't think there will be a next time, officer. I love my wife and I don't want to do anything to hurt her," Earl said. But I was still angry. Although he never hit me again, no matter how heated the debate, I never forgot it; what's even more important is neither did he.

Birdie used to say to me, "Don't tell other men what Earl did to you because they will only do it too."

"But why?" I would ask.

"Oh, I don't know," he would say. "Men are just like that."

If you ask me, I think it's part of human nature to turn on a person when you are very close. That is why it's important that the parameters of a relationship be clearly set and maintained.

One day early on in our marriage Burdette hit me; we were having an ongoing disagreement about his right to go out and mine to stay home. I heard him bragging to his mother and stepfather on the telephone that he was going to straighten me out on this. "I hope you don't hit that woman, because if you do, she will have you arrested," they cautioned him. But Birdie told his mother, "I'm not going to take it anymore." Somehow he felt compelled to have a showdown with me early one Saturday morning. I was in bed when I heard a loud roar and felt Birdie jump on me and pin me down with a bear hug to the bed. I wrestled him to the floor and he continued to yell and knock me off my feet each time I stood up. Like Earl, Birdie did not hurt me, but he did hurl me around the room in an alarming way. I wanted him to stop but he continued to yell and run into me and hold me in a bear hug. By the time his mother and stepfather arrived, we were rolling on the floor. I was disheveled and very embarrassed — especially since they disliked our marriage and would have been overjoyed to see it end. In a state of frenzy, I called the police. To our surprise, the policeman who came was Leroy, the best man at our wedding. "I want you to arrest Birdie for attacking me," I screamed when Leroy came in the door.

Leroy began "sweet-talking" us. "Now we're all friends and I was the best man at your wedding. How's that going to look if I take 'my man' in? You two come on and kiss and make up," Leroy pleaded. But Burdette was now so caught up in the act that he couldn't stop. He ran into me and caught me in a bear hug again — this time right in front of the officer. "Oh, man," Leroy said, "now I have to take you in. You made me a witness."

In the meantime my mother called. When she heard about the ruckus going on, she, too, rushed over. Now both of our mothers were there to see Leroy take Birdie off to the precinct. Leroy had

Mother and three grandchildren, 1962

planned to take Birdie down to the Tombs (the city jail) in his car but he was unable to do so, and it finally ended up with Birdie having to ride in a police wagon sandwiched between lice-contaminated derelicts, thieves, and murderers. (I have always wanted to hear the details of his experience that night, but he has never shared them with me.) Birdie hardly deserved such a fate, but what was I to do?

The night court judge was deadly serious. Birdie was too: in just those few hours he had been incarcerated Birdie already looked like a criminal. He had grown a stubble, his face and shirt were dirty, and he had a tough-guy smirk on his face as if he had been doing time at the "Big House." But the judge, a black man himself, didn't care that Birdie was a man with no history of prior arrest; he didn't like men hitting women. "Do you want to press charges?" the judge asked me.

"Well . . . ," I said, glancing at my husband, who was rearing back on his heels with his hands behind his back, just like James Cagney. "No, Your Honor," I said. "He has never done this before and I am sure he will never do it again."

"I want you to sit down and think about it and I'll call you back later. Maybe you'll change your mind," said the judge, pounding his gavel and moving on to the next case.

I took a seat on the bench in the courtroom knowing full well I would not press charges against Birdie. He had learned his lesson: if he ever hit me again, he knew I would call the cops. I had a feeling he would not try it again. (Although we have had some screaming arguments in our thirty-two years of marriage, he has never again resorted to violence.)

The judge warned Birdie that if he ever came before him again for hitting me, no matter what I said, he would lock him up. We went home that night in silence and, for many weeks thereafter, Birdie and I were cool toward one another. It took a few years before he could talk about the arrest. But later he admitted that I did the right thing.

Birdie was not a professional man. He belongs to the forties, when a good many black men opted to look for a job after getting a high school diploma. He found a position at General Motors in their automobile plant in Tarrytown, New York. Since 1956 he worked in the paint shop, the body shop, on the assembly line, the automobile repair maintenance crew, and so forth doing routine operations. Only in 1992 did he retire after thirty-six years. Like my father, he was depressed about his job, but he saw it as a way to support a family, and as the dues he had to pay for not having continued his education. Although his life had the outward look of prosperity — growing up as he did in "409" on Edgecombe Avenue — it lacked real security, the kind that enables a kid to get ahead in school. I once asked him, "Birdie, how did you like the way you were raised?" (He was an only child and was brought up by his aunt and uncle, not his mother.) He answered without hesitation, "I raised myself." Not many people can do that successfully, but he did.

Birdie and I are different yet we are also very much alike. We were brought up at the same time (he is one year older than I am) and in the same neighborhood. We know and admire many of the same people, places, and things. Throughout all of our problems and our long marriage loyalty is what has kept us together. (My stepfather may have been right when he said that loyalty to others brings happiness in life.)

CHAPTER 4: MY MOTHER WAS PERFECT, OR SO SHE SAID

Mother posing, 1945

My mother was a treasure. I openly adored her. Not only did she raise me carefully and lovingly but she was also my best friend. She was intelligent, forceful, and physically and mentally agile. She could do a split, a headstand, and she even learned to swim at seventy. Her career as a Harlem fashion designer in the 1950s and 1960s was brilliant and made her an unsung pioneer in black fashion. Later, when she became my collaborator, she inspired my new medium: the quilt. We made our first and only quilt together in 1980. Since then, with the wealth of knowledge and skills she imparted to me, I have made eighty-five or more quilts. There was nothing Willi Posey Jones could not do once she set her mind to it.

The Poseys, my mother's family, came from Jacksonville, Florida, to New York City in the early 1900s. Uncle Cardoza, my mother's oldest brother, was the first to arrive in 1918. After completing his army service in World War I, he had settled in New Jersey, where he got a job in the post office. As was customary with families who migrated from the South, he then helped bring the rest of his family North. My aunt Bessie came next (she was the oldest of the four sisters); then Mother, Grandmother Ida, and Uncle Hilliard (the youngest of the Posey children) and so on until they were all here. The family settled in Harlem, got jobs, went to school, married, and raised their children within blocks of one another.

The Joneses, my father's family, were also from Florida. My father was the only member of his family who came to settle in New York City. He had been brought up in

Tampa and came in 1921, when he was eighteen years old. Young men often got a job on a boat to get here and Daddy came North that way. To my knowledge, he never went back to Tampa, not even for a single visit.

One of my favorite diversions as a youngster was looking at my mother's old photograph albums. The pictures of my mother and father always seemed funny to me then; now, of course, they are among my most prized possessions and give me a sense of family history I would not otherwise have. The scene within the photographs is often taken from a rooftop, with my parents posing dramatically, like actors in silent films. They are dressed in old-fashioned clothes. My father is decked out in pin-striped suits, spats, and black-and-white spectator shoes. Mother wears lacy dresses with low waistlines and satin sashes, silk stockings, and pointy-toed shoes with T-straps. Their beach pictures show them wearing long-legged bathing suits that look like heavy thermal underwear with stripes. In one picture that I love, Mother is wearing knickers and a large cap. She looks as if she is going horseback riding, but it was just the style at that time. From the pictures of them on the rooftop, I discovered both Mother and Daddy took violin and tap dancing lessons.

I wanted to know everything about my mother; she was, after all, a model for me. As I grew up, I began to criticize her flamboyancy, yet, even so, I always admired her personality, strength, and courage. Most people will believe whatever we say about our parents. It is my responsibility to keep my mother's truths and pass them on — one day I hope my daughters and granddaughters will do the same for me.

My mother was a very little girl when her father died in Jacksonville. Grandpa Bunion (Mother always referred to him as Professor B. B. Posey) was a highly regarded teacher and school principal. His wife, Ida Bingham Posey, was a teacher in his school and she and their six children moved with him around the South, where he set up a series of schools. From everything I have heard of him, it's clear to me that my grandfather was his own man and had a positive influence on everyone around him. Grandpa Bunion, a dominant nineteenth-century black man, was the son of slaves. He knew Booker T. Washington; indeed, he had introduced Booker T. to the townspeople of Palatka, Florida, when he came to speak there. He also knew and worked with Mary McLeod Bethune. Thus, he knew the great black educators of his time and played a role in nineteenth-century southern black history.

I never met my grandfather, but I have inherited his tradition of teaching. I have copies of his teaching certificates issued in 1887 from the states of Florida and South

Carolina. We are a family of teachers. From their earliest years, my daughters also displayed a natural facility for communicating knowledge and ideas. I have always encouraged them to share what they know with others, and they have been teaching for almost as long as they have been learning.

Ida Bingham Posey, my mother's mother, was a mild-mannered woman and a lady. After Grandpa Bunion's death in 1910, she moved to New York City, where she earned her living making clothes for friends. Her life without her husband was a lonely one, and she died in Mount Sinai Hospital in 1927 at the age of fifty.

My mother was devoted to her mother, and I suspect that in many ways they were very much alike. Grandma Ida's parents, Peter and Betsy Bingham, had been slaves who had acquired land and property in Palatka, Florida, after the Civil

Mother, circa 1918

War. The earliest traceable member of the family is my great-great-grandmother, Susie Shannon, Betsy Bingham's mother. Susie was half Cherokee Indian, and in her youth had long black hair that we kids were later to admire when growing up in Harlem in the thirties. At the movies we saw Native Americans fighting to reclaim their land, but none of us had ever seen a heroic African. The movies we saw portrayed bogus Africans who willingly submitted to the white man's domination and — what's even more absurd — lived their lives in total terror of the jungle they were born in. Alex Haley's African roots would have been a revelation to us then.

Mother and I disagreed about many things. For example, Mother was a bit of a prude, although to look at her you would never have guessed it. She wore tight-fitting clothes and short skirts, which revealed her youthful legs — Mother had the body of a much younger woman. Her opinions about s-e-x, however, were straight out of the nineteenth century. Had she practiced what she preached to us while we were growing up? Was she really as pure of mind as she made us believe? Was she a virgin when she got married? Did she enjoy sex with my father? My mother would have sooner told her age than answered such questions. I am no sexual militant, but at the same time my best-kept secrets are not about sex. (I tell my age, too.) So there marks a big difference between my mother and myself.

One thing I was never able to do was to catch my mother in the wrong. She should have been a magician, because right before your eyes she could turn wrong into right. For example, one day I asked her: "Mother, what do you consider your worst fault?"

"Well, I don't think I have any faults," she replied, trying to appear humble.

"No faults?" I exclaimed. "How come? Are you perfect?"

"Oh no, I'm not perfect," she answered with a coy smile, "but you know what I mean?"

"No," I declared, "I don't know what you mean. If you are not perfect, what do you consider your faults? Tell me one."

"I don't know what you're getting at. You tell me what you think my faults are," Mother barked. She then stormed out of the room, thereby ending the conversation.

When I started (in the late 1970s) to write about Mother, I decided to call her on the telephone and try once again to question her. My mother was now married to a very fine man (they had married in 1977) and her life had changed — maybe her answers had, too.

"Mother," I said, "what are your faults?"

"Being too sympathetic, too giving from way back . . . too understanding . . . too friendly . . . but then there are some people I don't go near. Sometimes I know I'm too sympathetic. I have to fight myself to stop before I get hurt. You can do too much, you know? That's my biggest happiness," she said, responding in a stream-of-consciousness mode, never taking a breath.

"If this makes you happy, how could it be a fault?" I asked her.

"Well, yes," she said, "I don't have any bad habits: no smoking, no drinking, no . . ."

"Well, tell me, Mother, " I said, "have you made any mistakes?"

"Yes, I've made mistakes in raising you all. But that's natural. You can't help that, if you are so sympathetic as a mother," she answered smugly.

"Are you a happy woman, Mother?" I asked.

"Yes," she said. "I have a nice husband. . . . I am a very contented, happy woman. We live well. We get mad. We fight. We think any minute we're going to have a divorce. . . . We have food, shelter, and money to do whatever we want to do. We have complete freedom. He doesn't want to travel, but other than that I'm happy in my older years. I don't need anything I can't get."

"Okay, Mother," I said, "what are your strong points?"

"Sharing," she quipped. "I am too generous. That's it, I've always been like that."

I decided to ask Pop-Pop (my stepfather's name was Thomas H. Morrison Sr., but we all called him "Pop-Pop") the same question to see if their responses were alike. "Do you have any faults, and if so, what are they?"

"I do have faults, because I like things orderly. I like to know where things are," he responded quickly. "However, I don't think I have any outstanding faults. I don't drink or gamble and these are the biggest faults a man has to worry about."

"Pop-Pop," I asked, "what are your good points?"

"I'm very strong on details," he announced rather proudly. "That's why I have been stuck so many times with being the secretary in organizations. In the Masons I was secretary for twenty-six years and in the Elks for eighteen years . . . because of precision. Credit it to the Army."

"What do you mean?" I queried.

"I was in the National Guard from 1932 to 1960 when I retired as a captain."

"And your job in the post office?" I probed.

"I was a vehicle analyst and assistant superintendent for the last fifteen years, and never lost a case," he boasted.

"Are you a happy man, Pop-Pop?" I pried further.

"Yes," he answered, "because I don't have anything to worry about. If I can't do anything about something, I don't worry about it. That's my secret."

We ended our discussion with his thoughts about why he and Mother were so happy. "Loyalty and consideration for other people. We don't live our lives just for ourselves," he responded thoughtfully and complacently.

Mother began sewing when I was a very small child. We had an old-fashioned, foot-pedal Singer sewing machine that had belonged to Ida Posey, my grandmother. Mother learned to sew on it and so did I. When I was a child I had a lot of fun on that old sewing machine and, until recently, I still sewed on it. Mother would give me scraps of fabric or pieces of patterns she had discarded and I would sew them together in an attempt to make outlandish-looking shoes and pocketbooks — once I even tried to make a brassiere. I never thought I was making art, and though I loved the process, I never liked the results because they always looked so homemade.

Mother with National Association of Fashion Designer friends at her birthday party, 1957

Mother, on the other hand, was never critical of herself. By the time we moved to Edgecombe Avenue in 1940, Mother was already designing and sewing professionally. Over the years, I observed the pride she took in her work. When she got a job in a factory making children's dresses in the late forties, her skills became more refined. She went to the Fashion Institute of Technology (FIT) to learn how to cut and make patterns. She was so talented and creative with fabrics and not at all afraid to take risks in her new field.

Mother had been very sociable in her early years when she first came to New York City and had belonged to a club called the Aristocratic Eight. After marrying and having children, however, she lost contact with her friends and the clubs. Now, in the early fifties, we were all grown up and Mother was free to pursue a career as a fashion designer and make social contacts with other women. She joined the Association of Negro Business and Professional Women's clubs and the National Association of Fashion and Accessory Designers (NAFAD), the black fashion designers' organization. She participated in their annual fashion shows and met many Harlem designers who became lifelong friends. Among them were Barbara Mayo, Margaret Floyd, and Lois Bell. These women designed beautiful clothes but were largely ignored in the fashion industry. They showed their collections, accordingly, in rented ballrooms at the Waldorf Astoria Hotel downtown and the Theresa Hotel on 125th Street in Harlem. Their customers were fashionable Harlem women who wanted their clothes custom-made.

Mother gave her first fashion show in 1950. I was the emcee and I will never forget the experience. Mother rented a small club on 125th Street for the show but its dressing room was so small that Mother's seven or so models had to undress in the hallway and in the bathroom. Although the models had rehearsed their appearance, it was all Mother could do to get each one dressed and out on the runway. I was also a wreck because the models appeared out of order with the written account of their garments — so I had to describe their outfits from memory. Fortunately for me I knew the clothes, having assisted Mother with the hand-work. It was my first time speaking to an audience of any kind and I was terrified. Mother came up to me during the show and, holding her hand over the microphone, said, "Your hands are shaking. Stop it, and speak into the microphone." After that she made me rehearse at home using a tape recorder.

Sometimes when I would model myself, Mother was the emcee, often lapsing into song whenever there was a lull between models coming onstage. She was really good at it too, even though Barbara and I were embarrassed by her overly relaxed manner onstage. Mother had studied tap dancing when she was a kid and wanted a career on the stage, but her father had been against the idea of stage work. In those days, show business was considered a sure road to hell. But through her fashion shows, Mother got her chance to be in front of an audience, something she obviously felt comfortable doing and totally enjoyed.

Among Mother's many professional models were the beautiful Ann Porter and Yvonne Mullings. These early black models never had the opportunity to make it big in the fashion world — unlike the black models of today. My sister, Barbara, although she was not professionally trained, was also one of Mother's best models; she was no longer working as a dietician but

Madame Willi Posey attending a bride and her father, circa 1950

Me modeling for Mother, 1950s

was teaching home economics in public school. I modeled for Mother, too, and so did my cousin Freda (the daughter of Aunt Edith, my mother's sister) and my two daughters, Barbara and Michele. It was quite the family business!

In the late sixties, as I began to gain weight, I stopped modeling and became Mother's emcee for all her shows. I had been teaching art for many years by then, so appearing in front of an audience was no longer the challenge it once was. Now I enjoyed this "Master of Ceremonies" role almost as much as Mother did.

Mother's specialty was weddings; she would make the bride's dress and trousseau, and the bridesmaids' gowns. She enjoyed weddings most because she could get involved with the family and the festivities. Mother loved people. If I had had my wish, I would have set her up in an elegant boutique on Madison Avenue where her clothes would have been available to smartly dressed women everywhere. But, alas, I was only a struggling artist throughout her entire life.

In the late sixties Mother went to Ghana and Nigeria in West Africa and came back with a wealth of African-inspired fashion ideas, together with African fabrics for her Harlem clientele. There was now a thriving market for African-inspired clothes in Harlem. By the seventies, Mother was no longer giving fashion shows but she still had her regular customers who needed elegant gowns, new outfits, or whole wardrobes.

I guess I took it for granted that Mother would always keep me fashionably dressed in clothes that fit me perfectly. Mother's clothes had a distinctive look and were almost always ensembles — two or more pieces that were worn together. Sometimes she would make a wrap-around skirt or a coat that wrapped around and tied, instead of button-down. She made short-sleeved coats with deep-cut necklines, to be worn with a high-neck, long-sleeved dress. After going to Africa in the mid-1970s, she often combined several prints together to form a single garment — like a patchwork quilt. The seams in Mother's garments were turned in and clean-finished so that there were no raw edges; she called them French seams. She prided herself that her garments were as beautifully made inside as on the outside. She used only the best fabrics and took much care in selecting them from wholesale dealers in the garment district. Her trips to Europe, and later to Africa, inspired her, but her approach, as with the tankas she made for my paintings, always had her own special touch. She made Michele a white lace pantsuit for her high school graduation in 1969 that was unique at the time. By the mid-1960s Mother's clientele had changed from young brides to older women, and so she began to specialize in larger sizes. She could cut a pattern from a person's measurements that would fit like a glove. Mother could make a person who might otherwise be difficult to fit look great. She had learned to do this at the Fashion Institute of Technology.

My sister Barbara modeling in wrap-around skirt, 1950s

For years after her death I rambled around trying to find clothes I could wear. Now I buy designer clothes from small boutiques mostly in California, but I'm still always looking for designs that remind me of Mother's. Recently I found a California designer who made a suit jacket with a peplum that looked like one of Mother's designs from the 1940s — I bought four of them in different colors.

If Mother had been a rich woman she would have been a philanthropist, because she gave a lot of time and money to community causes. At Christmastime she would go with a group of her models to visit needy patients at Harlem Hospital, taking them useful but beautifully wrapped gifts. Mother also made annual donations to the Mission Society for Camp Minisink, a summer camp for Harlem youth. These donations were presented at her fashion shows.

In 1972 Mother began to collaborate with me by making the tankas for my Slave Rape Series and the costumes for the Family of Woman Mask Series. What was so wonderful about collaborating with her was her ingenious solutions to design problems. For example, I was not sure how the tankas should look for the Slave Rape

*Ann Porter, sister Barbara, Barbara Murray, and
Mother giving Christmas presents to needy patients
at Harlem Hospital, 1950s*

Series. The Tibetan tankas I had shown
Mother were cut out of a single piece of cloth
and were not patched. When she was a little
girl growing up in Florida, Mother had
learned quilt-making in the free-hand piecing
technique her grandmother, Betsy Bingham,
had taught her. The result was that Mother's
tankas were an amazing and original blend: a
tanka that was Tibetan and African inspired,
and yet also drew heavily from the African-
American women's pieced quilting tradition.

In 1980 Mother and I collaborated on our
first and only quilt, *Echoes of Harlem,* for an
exhibition titled "The Artist and the Quilt."
There were twelve women artists in this show,
including Alice Neel, Joyce Kozloff, Betye Saar,
Miriam Schapiro, Marilyn Lanfear, Isabel
Bishop, and Charlotte Robinson. Each artist
was to collaborate with a quilt-maker. For me,
the most natural person to collaborate with
was obviously Mother. I told her that I would
paint a series of portraits for the center of our
quilt. Mother wanted to piece together basket shapes with triangles cut (free-hand) from
fabric pieces to make a quilt border around these painted portraits. I was aghast because
I thought free-hand cut baskets and triangles of different sizes would look unprofession-
al. Today I wish Mother had made these because they would have looked wonderful. But,
not knowing at that time anything about the tradition of African-American quilts, I
didn't realize where my mother's free-hand design approach was coming from. I reluctantly made a drawing of her quilt idea for the two of us to ponder, but I wish now we
had followed it through and incorporated it into the actual quilt design.

Mother died on October 28, 1981. People say she died a beautiful death because she
was not sick; she just went to sleep and didn't wake up. At the time my daughter
Barbara was pregnant with her first child (Faith Willi was born in March 1982), and
Mother was making Barbara a winter maternity coat. The ironing board was up and the

coat pieces, freshly cut, were waiting for Mother's hands the next morning. But Mother had a heart attack that night and never woke up again.

We had just finished working on the International Ringgold Doll Collection and a doll kit. Mother had made all the clothes for the dolls. And, although I had only requested one outfit for each of the twenty-four dolls, Mother actually had made many more — it was as if she wanted to make sure that I would never run out. The doll kit was an idea I had to satisfy a growing request for people to make dolls like mine. The kit was made of two flat pieces of cloth with the doll image printed on them, and sold for ten dollars. Mother had helped me pack these doll kits and the instructions, but this turned out sadly to be our last project together. Accordingly, I have always regretted that it was not more successful.

Mother left me with a rich endowment of ideas and memories. If I live to be as old as Susie Shannon, my great-great-grandmother (who was one hundred and ten years of age when she died), I would never need more. Not a day passes that I don't wish I could tell my mother about all the many wonderful things that have happened to me since she died: a twenty-year retrospective at the Studio Museum in Harlem; a twenty-five-year retrospective that traveled to thirteen museums; a senior professorship at the University of California at San Diego; seven honorary doctorates including one from my alma mater, the City College of New York; five children's books that I authored and illustrated; this autobiography; over a hundred awards, honors, citations, and grants, public and private commissions (including two thirty-foot mosaic murals to be installed in New York's 125th Street IRT subway in 1995); an increasingly happy marriage; two wonderful daughters; three beautiful grandchildren; and many, many new friends.

In 1981 when Mother died I was in a slump with my career and I don't believe Mother ever thought I would achieve my dream. She knew so well the obstacles I struggled against. I knew when Mother died that I would have to reach out and find new friends to fill her void.

I had planned to do another quilt with Mother before she died. We had discussed making a doll quilt, but she died before we could get it off the ground. However, she had cut out all the dolls' dresses from a beautiful printed fabric and left them for me to decide on a composition. Finally I came up with the image of a mother and children and went on a quilting marathon. I finished *Mother's Quilt* in just two days. The quilt is made of eight doll shapes (a mother and seven daughters) cut out of black satin fabric (they each wear a doll's dress designed by Mother) and appliquéd onto a bright red cloth background. The faces have painted and embroidered details and the hair is made of red, orange, and blue braided yarn. *Mother's Quilt* is one of my favorite pieces and I decided never to sell it — it's in my private collection.

After that I planned to make a quilt each year in Mother's memory. From 1980, when we created *Echoes of Harlem* together, through 1994, I have made over eighty quilts. Obviously I needed help with this; since Mother's death I have had some very gifted artist assistants. My first was Barbara Pollack, a lawyer-turned-artist who came to assist me in 1985. At this time I was making my third quilt, *The Street Story Quilt.* This large three-part quilt measured ninety inches high and one hundred forty-four inches wide and marked the beginning of my working with assistants other than Mother. The story, painting, and quilting on this work were so extensive that it took a year to complete. Lisa Yi, my second assistant, was a graduate student at Columbia University's School of Art, and began to work with me in 1986. She helped me with *Faith Ringgold's Over 100 Pound Weight Loss Performance Story Quilt* (my weight-loss quilt and performance costume) in 1986 and with *Tar Beach* from the Woman on a Bridge Series in 1988, together with all the other quilts I did in this period. Yi also helped edit my stories and made wonderful nutritious and calorie-conscious lunches. It was during this period that I lost a hundred pounds and Yi's cooking helped keep it off. Yi, a painter now, has since become a fine quilt-maker too. Denise Mumm has been with me since 1989. She just recently quilted my two largest works, a nine-by-seventeen-foot quilt commissioned by De Hostos Community College in the Bronx, and a nine-by-twelve-foot quilt commissioned by Percent for Art for Public School 22, an elementary school in Crown Heights, Brooklyn. Mumm, a dressmaker as well as a wonderful mixed-media sculptor, has been with me for five years and in that time she has learned how to create borders, make backings, and quilt from my detailed drawings. In 1993 Mumm restored the 1973 Slave Rape tankas mother had made. I have often thought how pleased Mother would have been if she had been able to see how faithfully Mumm maintained the original designs.

In June of 1982, just shortly after Mother's death, I was awarded a fellowship at the MacDowell Colony in Peterborough, New Hampshire. I never wanted the isolation of an artists' colony in Mother's lifetime because I needed to be near her for our collaboration. But now it seemed like a good idea to leave my family and be alone with my grief. At this time I decided to do a series of works in tribute to Mother titled Baby Faith and Willi. (Mother had died just a few months before my granddaughter Baby Faith was born, so it seemed natural to portray them together in art as they hadn't been able to meet in life.) The imagery in this five-part abstract series represents children. Above the children in each painting is a solitary hovering-flying figure (my first), which I think suggests the presence of Mother. I referred to these works and others of this period as "painting the inside of my head." Up to that point my art had always been about specific people and issues. During this period of mourning, however, I wanted just to paint and not think about what or why. That summer at MacDowell Colony I began another series of sixteen paintings titled the Emanon Series. ("Emanon" was a name I got from a jazz piece by Dizzy Gillespie which spelled "no name" backwards.) In order to produce an abstract image in my painting I positioned myself close to the canvas and made strokes of color all over it, one color at a time, until I had covered the whole surface. When I finally moved away from the canvas, I was surprised and excited by the abstract composition I had created. There were all sorts of strange images there, so I was satisfied that I was indeed "painting the inside of my head" and not anything else. I made borders painted in gold or silver for these works from glued-on canvas. Had Mother been alive to collaborate with me, she would have made a beautiful tanka for each of the paintings. In 1983 I painted four abstract paintings which I named the Dah Series. They appear to be unframed because the glued-on borders are included as part of each painting. They got their name from Baby Faith, who was only one year old when she was asked what she thought of these paintings. She responded with "Dah." We had always thought "dah" was short for "da da" or daddy but maybe my granddaughter was showing an early appreciation for art. At any rate her title stuck.

I painted another series titled California Dah while at the University of California in San Diego (where I was now teaching) in the winter quarter of 1984. The five paintings of this series were bordered on the sides and bottom by long lengths of hanging raffia. As they were intended to be used as a backdrop for my new storytelling masked performance piece titled *The Bitter Nest,* I inserted grommet holes on the tops so they could be hung up onstage.

In 1990 I went to Paris and la Napoule in the South of France to create the most ambitious of all my tributes to Mother — The French Collection, a twelve-part, painted story-quilt series. After our initial trip to Europe in 1961, Mother had returned several times to Europe to visit the couturiers in Paris and Rome. (I would write on her behalf to request invitations to see the private showings at the salons and Mother would come home bursting with ideas for her next season's collections.) She kept a scrapbook of her invitations and sketches of the designs she saw. Mother was a good traveler and going to Europe in the 1960s and to Africa in the 1970s not only brought her a rich reservoir of fashion ideas, but also many new friends and associates. If only she had been able to go to Europe in the 1920s when she was young — like Willia Marie Simone, heroine of The French Collection — who knows what Mother could have done.

Willia Marie Simone is a woman of courage, originality, and creativity but, unlike Mother, Willia Marie was able to do things that no African-American woman artist had ever been able to do in Paris or America. In this sense, Willia Marie is my alter ego. For her character I had to rewrite history using Mother's beloved Paris as the setting.

In The French Collection Series I seized the opportunity to paint in the manner of Van Gogh, Matisse, Monet, and Picasso, as I had tried to do when I was a student. But now I had a story to tell about a young black woman who went to Paris at age sixteen to become an artist and never to return to America. As the story goes, Willia Marie becomes a successful artist and makes a name for herself in the modern art movement and exchanges ideas with the great artists of her time.

In *Dinner at Gertrude Stein's,* a young Willia Marie listens to the lively after-dinner discussion between Gertrude Stein, Alice B. Toklas, Pablo Picasso, Ernest Hemingway, Leo Stein, Richard Wright, James Baldwin, Zora Neale Hurston, and Langston Hughes. In *Le Café des Artistes,* Willia, now widowed and the owner of a café, asserts herself in "A Proclamation of the Colored Woman's Art and Politics," a discussion of the contributions of black women to modern art, culture, and politics. *Matisse's Chapel* embodies my dream of seeing Mother again; but equally it seeks to expose the treacherous history of slavery. (I chose Matisse's Chapel as the cover for this book and you can read the text for it at the back of this book on page 273.) In it Willia Marie has a dream that all of the deceased members of her family have assembled in the church in Vence, whose windows, altar, and wall decorations had been designed by Henri Matisse. She goes there and finds them listening to my great-grandmother, Betsy Bingham, telling a story about slavery as told to her by her mother, Susie Shannon (my great-great-grandmother, who had been born into slavery but had never wanted to discuss it). Portrayed here are all the deceased members of my own family. If indeed my mother were to reappear and I could talk to her, what would she say about my story of Willia Marie? She always had the answers for me before, so it is reasonable to expect that in death she would be even more perfect than in life.

Chapter 5: Parental Politics: My Daughters and Me

Michele and Barbara in baby carriage, circa 1954

For the first twelve years of their lives, my two daughters were the most beautiful, lovable, personable, and smart children a parent could hope for. Barbara seemed to have come into the world smiling. Although Michele was a hell-raiser right from day one, she was also a joy. People used to stop me in the street to marvel at my beautiful babies. My mother used to say: "Today they are around your feet; tomorrow they'll be around your heart." However, it never occurred to me that they would ever change. But don't get me wrong: they are still beautiful, personable, and smart, and although we don't have the same bonds of friendship my mother and I had, we continue to try.

As a young mother I thought if I gave my girls lots of love and attention, a good home and education, and a wealth of cultural experiences, they would be trouble-free. But there is no guarantee of what kids will pattern their lives after. There is only one certainty in the mother-daughter relationship: No matter how hard you try, mother will make mistakes and daughter will, too, but the mistakes daughter makes will probably all be "mother's fault."

In the summer of 1969 I sent the two of them to the University of Mexico on a study-vacation and things have never been quite the same since then. I was thirty-eight at the time and Michele and Barbara were sixteen and seventeen respectively. I thought we all had a lot more sense than we did.

Barbara and Michele modeling for Mother at the Royal Manor, 1962

We are big talkers and debaters in our family, so as you might guess we have been over this summer many times but never without a fight. Both Michele and I have written about it: first Michele in *Black Macho and the Myth of the Superwoman* in 1979, and then me in *Confirmations: An Anthology of African American Women Writers* in 1984. I might add we have such totally different recollections of the events of that summer that I sometimes wonder if we are writing about the same incidents.

The rift between us began in the middle of the 1960s, when I was in my mid-thirties. As I look back, the sixties provided a fantastic revelation, an inspiration, and a milestone in my development as both a woman and an artist. For my teenaged daughters, however, the 1960s involved a youthful power blast. The world was looking at youth, listening to them. "What the young people are saying" prefaced everything that certain adults had to say. I, on the other hand, was outraged when I first heard my daughters announce, "But, Mother, everybody is . . ." — as if this youthful viewpoint was the criterion upon which we should all judge our actions.

The summer of 1966 was our last summer to go on a family vacation. Barbara and Michele were thirteen and fourteen years old at the time, and we had just received the news of their father's death before we left home for Provincetown. I feared because of Earl's death that our summer would turn sour. Birdie loves the water, so he was in a boat and swimming in the ocean every day; he barely put foot on dry land. Even when he went into town, he went by boat. The girls stayed all day with Birdie in the water and on the beach, while I had my painting and general housework to do in our rented apartment. In a week's time Birdie was back at work. Everything seemed fine until he went home. It was then I recognized that whatever I said was taken much more seriously by the girls if it was repeated by Birdie. The remainder of the summer was fraught with discipline and rebellion.

The following year Mother offered to take the girls to Europe so that I could paint. I was going to have my first one-person exhibition in New York City in December 1967. The news from Europe was that Barbara and Michele were disobeying Mother, who wrote me all the details about it. I felt guilty for shunting my responsibilities off on her so that I could have a summer to paint, especially since I knew that she had planned a tour of the couturiers' salons in Paris and Rome. I wrote to the girls, pleading with them to enjoy the summer abroad, reminding them how hard we all worked

Barbara and Michele kissing me at my wedding to Birdie in 1962

to make a good life for them — and that their grandmother and I need not be their enemies just because we were women. But how could they understand? Their rich classmates at the New Lincoln School had nannies and took European vacations for granted. Having been born in the depression years, I tried to explain to Barbara and Michele our financial situation: "Even though you girls have had many advantages in life, you must understand we are not rich people like many of your classmates at the New Lincoln School. We are poor people struggling to see that you — "Michele interrupted me: "The only one who has ever been poor here is you."

Now in this summer of 1969, I was once again preparing for a one-person show and desperately in need of time to paint. But there was no telling what this summer would produce: the girls were in open rebellion by this time. Michele was the friend of a white girl whose mother had a black boyfriend, a jazz musician, and they all got high together. My kids thought that was great family unity. "You're too emotional on the subject. Everybody who uses drugs is not a drug addict," the girls informed me. I was outraged. Earl's and Andrew's deaths (Andrew had died in 1961) flashed through my mind. The girls standing before me were just a blur.

Birdie cautioned: "Don't talk anymore, leave them alone. They're just trying to taunt you," he said. "They're young and crazy. They don't understand."

One day I heard them discussing some so-called revolutionary remarks Stokely Carmichael had made in a lecture, "The only position for women . . . is prone." "But how do you feel about this?" I asked them, trying not to reveal the horror I felt that they could just repeat this statement without recognizing the horror themselves. Michele was objective, announcing that it had nothing to do with how she felt. Barbara had not been present at the theater group when Stokely spoke, so she couldn't really comment. "Please don't allow yourselves to be used by anyone, male or female," I begged them. "If you lay your heart out there, it is sure that some creep will come along and step on it. Defy his ideas as you do mine." But Michele had a super crush on Stokely Carmichael, and Barbara was excited just to hear that she had met him. "What's he like?" Barbara asked her sister. It was obvious neither girl had heard a word I said. They had already been told by movement leaders that mother was the undisputed enemy of all revolutionary ideas. My daughters didn't seem to sense the contradictions. "Have a baby for the revolution!" was a supposed battle cry for women of the movement. Would they then be revolutionary mothers — or merely women, with the added burden of a child to bring up, possibly alone?

Birdie was very expressive on the baby issue. "We don't want a baby, Barbara or Michele. If we did, we could have one ourselves. Your mother and I [now aged thirty-five and thirty-six] are not as old as we seem. Hold those boys off. The revolution, my ass! All they want to do is fuck and run."

"But, Daddy," Barbara argued, "you don't know the boys of today. They are honest. We're not into the lies of your generation."

"We who? You'd better speak for yourself. You don't know what those little mother-fuckers are into!"

Come 1969, we could no longer take a vacation together, but I got an idea I thought they would like: summer study abroad at the University of Mexico in Mexico City. They could both study their favorite subjects — Barbara, Spanish and Portuguese; and Michele, art and literature. Though Mother disapproved of my allowing the girls to go to Mexico by themselves, she admitted that they really had enjoyed studying French when they had been in Paris with her. It was what had saved the trip from being a total disaster for Mother. Although Birdie and I were separated, I knew that if I were to call him now, he would caution me: "Don't let those girls go away alone. Keep them with you and give up your art. Postpone the show. They'll be back in school in a few months anyhow." But then, so would I.

In Mexico they could live in a student house where they would be supervised, but still be somewhat on their own with other young people. A sense of freedom was apparently what they yearned for. Maybe that was just what they needed: an opportunity to show how mature they really were. I thought the trip would be a good test, at any rate. They could no longer say that I had babied them and never allowed them to make decisions on their own. The trip would also be a high school graduation present for Michele and an introduction to college life. (She was due to go to Howard University in the fall.) Though Barbara was only in her senior year in high school, she was in the fourth-year class in both French and Spanish. She had a facility with languages like Earl's father, Grandpa Bob.

Before the girls left for Mexico I gave them a thorough briefing: "Remember to lock your door . . . be careful when you meet strangers . . . stay together, and most of all look out for each other." Michele was the older by eleven months; therefore, she was to be responsible for Barbara.

I began to assemble my canvases and paints to start work. For the first day or two I did nothing else and before long I was totally absorbed in my art. The girls had called to tell me that they had safely arrived in Mexico and were starting school the next day. Everything seemed perfect. A pattern for my summer was set up.

The girls had been gone less than three weeks when, at 2 A.M. on a hot July night, Barbara was on the phone. She was in New York at Kennedy Airport on her way uptown in a taxi. "I'm all out of money. Be downstairs to pay the taxi driver," she demanded, and hung up. I waited in front of the building for Barbara. I was far away, out of my mind with worry. "Barbara home . . . barely two weeks . . . Where's Michele? Out of money . . . oh, God, what has happened . . . ?" When her cab arrived, I embraced Barbara. My baby looked adorable, acting so grown up in a new white Mexican dress with embroidery on it. I wanted to hold her and kiss her again and again, but she wasn't for it. She was cool and in a hurry to get the greeting over with. She had on her "cut-the-kid-stuff-I'm-a-woman-now" face.

Finally Barbara got down to the story. She and Michele had met some Mexican "revolutionary" students the first day of classes and decided to go and live with them at their commune in the suburbs of Mexico City. There were three men and two

Michele, me, Barbara, and Birdie, circa 1968

women, all in their middle to late twenties, and Ramos, the leader of the commune, who was thirty-two years old. Michele would not be coming home. She had fallen in love with a South American revolutionary who had joined the movement. They intended to live at the commune and be happy forever after. Michele had turned over all of her money to Ramos, who would take care of everything. Barbara came home because she didn't fit in. As for the nature of these revolutionary activities, the story was vague. They were doing some takes in the nude for a movie. Otherwise they smoked a lot of pot. The "girls" did housework, though there was a maid, and the men "worked" one day a week in town.

I called Michele immediately, ordering her to come home. I could feel her coolness through the phone. "As far as I am concerned, I am home," she informed me. If I'd feel any better about it, I could send permission so that she could get married. That was all she had to say. Ramos was there to explain matters further if I didn't understand.

Ramos then got on the phone and proceeded to inform me that I was "a reactionary individualist artist, a domineering self-serving woman, a pawn of the capitalist system who had to be destroyed." I was a menace. My children should leave me because I was a dangerous negative influence. People like me were beyond hope.

A lifetime of careful speech and whitey-fied intonations went right through the window. I reached back to my native Harlem street language and racial epithets, and cultural slurs came out like a river. "Me? You motherfucking . . . bastard, son of a honky bitch. You have taken advantage of my child. Whoever said a white racist full-of-shit creep like you could —"

He was very upset. I could almost feel his hot breath coming through the phone. "Mrs. Ringgold," he said, his Mexican accent seeming heavier now and his voice out of control, almost cracking. ". . . Your daughter has left you —"

"Let me warn you," I screamed, "you're not fucking with a fool. Your honky ass will be hotter than hell if —"

"Mrs. Ringgold," Ramos interrupted me again, "there is nothing you can do. Michele is —"

"Listen, you murky-white cracker junky half-ass revolutionary pimp motherfucker, what have you given her? Some of your dope? Barbara tells me you have a fucking drugstore there. Well, you dopy freaked-out sack of shit, you'd better not take me lightly. This black capitalist bitch will cause you more trouble than it's worth. What kind of revolutionary are you, you freak? You haven't seen no revolution! The best you can do, you motherfucking drug addict bastard, is send my daughter home or —"

"Good day, Mrs. Ringgold," Ramos said, and hung up the phone. Later, Michele told me Ramos's face was beet-red and he was trembling uncontrollably. She had never seen a man so afraid before or since. On my side, I had never been so angry in my life.

I called the American embassy in Mexico. The ambassador was conveniently out of town, but his assistant spoke with me. I told him the story, and that I was rescinding my permission for Michele to be in Mexico, waving in my hand a copy of my letter of consent (which he of course could not see). The assistant attempted to explain to me that it would not be possible to make Michele leave Mexico unless she was doing something unlawful. "Unlawful?" I screamed. "What do you think they are doing over there? Watching the sun set?"

"I don't know, Mrs. Ringgold," came the disinterested voice of the assistant.

"And you don't care either, do you? Well, if you know what's good for you, you'll get your ass over there and see what they —"

Suddenly I realized I was raving to a dial tone. The assistant had hung up on me. I had to get a grip on myself. I called the State Department in Washington, D.C., and I called the White House and tried to get through to President Nixon. Then I sent the following telegram to all the appropriate officials:

MY DAUGHTER IS A MINOR BEING HELD IN A MEXICAN COMMUNE AGAINST MY WILL. I AM HER MOTHER AND A BLACK WOMAN, AN AMERICAN CITIZEN, A REGISTERED VOTER, AND A TAXPAY-ER, AND I DEMAND IMMEDIATE ACTION OR ANY HARM THAT COMES TO HER IS THE RESPONSI-BILITY OF ALL OF YOU WHO DO NOT ASSIST ME IN BRINGING HER HOME IMMEDIATELY. SHE HAS A RETURN FLIGHT TICKET. I EXPECT HER IN AMERICA BY SUNDOWN TOMORROW.

Now the assistant to the ambassador was calling me. He was at the commune. And he wanted to know what Michele looked like. "She's black!" I bellowed. "Can't you see? Now what are you going to do?"

"Well," he said, "everything here looks all right to me."

"Save your comments," I said. "I'll be there in the morning. At that time you can tell them to the proper authorities. You can be my witness, since you're there and you see what's going on."

He hesitated. His voice softened. "Well, what do you want me to do?"

"Take her out of there right now. Put her in a hotel where she will be safe for the night, and tomorrow put her on the first flight home. That is all. Don't leave her there. She doesn't even speak their language. Can't you see they are adults, taking advantage of a young black girl?"

The next day Michele flew back to America, with no ticket, no identification or papers of any kind, and no money. When she arrived in New York, she was sent immediately through a little gate to the side and hustled into a taxi headed uptown.

When she arrived home, Michele looked pretty much as Barbara had: dressed in a beautiful white, hand-embroidered Mexican dress that seemed made for her. She was a little thinner but she looked pretty and healthy. She was very hostile, however, admitting nothing about the drugs. As far as she was concerned, I had destroyed her chance at happiness; and like Barbara, she had nothing but contempt for me. As soon as her friends from Mexico came for her, she announced defiantly, she would be off again to the commune.

I wanted both Michele and Barbara examined for drugs and mental and physical health. I searched the Yellow Pages for family services, someone to talk to who knew more than I did about all this. I found the name of an agency I recognized and called. "I'm having trouble with my daughters and I'd like to talk to someone about it. They have just come from Mexico where they joined a commune and I don't know what . . ." There was an accommodating silence on the other end. Embarrassed, I rambled on. " I don't know why my daughters did this. . . . I thought we all knew what our struggle was, and what we should be. . . . I didn't think young black people had time for . . . We have so many other important — "

She cut me off. "Mrs. Ringgold, please come down to see us. We will talk." From the way she responded, I knew she must be a black woman and I could feel that she understood what I was going through. The wait through the night began. A quiet desperation crept over me. What would become of us?

Back in Mexico at that very time, hundreds of young white Americans were being arrested on marijuana charges. Many were later forced into heroin addiction in Mexican prisons, their parents compelled to send thousands of American dollars each year to maintain drug habits forced upon them by unscrupulous prison personnel. A large group was released in 1979 in exchange for Mexican prisoners serving time in American jails. So I was lucky I got my girls out of there, although I didn't realize how lucky then.

At the social service agency we never saw the black woman I had spoken to on the phone. Instead, we were greeted by a cold, pale white young woman from the old school of social workers. She established my ability to pay and then fell into a dead silence. She had us all figured out. When she finally spoke, she advised us to go home and wait for all hell to break out. Only then, I surmised, would she feel comfortable talking to the police and hospital caseworkers and perhaps placing Barbara or Michele with another member of the family — while I did time for hurting them or they did time for hurting me.

I needed immediate help. Michele had to be placed somewhere, because she clearly couldn't stay with me and there was no one else who could keep her. She was going to Howard University in September. If she wanted to leave from there and go back to the commune, so be it — I wouldn't even have known when she left. But for now I wanted her to be somewhere else. More than pain, I felt anger for the waste of energy, time, and resources. It is the "feminine ghetto" that drives so many young women, no matter how richly endowed and carefully brought up, to seek out the enemy and give themselves over to him. Why can't we ever disappoint the bastard and leave him standing there as we sashay on by?

At my request, Michele was put in a Catholic girl's home where she had to remain until it was time for her to go to college in five weeks' time. If she promised not to run away with the Mexicans, she could come home and we would try again. She refused.

At Howard University, Michele took to spending money recklessly and not attending classes. The Mexicans followed Michele to Howard and tried to get her to go back to Mexico with them, but by then she had made her decision not to go. Birdie went down to see her and then came to see me. He was concerned about Michele's education. He felt she was jeopardizing it by her casual "party" attitude, which he was able to detect easily in his one short visit. I was very glad he came to see me. We had not been together for almost two years. The girls demanded too much of my time to share myself with anyone; only Birdie could understand what I was going through. At that point all I could do was teach and try to get a little painting done in between bouts with Barbara and late-night calls from Michele demanding money.

Now it was Barbara's turn to act out at school. I guess we were lucky she chose her senior year in which to do it. Her SAT scores placed her in the upper 99th percentile of graduating high school seniors, and she was selected to be in *Who's Who among High School Graduates for 1970.* Several Ivy League colleges requested her application, but she was — in keeping with the mood of the 1960s — ready to "turn off and drop out." Although we were proud of her achievement up till now, her rebellious spirit hardly gave us a chance to enjoy it.

The kids at the New Lincoln School were experimenting with drugs, and for the first time some students in the senior class were not intending to go on to college. Barbara had begun to cut school and argue with me. "What's the sense of going to college, or even finishing high school?" Later I discovered she had taken LSD and was giving her teachers a bad time. Because of my well-known aversion to children experimenting with drugs, I was not told, and this information was kept top secret. But I knew something was very wrong with Barbara.

Well-meaning parents were as much confused about drugs as they were about the white power establishment, the black man, the poor, the war in Vietnam, and everything else. They were reluctant to guide, restrict, or set standards for their children. They practically pushed the kids to rebel, as if through their children's actions they could achieve some form of redemption for being rich. My children were no better off despite my standards of appropriate dress, behavior, and developing ghetto smarts. What I had to say, as far as my children were concerned, just didn't count.

Some girls at the New Lincoln School were coming to school barefoot and wearing their nightgowns as dresses. A meeting of parents and teachers was called to determine what guidelines, if any, should be provided for student dress. The meeting was a sham and ended in even more confusion, because nobody wanted to say anything authoritative. Some kids at the meeting sported filthy and tattered jeans and matted hair (in order to identify with the oppressed masses); their faces were lined with dirt. This dirty, ragged, disheveled look was political chic. The richer the kid, the more authentic the look.

Birdie and I were officially back together again. He was very supportive, and acted as a buffer between me and the girls, shielding me from their constant tyranny. He listened to their recklessly youthful ideas and became a sounding board for their madness. Birdie told me to ignore them: "Cut the cord or they will destroy you." Yet he was ambiguous about how to do it. I was still "Mommy Faye" (my girls' name for me), and the ultimate burden was still mine. He could only make the pain more bearable. Even my mother couldn't help me now. The sixties youth said "no no" to extended families.

It was a rough year, but somehow Barbara managed to graduate. She entered Lehman College in the fall of 1970, which was the first year of a new program for disadvantaged youth called Open Enrollment. The City Universities in New York were open to all graduating high school students for the first time. A new program, Search for Elevation in Education and Knowledge (SEEK), was developed to provide funds and remedial instruction, making it possible for these students to pursue a college education. Barbara identified strongly with these students. She made a statement to me that I will never forget: "They have everything. I wish I were SEEK." But she was just the opposite. She could have gone to any college she wanted to, but she chose Lehman. Her explanation was that she had never gone to school with her "brothers and sisters," and that always having gone to a private school had cut her off from her grassroots.

Barbara's first year at Lehman was a disaster; she cut classes and was thrown out of school for a year, which taught her a lesson she needed to learn — they don't fool around with you in college. Either you keep up or get out. Barbara worked that year at the National Biscuit Company (Nabisco) as a legal file clerk librarian. She was what I'd call a "hit and run" sometime-activist. But I am still proud of the "hits" she's made. For

Barbara at the University of Illinois Linguistic Conference, 1978

example, at Nabisco she read in an in-house journal that Nabisco was increasing their business in South Africa. Barbara wrote a letter in protest and hand-delivered it to the president of Nabisco. (She was nineteen at the time.) He chided her for making public use of company business, but promised to look into the matter. Barbara's job was actually reading and updating legal journals, a job she thoroughly enjoyed (and put to use on two other occasions several years later when she filled out a prepared divorce form bought at a stationery store and filed for and won a divorce decree — twice — costing her only the filing charges of $90.00 each time). After the year at Nabisco, Barbara returned to Lehman College and her usual straight A average.

In 1974, when she left Lehman College to spend her senior year abroad at the University of London, she wrote me exhilarating letters about the education she was receiving. It was what she had been used to at Our Savior and the New Lincoln School — real work in a challenging environment.

After receiving her undergraduate certificate from the University of London, Barbara enrolled in the doctoral program there and began her studies in Swahili, English semantics, Anglo Saxon, medieval English, and English dialectology. The dialects she studied included Public School English, the language of the upper class; the Queen's English, which identifies members of the royal family; and working-class dialects. Barbara had also won a residence scholarship for room-and-board at Crosby Hall, whereupon she met the Queen Mother (a patron of Crosby Hall) at a dinner in her honor. Barbara had been appointed the student president of the residence and was therefore introduced to the Queen Mother and shook her hand when she extended hers. In a brief exchange with the Queen Mother, Barbara remarked about the beauty of England and the hospitality of the English people. Her picture with the Queen Mother appeared the next day on the cover of one of the London daily newspapers. I must say this went over big with the Jamaican side of her family.

"If I don't pass my second exams, I will take a diploma and come home," Barbara wrote to me one day. I'd been told there was a young man in the U.S. with whom she was in love and was intending to spend "the rest of my life with." I'd heard that before. My answer was "Come home when you're ready to support yourself, Barbara. You are twenty-five years old with two master's degrees. You can get a job now." But Mama T (Earl's mother and Barbara's paternal grandmother), who always said yes when I said no, offered to give Barbara free room and board if she came back.

Finally Barbara arrived in the U.S. in October of 1977 and enrolled in the City University doctoral program in generative linguistics with a concentration in East African linguistics. She had first become interested in sound and syntax in East African languages while doing research at the British Museum Archives of African Languages; later she won a summer fellowship to attend a linguistics conference where she made contact with other East African linguists at the University of Illinois in Champagne-Urbana. In 1980 Barbara won another fellowship from City University to do research on East African languages at the Yale Library, where she read in Italian and German all they had on the structure, sound, and syntax of East African languages. Despite all this advanced study and three master's degrees in linguistics, Barbara never completed her doctoral thesis. She now teaches — she is a brilliant and inventive fourth-grade teacher in an elementary school in Harlem — and has three beautiful daughters.

Burdette, Barbara, and me at Barbara's graduation, 1981

In the late 1970s I wanted to stay close to Michele to help and guide her, but we had a very bitter argument at home that I could not ignore. There were witnesses who heard the harsh way in which she spoke to me. I asked her to move out by a certain date and she did, finding a studio apartment in Greenwich Village. She had begun teaching journalism at

New York University in the fall of 1976. At this time she was already writing *Black Macho and the Myth of the Superwoman,* her book on black feminism. I guess it was difficult for her at twenty-four years old to live with me while writing a book that would deny my presence as a feminist role model in her life. (I was only to discover this, however, when the book was published.)

If I had found 1969 difficult, 1979 was worse. Michele's book was published, and I received a bunch of negative public attention. It was payback time for Michele. I remember tuning into a national radio program just in time to hear the interviewer announce that she was talking to Michele Wallace, "the woman whose mother had put her in a home." "And what was a nice middle-class girl like you doing in a girls' home?" she asked Michele. In her book Michele "whitewashed" the Mexican commune incident and made me look like a controlling stereotypical black matriarch whose daughter became a feminist in spite of her. She gave me no credit as a role model for learning how to be both a woman and a political activist. There is no greater defeat to a woman who is a mother than to have her value as a mother denied. I had produced two very talented children; why not give me credit?

What most angered me was that Michele made no mention of the fact that I was an artist, an activist, or a feminist. A caption to a photograph of Michele, her two grandmothers, and me appeared in *Ms.* magazine to accompany an article about the book. It was a quote from Michele's book: "By the time I was fifteen there was nothing I dreaded more than being like the women in my family." Need I say more?

Michele had left Howard University in 1970 after the first semester and enrolled in the English Department at City College, where she studied with postmodernist fiction writers John Hawkes and Donald Barthelme. In 1974 she received a B.A. degree in English and writing. After publishing *Black Macho and the Myth of the Superwoman* in 1979, she enrolled in the Ph.D. program in American Studies at Yale. Feeling a need for a better grounding in black history after having written *Black Macho,* Michele studied history with John Blassingame, David Brion Davis, and David Montgomery. She didn't complete her doctorate at Yale in 1982, because of illness, but she is now working on a Ph.D. in Cinema Studies at New York University's Tisch School of the Arts.

Michele had now been writing seriously since the age of sixteen and, by the early 1970s, had become a wonderfully gifted writer. Over the last twenty years, beginning with the publication of *Black Macho,* through her prolific writings and public presentations — as

a teacher, lecturer, and a much-sought-after conference participant — she has become a major
presence nationally in the articulation of cultural
criticism. She is an associate professor of English
and Women's Studies at the City College of New
York and the City University Graduate Center
CUNY. Michele authored her second book in
1991, a collection of essays titled *Invisibility Blues:
From Pop to Theory.*

In 1991 Michele organized "Black Popular
Culture," a conference to explore new and criti-
cal approaches to cultural production through-
out the African Diaspora. Among those she
invited to this three-day event were Angela
Davis, Isaac Julien, Houston Baker, Marlon
Riggs, Henry Louis Gates, Jr., Hazel Carby,
Manning Marable, bell hooks, Manthia
Diawara, Lisa Kennedy, Stuart Hall, Valerie

Michele, 1979, jacket photo for her book Black
Macho and the Myth *of the Superwoman*

Smith, and Coco Fusco. Despite the fact that the conference opened at the Studio
Museum in Harlem, smack-dab in the center of a mesmerizing exhibition of the museum's contemporary African art collection, there was depressingly little said about black
art. The Studio Museum was a cosponsor of the conference along with Dia, a SoHo-
based contemporary arts center known for, among other things, never having exhibited
a black artist. On the final day of the conference, I sat proudly in the audience as my
daughter delivered her groundbreaking presentation in the Dia space on "Why Are
There No Great Black Artists?" (inspired by Linda Nochlin's polemical 1971 essay "Why
Are There No Great Women Artists?"), which addressed the problem of visuality in
African-American culture. Michele as the last speaker — feeling not only the strains of
fatigue from this grueling one-woman responsibility but also the recurrent (as of that
time undiagnosed) effects of lupus — took on the canon of black popular culture for its
benign neglect of visual artists of color, many of whom had attended the conference. It
is moments like this in which a mother can feel real proud of a daughter, and know for
sure she's done something right.

I've been told I am demanding and I don't deny it, but I am also generous and giving of my time, love, energy, and resources. My mother made many demands on me and I complied. She would have been devastated if I had ever shown disloyalty toward her. Lack of trust was unthinkable in our relationship as mother and daughter. In my relationship with my daughters I feel my demands, even of loyalty, have often been a burden on them.

To make up for some of the closeness I missed in my relationship with my daughters, I made a number of works of art. Through art I tried to create the peace we could not achieve in real life. (There is a kind of eternal insidious competition between me and my daughters — a women's war that never seems to end.) In my Couples Series I created wedding installations for each of my daughters, in an attempt to resolve a charged issue that confronts so many mothers and daughters, that is, daughters' love relationships. In another series, the first Slave Rape Series, I created portraits of Barbara, Michele, and me: Barbara in *Fear: Will Make You Weak,* Michele in *Run: You Might Get Away,* and me in *Fight: To Save Your Life.* Michele mentioned recently that I had once said that all of the women in my paintings were based on the likeness of one of the three of us. I don't remember stating this, but I do know that all of my story quilts about families have been in some way based on my own experience of family.

The text of my performance/five-part story quilt *The Bitter Nest* (which I created in 1985 and 1987 respectively) is a fictitious response to our mother-and-daughter feuds. In the story everything is resolved in the end with the death of the family patriarch, Dr. Prince. Although there is no reigning patriarch in our own family, the men in my daughters' lives have been a continuing issue over which we have struggled. Michele's happy marriage in 1989 to Eugene Nesmith, a talented actor, director, and theater professor, has done a lot to relieve some of that old tension between us and has helped us to be closer than we have been in years. Barbara's three children, my glorious grandchildren, have welded Barbara and me together. Despite the fact that we sometimes pull apart, we have Faith, Theodora, and Martha, the next generation, to give us hope and keep us together.

The Flag is Bleeding, 1967
Oil on canvas
72 x 96 inches
Artist's collection

Flag for the Moon: Die Nigger, 1967–1969
Oil on canvas
36 x 50 inches
Artist's collection

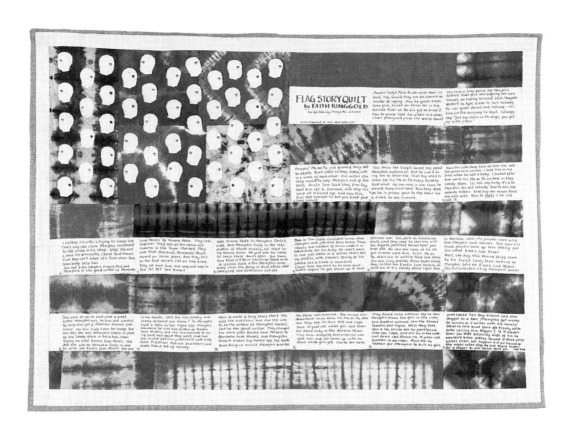

Flag Story Quilt, 1985
Appliquéd, tie-dyed, and pieced fabric
57 x 78 inches
The Spenser Museum

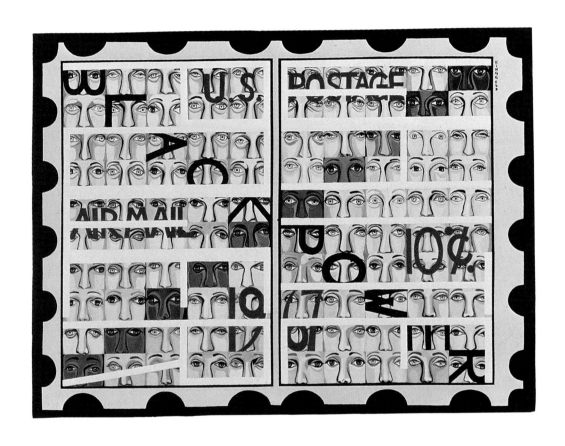

U. S. Postage Stamp Commemorating the Advent of Black Power, 1967
Oil on canvas
72 x 96 inches
Artist's collection

Die, 1967
Oil on canvas
72 x 144 inches
Artist's collection

Echoes of Harlem, 1980
Acrylic on canvas; dyed and pieced fabric
96 x 84 inches
Collection of Philip Morris Companies
Collaboration with Willi Posey

Who's Afraid of Aunt Jemima?, 1983
Acrylic on canvas; pieced fabric with sequins
90 x 80 inches
Collection of Fred Collins, Esq.

Mrs. Jones and Family, 1973
from the Family of Woman Mask Series
Acrylic on canvas; embroidered and pieced fabric
60 x 12 x 16 inches
Artist's collection
Collaboration with Willi Posey

Mother's Quilt, 1983
Acrylic painted, appliquéd, and embroidered fabric with sequins
58 x 43½ inches
Artist's collection

Street Story Quilt Parts I-III, 1985
The Accident, The Fire, and *The Homecoming*
Acrylic on canvas; dyed and pieced fabric with sequins
90 x 144 inches
The Metropolitan Museum of Art

The Dinner Quilt, 1986
Acrylic on canvas; dyed and pieced fabric with sequins and beads
48¹/₂ x 66 inches
Private collection

Change: Faith Ringgold's Over 100 Pound Weight Loss Performance Story Quilt, 1986
from the Change Series
Photo etching on silk and cotton; printed and pieced fabric
57 x 70 inches
Artist's collection

Change 2: Faith Ringgold's Over 100 Pound Weight Loss Performance Story Quilt, 1988
from the Change Series
Acrylic on canvas; photo lithography on silk and cotton pieced fabric
62 x 62 inches
Artist's collection

Change 3: Faith Ringgold's Over 100 Pound Weight Loss Performance Story Quilt, 1991
from the Change Series
Acrylic on canvas; pieced fabric border
73½ x 80½ inches
Artist's collection

The Bitter Nest Part 1: Love in the Schoolyard, 1988
Acrylic on canvas; printed, tie-dyed, and pieced fabric
75¹/₂ x 92¹/₂ inches
Artist's collection

The Bitter Nest Part 2: Harlem Renaissance Party, 1988
Acrylic on canvas; printed, tie-dyed, and pieced fabric
94 x 82 inches
Artist's collection

The Bitter Nest Part 3: Lovers in Paris, 1988

Acrylic on canvas; printed,
tie-dyed, and pieced fabric

96 x 83 inches, Artist's collection

The Bitter Nest Part 4: The Letter, 1988

Acrylic on canvas; printed,
tie-dyed, and pieced fabric

94½ x 84½ inches, Artist's collection

The Bitter Nest Part 5: Homecoming, 1988

Acrylic on canvas; printed, tie-dyed, and pieced fabric

76 x 96 inches, Artist's collection

Subway Graffiti, 1987
Acrylic on canvas; tie-dyed and pieced fabric
50¼ x 62 inches, Private collection

Subway Graffiti #2, 1987
Acrylic on canvas; printed, tie-dyed, and pieced fabric
60 x 84 inches, Artist's collection

Subway Graffiti #3, 1987
Acrylic on canvas; printed, tie-dyed, and pieced fabric
60 x 84 inches
Artist's collection

Sonny's Quilt, 1986
Acrylic on canvas; appliquéd, printed, and pieced fabric
84¹⁄₂ x 60 inches
Collection of Barbara and Ronald Davis Balsar

Woman Painting the Bay Bridge, 1988
from the Woman on a Bridge Series
Acrylic on canvas; printed, dyed, and pieced fabric
68 x 68 inches
Collection of Joanne and John Spohler

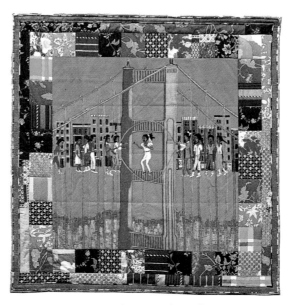

Double Dutch on the Golden Gate Bridge, 1988, from the Woman on a Bridge Series
Acrylic on canvas; printed, dyed, and pieced fabric
68½ x 68 inches, Private collection

Dancing on the George Washington Bridge, 1988, from the Woman on a Bridge Series
Acrylic on canvas; printed, dyed, and pieced fabric
68 x 68 inches, Collection of Roy Eaton

The Winner, 1988
from the Woman on a Bridge Series
Acrylic on canvas; printed, dyed, and pieced fabric
68 x 68 inches
Harold Washington Library

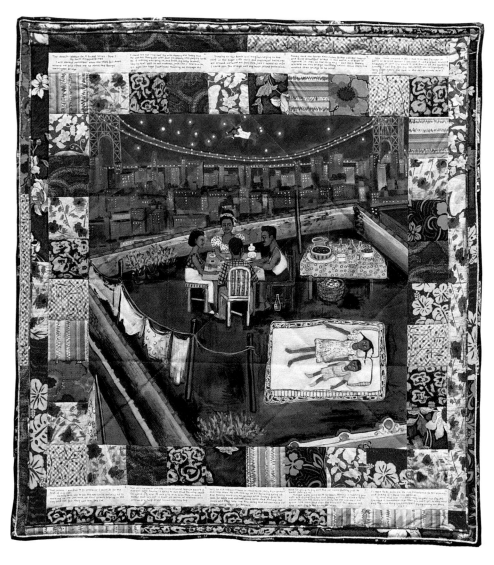

Tar Beach, 1988
Acrylic on canvas; pieced and painted fabric
74 x 69 inches
Solomon R. Guggenheim Museum

Tar Beach 2, 1990
Silk screen on silk
66 x 66 inches
Philadelphia Museum

The French Collection Part I: #1, 1991
Dancing at the Louvre
Acrylic on canvas; pieced fabric border
73½ x 80½ inches
Artist's collection

The French Collection Part I: #2, 1991
Wedding on the Seine
Acrylic on canvas; pieced fabric border
74 x 89½ inches
Artist's collection

The French Collection Part I: #3, 1991
The Picnic at Giverny
Acrylic on canvas; pieced fabric border
73$\frac{1}{2}$ x 90$\frac{1}{2}$ inches
Collection of Eric Dobkin

The French Collection Part I: #4, 1991, *Sunflowers Quilting Bee at Arles*
Acrylic on canvas; pieced fabric border
74 x 80 inches, Private collection

The French Collection Part I: #5, 1991, *Matisse's Model*
Acrylic on canvas; pieced fabric border
73 x 79¹/₂ inches, Artist's collection

The French Collection Part I: #6, 1991, *Matisse's Chapel*
Acrylic on canvas; pieced fabric border
74 x 79¹/₂ inches, Artist's collection

The French Collection Part I: #7, 1991, *Picasso's Studio*
Acrylic on canvas; pieced fabric border
73 x 68 inches
Artist's collection

The French Collection Part I: #8, 1991, *On the Beach at St. Tropez*
Acrylic on canvas; pieced fabric border
74 x 92 inches, Artist's collection

The French Collection Part II: #9, 1993
Jo Baker's Birthday
Acrylic on canvas; pieced fabric border
73 x 78 inches, St. Louis Art Museum

The French Collection Part II: #10, 1991
Dinner at Gertrude Stein's
Acrylic on canvas; pieced fabric border
79 x 84 inches, Artist's collection

The French Collection Part II: #11, 1994
Le Café des Artistes
Acrylic on canvas; pieced fabric border
79¹/₂ x 90 inches
Artist's collection

PART III

MAKING ART, MAKING WAVES, AND MAKING MONEY

CHAPTER 6: A EUROPEAN TRIP ENDS WITH A DEATH IN THE FAMILY

Michele and Barbara in our cabin on the S.S. Liberté, *July 1961*

In 1961, the girls, Mother, and I went to Europe for the first time. They were on a sight-seeing vacation and I was on an expedition to seek out the great masterpieces of European art, which so far I had seen only in reproductions. I was also questioning my future as an artist. Somehow I felt that being in Europe — where Picasso, Matisse, Monet, and the other great painters had lived — would lead me to the answer.

We sailed for France aboard the S.S. *Liberté* one cool morning in mid-July. The *Liberté* was on its last voyage, and we reaped the benefits of its final gust of glory: sumptuous French feasts replete with wine three times a day. Mother liked her food plain and felt that wine was for winos. Our first meal began with soupe à l'oignon gratinée. Although she spoke no French, Mother animated her way through the language, waving her hand over the waiter's tray as if the gesture could make the whole thing vanish.

Our waiter had a beautiful smile but spoke only a few words of English. He returned with escargots. "Madame is pleased?" he asked, and then trailed off in a profusion of French. But Mother's eyes were closed now, her face passionate with resignation. "Please, please listen to me," she said slowly and clearly in her most articulate English. "I want just a little plain broiled chicken." Our next course was beef fillet with Madeira sauce. The waiter appeared smiling again, but Mother did not. The girls were enjoying it all.

Using her hands and face in a dramatic presentation of "perfect" slowly articulated English, Mother fluttered her hands like a bird and then took on the posture of a broiled

Michele, me, Mother, and Barbara on the S.S. Liberté *to France, July 1961*

chicken in a pan. Mother "spoke French" to the waiter. Finally he understood and was delighted. She got what passed for "a little plain broiled chicken" twice a day for the duration of our trip.

Barbara and Michele refused Mother's "Franco-American diet," preferring to pick and choose among the courses, always ending every meal except breakfast with a dish of ice cream. They were eight and nine years old on this first trip to Europe, and the boat was made for them. There is something very carefree about the ambience of a boat at sea, and the children picked it up immediately. Before we were an hour out at sea, they had met up with a marauding band of children whose parents allowed them total freedom from morning until night. The children had a great time swimming and plotting a scheme to find Bob Hope, who was also on the boat. Each morning the kids got together with a new plan to catch at least a glimpse of the famous comedian — and perhaps get a signature, too. But Bob Hope stayed out of sight in his suite of rooms, hidden on the other side of the boat where the public was forbidden to go. I wonder if he knew there was a group of children (two little black girls among them) who were looking for him? They never saw him, but the hunt filled their days and nights with anticipation, and mine with peace.

At mealtimes, I would watch all the gaiety at the surrounding tables — which were littered with empty wine bottles. Finally, I requested the waiter open the wine on our table just to see what it was all about. After all, in Harlem wine was for winos, but could all these nice-looking white people be winos? "No," I thought, raising my wineglass for my first taste. "Is madame pleased?" the waiter inquired. "Oh yes, it's fine," I said, evading my mother's disapproving glance and trying not to seem like a wino. The discovery of "wine with meals" and the peace and quiet of lemonade on a shaded sun deck supplied me with an afterglow that floated me to Europe.

In Paris we took two rooms in a small hotel on rue du Four, just off the boulevard Saint Germain-des-Près. Barbara stayed in my room and Michele in Mother's. By day we did everything together in Mother's room, which was the biggest and sunniest and had the best balcony. The balcony overlooked the church of Saint Germain-des-Près. The magnificent spectacle of its Romanesque steeple and massive tower dating back to the year 1014 is something I will never forget. Every morning we had a typical French breakfast on the balcony — French bread piping hot from the bakery down the street, with fresh-churned butter and preserves, and coffee with goat's milk for Mother and me and hot chocolate for the girls. The girls took all of this very much for granted as they sat at a table on the old ironwork terrace dressed up in Mother's and my negligees over their baby-doll pajamas — pretending to be two ladies on the first leg of a world tour.

I wanted my daughters to know about art, music, and literature; to know about other people's culture and history as well as their own and to be well traveled. I wanted them to be little "continental colored girls" with a future — if they chose — outside Harlem or, indeed, America. Most of all, I wanted my daughters to have choices. Obviously high on the "to do" list in Paris was the Louvre. *Mona Lisa,* here we come — Mother, Barbara, Michele, and I, three generations of blackness from Harlem, U.S.A. The day we went to see the *Mona Lisa* at the Louvre was the same day the girls discovered a *glacé* (French for ice cream) wagon in the courtyard outside. The French ate very little ice cream at this time, so it was a rare thing to see someone selling it. "We have come to the Louvre to see the *Mona Lisa, The Death of Marat,* and certain other masterpieces, not to eat *glacé,*" I told Barbara and Michele, trying to sound warm but firm. After all, we had already begun to attract attention just by being there and I didn't want to cause a scene over anything as "American" as ice cream. A crowd was beginning to form around us, and the man selling *glacé* held out two containers in a vain attempt to connect with Barbara's and Michele's outstretched hands. "When we come out," I promised, and took their hands in mine, hurrying them into the Louvre against their will.

I had to almost drag Barbara and Michele through the museum; they knew all too well that my art museum tours could take hours, since they had already been on many museum trips to the Metropolitan and the Museum of Modern Art in New York. We were now followed by a crowd of curious French museum-goers. Mother pretended she was not with us, as the magnificent halls of the Louvre echoed with the girls' desperate pleas for *glacé*. Finally we found the *Mona Lisa,* whereupon I began to lecture the girls on "The Smile" and the history of this great painting. Our French audience was politely attentive but the girls were unimpressed. They found the smile as well as the painting too small, and its pursuit far too time-consuming a distraction from theirs — which was to get ice cream. The next time I saw Mother, she was outside the Louvre eating *glacé,* and shaking her head in disbelief.

That summer in Paris, on the campus of the Sorbonne, I met a medical student named Maurice Teplier. I was looking for art activities that I could attend. He had no answers but offered lunch instead at a nearby café. I accepted. Maurice was from the French Caribbean island of Guadelupe, and he was handsome and my height — don't go looking for a tall man in Europe. He spoke French and some Spanish, but very little English. I had studied Spanish in high school and college, so with some difficulty I could communicate with him. Within a few days I fantasized about becoming Madame Teplier. I could escape the problems of racist America, and bring Barbara and Michele up in Paris instead of Harlem. Wouldn't it be perfect to be the wife of a cultured French-speaking doctor, who was also black?

Maurice took me to see Bud Powell, the great modern jazz pianist who was playing at the Blue Room on the Right Bank. Bud was sitting at the bar as I came in. "You are Bud Powell, aren't you?" I asked, noticing how old and tired he looked. "No," he said, displaying a toothless grin, "I'm Harry Truman." I laughed and introduced him to Maurice, who was impressed. A fan of modern jazz, he had planned to surprise me with Bud Powell. The show made me sad. Although he still played masterfully, Powell had frequent lapses and often spoke incoherently. He'd ask his bass player, "Do you love me?" I wanted to cry. "It is the drug," Maurice said in his heavy French accent, cupping his hand as if holding a wineglass and moving it to his lips a number of times. "They drink the wine like water," he commented, shaking his head and looking down at his glass of lemonade. "Is it harmful?" I asked, trying to act nonchalant about the fact that I was drinking wine myself. "They die of it," he said. "Well, they die happy," I responded,

jokingly. "They are happy?" he questioned, looking perplexed. "No," I said, searching for a way
to explain. This was typical of so many of our
conversations. Eventually we simply had to
change the subject because some fine point had
gotten hopelessly lost in the confusion of my
Spanish or his English.

One evening, we saw a parade of men, obviously not together but all going to the same
place and, as I found out later, for the same
thing. "Who are those men and where are they
going?" I asked Maurice. His face had that
broad-as-possible smile and all he needed was
to add the "ooh-la-la" and the picture was complete. As I moved a little closer, I could see
women lining both sides of the street. "Oh," I
said, "some old-fashioned international entertainment for the boys?" I also remember early
one morning when Maurice and I went for
onion soup at Halles Market, and seeing a

*Michele and Barbara at the hotel on rue du Four,
Paris, summer 1961*

rather young woman who stood under a streetlight, reading a book. "Is she one . . . ?" I
speculated. Maurice nodded and, noticing the perplexed look on my face, he added,
"but intellectual."

Maurice lived with his two sisters in a tiny apartment on rue du Four, not far from
our hotel. He invited me to dinner one night to meet his sisters and some of their
friends. The people I met there were all French-speaking from Guadelupe, so communication was difficult but lively. Maurice's sisters were office workers, though I never fully
understood what it was they actually did; I assumed they were secretaries. The men
were either doctors or medical students. They were all upset about what was going on in
America at the time. The French newspapers and magazines carried daily front-page
stories about the civil rights struggle erupting all over the South with photographs of
black people catching a lot of bullets, being sprayed with high-power water hoses and
beaten with police clubs. These pictures of snarling police dogs and menacing mobs of
whites were the first really frightening pictures of the struggle I had seen.

Me, Michele, and Barbara at the Louvre, Paris, summer 1961

Maurice and his friends wanted to know what I thought about all of this. It took the rest of the evening and a grueling headache to attempt to explain, have it translated, and then discuss it. They had a lot of opinions about what was happening to black people all over the world. The language barrier prevented me from exchanging ideas so that they could understand the subtle differences of opinion we had. The evening ended with admiring glances from the men and women in the group. They clearly liked me, but could I "make kitchen"? They all waited to hear my answer, but I laughed it off and gave no answer. What did they think I was applying for — a job?

On my last night in Paris, Maurice and I had our first and last rendezvous at his friend's flat in the student section of Paris. The decor was "student" modern, plenty of pillows and coverlets on a big bed. We found some wine (and lemonade for Maurice) in the cupboard, and cheese and bread in the tiny icebox. I was curious about what "it" would be like — after all, we were in Paris, and he was French and black. But ours was not an illicit affair — I could almost have told my mother about it. I was more concerned about the open window than I was about Maurice. He was a no-frills, matter-of-fact, rapid-fire lover. Maybe I had made him wait too long? Maybe I should have waited even longer.

The next morning Mother, Barbara, Michele, and I were off to Nice in the south of France on the *Blue Star*. The trains in Europe are great. Traveling by train is like sitting in your living room with a view passing by. We took up the whole compartment most of the time. Only when the train became overcrowded did anybody attempt to join us.

At night we would pull up a foot extension and stretch out to sleep. Mother was a perfect traveling companion. Barbara and Michele were good, too. They were just young enough to take the whole trip for granted and yet enjoy it for the daily excitement and exposure to new things. It was never a burden to look after them, since Mother did most of it anyway. She was always able to handle things like that with ease and proficiency.

In Nice we stayed in a pension overlooking the beach and the Mediterranean. We had a huge marble balcony and breakfast was served to us in our room. We had lunch and dinner in the dining room with the other guests. They were Europeans, all talking and discussing something on French television. Mother and the girls and I enjoyed the pleasure of our own company. The concierge was a lady and was typical of the people we met in Europe: cordial, hospitable, and seemingly color-blind. In no time we became accustomed to the strange absence of racism.

Michele and Barbara at la Cathédrale Notre Dame, summer 1961

Early every morning we went to the beach and back again in the evening, when the French came home from work with their bottles of wine and papers. Mother was amazed at their scanty string bikinis. They changed their clothes in full view of all who cared to see and this thoroughly fascinated the girls, but finally drove Mother off the beach.

We took a group bus tour to Monte Carlo to see Grace Kelly's palace. As I recall, it was all pink and needed renovation. The rest of our group went straight to the gambling casino in the center of town where Sammy Davis Junior was appearing in the evenings. We sat at a café across the street and ate ice-cream cones for the equivalent of one dollar a cone. We found Monte Carlo boring — the best part had been getting there. The French Riviera is a panorama of natural geographic splendor, and I felt spiritually elevated by the view. Yet I kept thinking about Maurice, and anticipating our meeting again when I returned to Paris. What if it turned out that he really did like me?

Everyone was aware that we were Americans, and we were particularly special because we were also black females. Europeans knew what was happening in America. The Italian radical press carried front page stories with large pictures of Freedom Riders and marching ministers in the South. We were not only three generations of a family, but heroines as well. Look what we had escaped in the United States.

In Florence, the girls discovered *gelato,* Italian ice cream. The morning that we toured the Uffizzi to see the Rembrandts was a repetition of the events of the Louvre. This time, however, we were encircled by monks staring in awe at the two little black girls who were passionately pleading for *gelato.* I found that the French were mere schoolboys when it came to staring, because the Italians not only stared and touched but also made tender remarks about the *"Bella Negras."* Could that have been an early "Black is Beautiful" in Italian ?

It was in Rome that we heard the tragic news of Andrew's death. I knew that it was bad news when the hotel's concierge at the Palazzo came for me to answer a call from the U.S.A. I finally heard the news that I had been dreading since the early fifties when I first discovered that my brother was on heroin. I had become aware of the changes in his character — the loss of pride and ambition — and knew it was a matter of time before he would die.

Andrew may have been doomed ever since that cold winter night in 1942 when he was beaten up by a gang of boys called the "Irish Dukes." He had just turned eighteen and was on his way to visit his friend Jarrett on St. Nicholas Terrace. The "Irish Dukes" attacked him viciously, beating him with a rusty iron pipe while the police held back the hostile neighborhood crowd. He was alone in a white neighborhood that was angry about the black families who were moving in. Jarrett's family was one of those families. However, on that cold night in 1942, he had been waiting for Andrew in order to celebrate Andrew's birthday. But Andrew never arrived.

Later that night, when Andrew rang the downstairs bell, I went flying to the door. Mother was in the apartment next door visiting with Mrs. Curry. I eased Mrs. Curry's door shut because I wanted to see Andrew first. Instead of his customary style of taking two and three steps at a time up the stairs, he came slowly. I almost fainted when I saw the bloody rag he held up to his head. "Don't tell Mother," he pleaded as he staggered past me into the bathroom. I ran in behind him. There was blood all over him. Barbara was crying. We could see him clearly now under the light — his skull was exposed and all his hair was matted with blood. There was no way we could keep this from Mother.

She knew as soon as I said, "Andrew. . . "

"My God, Curry, something's happened to Little Andrew," she shrieked, as she raced through the door to our apartment with Mrs. Curry right behind her. At that time Mother was still young and strong enough to withstand almost anything — even the inhuman treatment Andrew received at the small private hospital around the corner from our house that did not admit black people. The nurse bandaged Andrew's head that night and gave Mother six aspirins to give him in the morning. Instead, Mother rushed him into a taxi cab and up to the Medical Center Hospital on 168th Street. There he stayed for care and observation for the next several months, but he was never quite the same after that. Now Andrew was dead at thirty-seven — not from the brutal beating with the rusty iron pipe twenty years earlier, but from an overdose of heroin.

Mother took the news of Andrew's death calmly. Barbara and Michele were good, too. Within a few hours we left Rome on the next train to Paris, with the help of a strange little lady we had met just minutes before hearing of Andrew's death.

We were in a taxi coming home from the zoo, and the girls and I had been speculating about what appeared to be uncaged wild animals in a natural habitat. "How had they done that?" we kept asking each other. We decided there was a ditch covered over with fake landscaping so that if the animals attempted to escape, they would fall in. Mother was silent. She was considering the taxi driver's offer to take us on a tour of the city, as a kind of introduction to Rome. I had planned a tight schedule for our week in Rome — shopping at the flea markets, museums, the opera *Aida* at the Baths of Caracalla, and a full-day trip to the Vatican. As we were getting out of the taxi, Mother was negotiating the tour of Rome with the taxi driver when a little woman passing by stopped and introduced herself to Mother. "I am an American Indian from Wyoming," she announced. "I speak fluent Italian. I will take you to see whatever you want."

"Could you take us to see the Vatican?" Mother asked her. "We would love to see the Pope."

"The Pope is in his summer residence at this time, but I will find out when he returns, or if we can go out there to see him," responded the little lady. Mother thanked the taxi driver and told him that we would go with the American lady. "She speaks English and Italian," Mother explained apologetically to him. *"Si, signora,"* said the taxi driver, who drove away, leaving us standing there with this strange little lady whom everybody liked immediately — except me. We entered the inner courtyard of our hotel, the Palazzo, where we intended to have a leisurely dinner before our night tour of the floodlit monuments of Rome. The little lady followed us, and Mother, Barbara, and Michele started chatting with her as if she were an old family friend. So I decided that even though the lady appeared eccentric and strange, she must be all right.

Andrew, 1950

When the concierge called me to the phone, the little lady went with me. It was my sister Barbara telling me Andrew was dead. Before I could speak we were disconnected. The little lady took the phone and spoke in Italian to the operator and Barbara was back on the line in a few seconds, telling me to hurry home and to be careful about how I gave the news to Mother. Birdie and Daddy were with Barbara, so I didn't have to worry about my sister facing all of this alone.

It was the height of the summer season and the planes from Rome to New York were booked solid for the next couple of days. The best way to get home was to take the first train out of Rome to Paris, and then a plane from Paris to New York. We already had round-trip train tickets back to Paris, and the ride through the Swiss Alps was a welcome relief.

The strange lady stayed with us while we packed our bags to prepare to leave Rome. She went with us to the train station to get our ticket reservations for the train to Paris, and she came back to the Palazzo and stayed with us until it was time for us to catch the train out of Rome. Although we had only met this woman a few hours earlier that day, Mother and she were like old friends. We never saw or heard from her again, but Mother and I both knew that without her we probably would not have been able to leave Rome so soon. She seemed to know we needed her, even before we did. She was, as Mother put it, "God-sent."

We rode for more than twenty-four hours on a network of trains from Rome to Milan and from Switzerland to Paris. Mother was calm and pensive all the way home. Riding through the Swiss Alps was one part of our trip I'm glad we did not miss. How can I explain the feeling of riding through clouds on a train? It was like nothing I had ever seen before.

Arriving exhausted at the Gare du Nord we went to a little pension right next to the railroad station. What a relief that we didn't have to worry about whether or not the hotel would take us. How much more painful it would have been if we had been dealing with overt racism along with the grief we were feeling. The next morning we rose early, had our last breakfast in Paris, and went to the airport to catch the morning flight from Paris to New York. There was no time to call Maurice. My family was my only concern. I was rushing home to grieve over Andrew's death; Mother and my sister Barbara needed all my attention now.

We arrived in America without fanfare. We somberly approached customs: the children first, and then Mother and I following with a mixture of grief and apprehension. Mother usually saw to it that the girls' clothes were clean and neatly packed before each new stop on our trip. But this time Andrew's death had left her with little interest in appearances, and we never noticed that the girls had accumulated many dirty clothes since leaving Rome. The customs officer held his breath, slammed Barbara's bag shut, and waved us on. In minutes we were in a taxi laughing our heads off for the first time since we left Rome. We went straight to Barbara's house, where Daddy and Birdie were waiting for us.

We were glad to see Birdie again. He had looked after my sister while we were in Europe, and was there to assure me that Barbara was not alone. It was Birdie who brought the undertaker to see Mother for the arrangements about Andrew's funeral. Birdie was there when we needed him.

Andrew had been found nude on the floor in a vacant apartment where he was carried after his death. We were told by the neighbors that earlier in the day he had been with a young woman and a small dog. All the neighbors knew him. "Baron comes here all the time," they said. Andrew loved women and wherever he was there was usually a dog. He died "happy," too "happy."

Although Andrew's death had left Barbara badly shaken, she did not break down when they went to identify Andrew's body. It was Daddy who wept. Barbara could not accept what was right before her eyes. "Why are they letting him lie there like that?" she asked pathetically over and over again. Andrew was the first member of our small family to die during Barbara's and my lifetime. It was a long time before any of us got over it.

Nothing was further from my mind than Paris, when a letter from Maurice arrived in the mail. "Why did you not call me in Paris?" he wrote. "Please answer this letter," he continued. "I want to 'know' from you." The rest of the letter was in French, which I could have translated and learned some French in the process. I had agreed to write him in English for the same reason. Our correspondence continued sporadically for months, a letter every two or three weeks. I could not tell whether or not he intended to come to America, or if he was going to invite me to come back to Paris. When would he start his medical practice and where? There were too many unanswered questions connected with Maurice. And the language barrier made it difficult to ask questions, and too easy for him to avoid answering.

Birdie was back in our life again. When he had heard that we were in Europe, he confided in my sister that he was afraid of losing me. Later, Michele and Barbara told him about Maurice. Now he was afraid that I would return to Europe to live in Paris with the girls and marry Maurice. While we were away he often called Barbara to find out how we were making out in Europe. It was during one of those calls that he heard of Andrew's death, just in time to go with Barbara and Daddy to identify the body.

A year later, in 1962, I had to confront two other deaths, those of "Aunt" Helen and Aunt Bessie. The summer of 1962, when Birdie and I got married, we sent Barbara and Michele to Camp Craigmeade in the Catskills, which they had been attending off and on for years. Aunt Helen, the founder/director of the camp and an indestructible and marvelous woman, died at camp that summer. Barbara held vigil outside Aunt Helen's room, listening to her groans and watching the staff go in and out of the room. In the morning Aunt Helen was dead. I myself had just returned home from the annual parents weekend at camp when I received the news. When I left, Aunt Helen had been her usual self doing the work of ten ordinary people: running the camp, supervising the children, the counselors, and everybody else like a mother, and bathing all the children in a huge tub in the kitchen. That was the last thing I remember seeing her do. But now it was over. Aunt Helen's death struck a dismal end to yet another summer.

Within a few weeks, Aunt Bessie, my mother's sister, had a heart attack and was rushed to the hospital. She died the next day. Mother, who had been so strong the previous summer in Rome when we received news of Andrew's death, now had a complete collapse. Birdie, the girls, and I had to move into Mother's house. We stayed there and nursed her back to health. The doctor had prescribed the remedy: tender loving care. It was the loss of so much in so short a time that caused Mother to become deeply depressed. I had never seen her in this state before. Within a few months I had gotten married, her oldest sister had died, and just a year before had been Andrew's death. Mother lay in her bed in silence. She was now mourning not only her sister but also her son as she hadn't been able to do before. I also think she felt my getting married meant she had lost me, too. I had to prove it wasn't so, and that would be one of the hardest tasks I ever had to do.

Chapter 7: The 1960s: Is There a Black Art?

Me painting Flag for the Moon: Die Nigger, *1969*

In the early sixties, for the first time despite all the hell in my life, I decided to make it known that I was an artist demanding to be taken seriously. My pictures, which once suffered from muddy color and faulty brushwork, were now colorful and well defined. Their subjects were flowers, landscapes, and trees painted in the French Impressionist manner. I used a palette knife so that I could work in heavy impasto, and still keep my edges well defined in the thickly laid-on paint. If I wanted to remove an image, I could just scrape it off with my knife and lay on a new one without getting "mud," or having the underpainting show through.

I was now ready to look for a gallery on East 57th Street, a famous location for important art. In 1963, only one black artist showed there — Jacob Lawrence at the ACA Gallery. Since the thirties, Lawrence had been hard at work as a painter and was known for his series depicting the life and struggles of black people. Lawrence's series on Harriet Tubman, John Brown, Toussaint L'Ouverture, and the Migration of the Negro were works that I knew and loved. I finally met Lawrence in 1968 at a benefit exhibition for Martin Luther King Jr. at the Museum of Modern Art. I was delighted to be in this exhibition with him and to find that such a great artist was also a great human being.

I approached everyone I knew who might help me find a gallery to show my work. Louis Shanker, an artist, suggested that I try the Ruth White Gallery on 57th Street.

Accordingly, I packed up some of my paintings, called ahead for an appointment, and had Birdie drive me down and help me carry the paintings up to the second-floor gallery. Ruth White was there when we arrived. I introduced myself and proceeded to show her my paintings. They were all oil paintings of trees and flowers in "French" colors. Her face was expressionless as she carefully studied the art.

Finally she spoke. She said something to me that, whether or not it was meant to, helped me as an artist. "Do you know where you are?" she asked.

"Yes," I said, looking at Birdie out of the corner of my eye to see how he was taking this. He was a master of comprehending situations and people on the spot. Today, we call it street smarts — then, any black person who didn't have it was missing an essential part of their education. "I am on East Fifty-seventh Street," I answered.

She pointed to my "French " paintings. "You," she said, placing a stress on the word *you,* "cannot do this." I knew what she meant as I saw Birdie's eyes go immediately to the walls of the gallery where there were examples of work very similar to mine. I thanked her for her time, gathered up my paintings, and we left.

That summer of 1963 I took the girls to Oak Bluffs on Martha's Vineyard in Massachusetts. We had been invited to spend the summer there on the estate of Dr. and Mrs. Goldsberry of Wooster. Birdie could come up on the weekends if he started to miss us. And he did visit, twice. We had already spent several summers in a beach house in Provincetown in the late 1950s where I painted the houses and boats while the girls ran free on the beach. Birdie had financed those trips before we were married, and even bought our plane tickets for our first ride in an airplane. The girls loved the tiny eight-seater plane that took us from Boston to Provincetown, and Barbara, since she was the smallest, got to ride in the copilot's seat. Who would have guessed that Birdie, an avid bird lover, had a fierce fear of flying? On our way to Provincetown some years later in the late 1960s, I learned from him the true meaning of a white-knuckled flyer.

That summer of 1963 was the beginning of my mature work. I planned to paint five paintings in my new style, which I called "Super Realism." The idea was to make a statement in my art about the Civil Rights Movement and what was happening to black people in America at that time, and to make it super-real. I painted outdoors on the Goldsberrys' lawn. Painting outdoors has its own problems, not the least of which is the insects that fly into the wet oil paint and get stuck there. But I survived the insects and the sun, and produced the first of the twenty-odd paintings of my American People Series.

The first painting, *Between Friends,* depicting an uneasy meeting between a black and a white woman, was inspired by the women who came to weekday poker parties at the Goldsberrys' house while their husbands were in their offices in town. The Goldsberrys were lifetime members of the NAACP (National Association for the Advancement of Colored People) and entertained an interracial group of high-powered friends. I thought the white women were simply representing their husbands, and I could sense a lot of distance between friendship and what these women were sharing.

My other four paintings also seemed to ask "why" about some basic racial questions concerning American people. *For Members Only* recalls the open racial hostility I encountered as a child on a church school outing to Tibbets Brook in Upper New York State. A band of white men, carrying sticks, surrounded us kids and demanded that we get out and "go back to your bus." *Neighbors* was about the not-so-neighborly greeting of

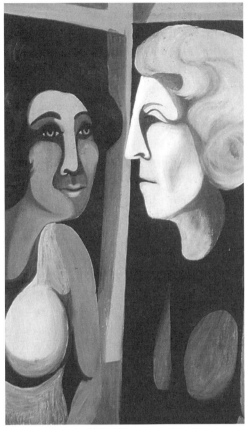

Between Friends, *1963, Oil on canvas, 24 x 40 inches, Artist's collection*

three generations of a white family living next door to a black family who had just moved in. *Watching and Waiting* shows a table at which a group of white businessmen are meeting. A black man stands at the door as if waiting for an invitation to sit down. (People often mistake the black man for a waiter, even though he is dressed in a business suit.) *The Civil Rights Triangle* referred to the church as both the power structure for change and its association with the white male establishment — which together made up the top structure of the Civil Rights Movement. By the time I came home at the end of the summer, these paintings were finished and I was planning to do many more in this series. Now I knew where my art was going. I had so many ideas that I barely had time to execute them.

Watching and
Waiting, *1963, Oil on
canvas, 36 x 40 inches,
Artist's collection*

James Baldwin had just published *The Fire Next Time,* Malcolm X was talking about
"us loving our black selves," and Martin Luther King Jr. was leading marches and
spreading the word. All over this country and the world people were listening to these
black men. I felt called upon to create my own vision of the black experience we were
witnessing. I read feverishly, especially everything that James Baldwin had written on
relationships between blacks and whites in America. Baldwin understood, I felt, the dis-
parity between black and white people as well as anyone; but I had something to add —
the visual depiction of the way we are and look. I wanted my painting to express this
moment I knew was history. I wanted to give my woman's point of view to this period.

We had now moved to a larger apartment on Edgecombe Avenue down the street
from where Birdie and I grew up. Dinah Washington had lived in our apartment
before us. She moved to Detroit with her new husband, Night Train, the football player,
and her two sons. Everyone in the apartment building had something to say about
Dinah. She was a legend in that building, with all the stories about her fancy clothes and

the midnight parties with live music played by Miles Davis and Count Basie and other famous musicians. Dinah was the Queen of the Blues and when she died suddenly in 1963, a few days after Christmas, Harlem mourned her death like a close relative. I kept her music playing, and on the weekends I often played it so loudly that my neighbors could hear. They never complained: Dinah was still the Queen.

I had a real studio now in one of our three bedrooms. Though it was small, it was my own space and I could work in it on weekends, holidays, and daily after school. During the week I often stayed up painting until two in the morning, when Birdie came home from work at General Motors and insisted that I come to bed.

I had given up the impasto strokes of the palette knife for a brush. My paintings were getting stronger. The brush was light as a feather in my hand and I liked the way I could paint flat colors in thin glazes. I had now control of both my medium and my subject; clearly it was time to go looking for a gallery again. I avoided Ruth White's gallery; after all, she only showed "French" paintings and I wasn't doing those anymore. Rather I was trying to find my voice, talking to myself through my art, and hoping that, if I could communicate with myself, I could also communicate with others. I desperately needed some opportunity to have meaningful dialogue with other artists. I was starved for this kind of exchange. I used to call friends and people I taught with, and endlessly talk on and on to them about being an artist and all the problems it entailed. I knew I was boring them, but the isolation was killing me. I got a lot of excuses like "My husband just came home," or "My doorbell is ringing." Nobody I knew seemed to have the time just to talk about ideas or problems, except my mother. She never got tired of listening. I know I worried her during those years, but she held on to me, and I to her.

Often older artists wrote my paintings off as "protest" art, sometimes even dismissing them as merely history painting or social realism. They were mostly people who had been badly burned during the Communist scare in the fifties and now wanted to keep their noses and palettes clean. Art for them was an abstraction, a fragment of an idea that nobody could understand, much less condemn. However, I had called my art "Super Realism" because I wanted my audience to make a personal connection with its images and the message. The older artists were cautious — "half-stepping," as they used to say in the sixties — trying to get by in the art world and not drawing attention to their blackness. "Art is art. Quality is the important thing. It doesn't matter what color you are" was their message. They knew there was little or no support for artists in the black community — so what could be gained by alienating friends and contacts in the white art world? On the

Mr. Charlie, *1964, Oil on canvas, 33 x 18 inches, Artist's collection*

other hand, I was not concerned with friends or enemies. Being unknown and a newcomer, I had neither. I was concerned with making truthful statements in my art and having it seen. Younger black artists objected to my paintings of white people. Some neither understood nor accepted my need to make images of anyone but black people. Others, I was told, felt that my steely-eyed white faces were going too damn far.

In the summer of 1965 I had heard that Harry Belafonte was interested in black artists and was collecting their work. I went to his offices on West 57th Street where his secretary told me that his business manager, Sy Siegel, bought all of his paintings for him. So I took several of my paintings from the American People Series to show to Mr. Siegel. One was *Mr. Charlie,* a large grinning head of a patronizing white man. Another, called *The Cocktail Party,* was a social gathering with one black person. The final canvas I brought was *The American Dream,* which presented a woman, half white, half black, showing off her huge diamond ring. Mr. Siegel turned red. He growled menacingly: "I don't know who these people are." Waving his hand at the paintings, he went on angrily, "And I don't know what they're doing." (He was looking at *The In Crowd,* a scene of white men piled up in a power pyramid with black men on the bottom.)

I tried to explain the scene to him. "You see this white man has his hand on this black man's mouth because he doesn't want him to speak out about the injustice in the black community. We call him 'Uncle Tom,' and we call him" — pointing to the grinning white face — " 'Mr. Charlie.' "

"Well, you wanted me to see them and I've seen them," Mr. Siegel thundered. He turned and left the outer office, slamming the door in my face.

I considered taking my *Mr. Charlie* painting down to the Broadway theater where James Baldwin's play, *Blues for Mr. Charlie,* was playing. Baldwin's secretary didn't think, however, that Mr. Baldwin would be interested in displaying my painting in the lobby of the theater. Baldwin himself was not available for comment one way or the other.

I never did see James Baldwin or Harry Belafonte, but Mel Tapley, an arts reporter for the *Amsterdam News* (a black newspaper and one of the largest weekly newspapers in the country), wrote an article about my attempts to find a gallery. He illustrated it with a big picture of me and the painting I'd tried to show Belafonte — without referring to the incident with Mr Siegel. This article appeared on May 16, 1964, and was the first article concerning my art to appear in print.

In the late 1940s I met black artists for the first time: Al Hollingsworth and Earl Hill. Earl Hill used to have life drawing sessions at his Bronx studio. Al Hollingsworth was a painter, illustrator, and cartoonist. He was a graduate of Music and Art High School and had been making a living as a syndicated cartoonist since he was twelve years old. I had met Al at City College, where we were the only two black art students in the art department. It was Roy, Al's brother, who introduced me to African art.

One Saturday we went on a group sketching trip to the Segy Gallery on Madison Avenue. I saw African masks and sculptures that both frightened and intrigued me. We attempted to sketch them, but Mr. Segy was entertaining collectors and we were in their way. He asked us to leave. Roy was indignant. He yelled out as we were leaving, "We fought two wars." I never knew exactly what he meant, but then I frequently failed to understand Roy — like the time he told me that I could no longer be a part of his art group because I was separated from my husband, Earl.

In 1964, for the first time in a long while, Romare Bearden was having a show at the Cordier and Eckstrom Gallery on Madison Avenue. He had developed a collage technique for his images of black life in the South and the Caribbean islands, using blown-up black-and-white photographs. I was delighted and very proud that Bearden had just been the subject of an impressive article in *Art News.* I wanted to visit his studio and join his group, Spiral.

Spiral was formed in 1963 in New York, the year I began the American People Series in Oak Bluffs. It was a black artists' group of thirteen men and one woman, Emma Amos. Romare Bearden, Charles Alston, Norman Lewis, and Hale Woodruff were the backbone of the group. They were "the old men of black art," as the painter Vivian Browne used to call them affectionately. Spiral was something like "The Club," a white artists' group that was also a men's group, with women by invitation only. I decided to call Mr. Bearden and try to get an invitation to join Spiral.

Bearden was polite but distant. "I saw your review in *Art News,*" I told him excitedly, "I really like your work. I am an artist, too. I wonder if it would be all right if I sent you some slides of my work?" He gave me his address and I sent off the color slides immediately with a letter in which I mentioned Spiral and emphasized my need to see and talk to other black artists. I also told him about how much trouble I was having finding a gallery to show my work. Within a few days I heard from Bearden.

Nov. 8, 1964

Mrs. Ringgold:

Thank you for your letter and for letting me see the reproductions of your paintings. I am returning them as soon as possible, because I know this type of material can be most valuable to you.

First off, let me state that I enjoyed seeing your slides. From what you tell me of your color combinations I can understand that your paintings are direct and forceable. It is hard to imagine them being produced by someone referred to as being so "petite."

Reading of your academic background and achievement in the teaching profession, I would hesitate to say anything more. However, since you have asked me to add a few suggestions I will make a few brief ones.

If you have not done so you might look at the work of George Grosz, Kathe Kollwitz, and, particularly in your case, Max Beckmann. Works of all these artists, I think, are available in the library. The placement of your figures, whereby the forehead of the upper most figure, when there are more than one, can be monotonous if you make this a habit. Place your figures in space whereby they can breathe and not be worried by having to hold the top of the frame on their heads. Look to the relations between the figures and/or the objects, so the eye can move in an easy way through the work. I have, in this connection, sent you a small reproduction of an old German painting, altho I hope you will not feel I only consider German artists; but in this work observe the variation in headdress, how the one on the right

The Cocktail Party,
1964, Oil on canvas,
42 x 24 inches, Artist's
collection (far left);
The American Dream,
1964, Oil on canvas,
36 x 24 inches, Artist's
collection (near left)

seems to go up above the frame, while the lady on the right is set down on the picture plane even tho all the women are the same height. The hands of the personages are all different. Everything, as a matter of fact, in this painting adds up to an exact and subtle statement. Since your desire, from what I read, is to do something of the same nature for contemporary life, just this one painting could be studied a long long time. Lastly, you might trace the dark area in the Cranach and you will find that the whole complex is as interesting a shape as that of the three figures. I think, should you agree this is valuable, you might simplify your background in some like manner.

I feel I have said enough of these technical matters. I hope my thoughts may prove helpful.

To conclude, let me hope that your paintings will eventually find their own friends. Most often, Mrs. Ringgold, this is a long process. I have friends whom I consider most talented artists, yet they are in the same dilemma as you are in seeking some place to exhibit their work. So, don't despair, just continue to work hard.

I hope you will forgive any syntactical and spelling errors you may find in this letter, I am poor on both levels. With best wishes for your continued success.

Very Truly Yours,
Romare Bearden

I was crushed. Oh, "Mr." Bearden, I thought I was trying to forget all those theories about composition and asymmetrical balance, subtle harmony and subdued colors. It didn't apply to what I was doing. And, furthermore, I had wanted to join Spiral, and talk it all over with the old men of black art, and the one young woman. Bearden's letter made it abundantly clear, however, that he was not going to include me in this circle, and I was not about to pursue an outright spoken rejection. At least Romare Bearden had seen my work, and answered my letter. He knew I was around.

Amiri Baraka, then known as Leroi Jones, a brilliant poet and playwright, was a model for poets and performance art since the 1950s. He wrote reviews of jazz and art, and in the late 1950s was a regular at the Cedar Tavern, where the artist Larry Rivers and other white artists and poets of the Beat Generation gathered. In the summer of 1966, Leroi Jones, who had now split with the Beat Generation, founded the Black Arts Theater in Harlem. I discovered the theater while riding on the Seventh Avenue bus. What caught my attention was the Marcus Garvey red-black-and-green flag hanging from the window of a brownstone. I got off the bus and found a three-story building that featured a program of activities in all the arts, plus a theater performance of *The Dutchman,* one of my favorite Leroi Jones plays. I promptly registered Barbara and Michele in the African dance classes, and myself in the silkscreen workshop. Ed Spriggs taught this class. He was new to New York from California and was on his way to making a name for himself in black art circles as the future director of the Studio Museum of Harlem.

The black community was the new power structure for black artists. Everybody was writing a grant proposal but, like the downtown white establishment, you still had to be somebody or know somebody to get a piece of the action. Haryou Act, a poverty-based program in Harlem, was the first to get large sums of money to research poverty and to promote culture and education. Adam Clayton Powell Jr. was the originator of this program. Money was flowing like water, and Leroi Jones got some of it for his Black Arts Theater.

Maybe the Black Arts Theater would provide a place for me to show my work, and give me the opportunity to have some meaningful dialogue with other black artists. Maybe I could rap with Leroi Jones, woman to man. I had just discovered that Leroi lived downtown in Greenwich Village — he was just commuting to Harlem like everybody else who worked there.

Leroi Jones's Black Arts Theater was to sponsor a traveling exhibition of black artists that summer. The intent was to take art to the people of Harlem by caravan, set up in parks and empty spaces. I heard about these plans the first day I went to the Black Arts Theater because a man in the office had filled me in on all the center's activities. When he found out that I was an artist, he told me all about the exhibition, which was to include Jacob Lawrence, Richard Mayhew, Norman Lewis, and Romare Bearden, among others. The man told me to bring my slides for Leroi to look at, and so I brought the same slides I had showed Harry Belafonte's business agent, Sy Siegel: *Mr. Charlie, The In Crowd, The Cocktail Party,* and *The American Dream.*

I was about to leave the theater's office when four men entered. The man who had encouraged me to submit my work greeted them warmly saying, "Leroi, you should see this sister's paintings. They're coming from the same place you're coming from, man. I know you're gonna dig 'em." I turned to see what Leroi's reaction would be to such a remark and was shocked to see a little man, not even as tall as I was. Obviously out of my milieu, I heard myself blurting out, "What, you're Leroi Jones? I thought you were . . ." My voice trailed off when I realized what I was about to say. My incomplete statement, however, had caught the great man's attention.

His moon-shaped eyes took in my straightened hair pulled back with a fall. My clothes, custom-made by my mother, were black "middle class" — a white, polished cotton dress fitted my ample hips. I was not wearing the 1960s hip uniform of dungarees, and I didn't have a "fro." "You thought I was what?" he asked. I sensed his mounting hostility, but responded recklessly: "I thought you would be a big man." He looked at me with disbelief. Narrowing his eyes, he asked, "Big, how?" The tiny office was static with expectation. "What is this jive-time chick talking about?" seemed to be the question on the faces of the other three men, who stood there watching this exchange with rapt attention. "You know . . . big," I said, stretching my arms above my five-foot-five-and-one-half-inch height in my two-and-one-half-inch heels. I pointed at the men in the room, all of whom were looking down on both of us. "Tall and big," I repeated, this time alluding to Leroi's weight as well as height. The conversation ended with my arms bent at the elbow, with both hands turned in touching my hips in a gorilla pose to show Leroi what seemed so hard for him to understand. I was a fool, but he was a little dude with a big man's rap and that was all I was trying to say. He was not pleased. But I dare say, he did not forget that "we talked." To my surprise I was included in the Black Arts Theater show; Betty Blayton Taylor organized the caravan, and the exhibition toured the streets of Harlem. Unfortunately I was on vacation in Provincetown with the girls when the exhibition opened in August of 1966, but I heard it was a great success.

My first gallery appearance was in the fall of 1966 in a group show entitled "Art of the American Negro." It was the first black art show to be held in Harlem since the thirties and was curated by Romare Bearden and sponsored by the Harlem Cultural Council. Carroll Greene, a black art historian, held the reception for the artists and patrons of the exhibition at his apartment in Kips Bay. It was my first time hobnobbing with the royalty of the black art scene and I was thrilled to be in the show and meet Bearden.

My art was changing. In the backgrounds of my canvases, stop signs and arrows had been supplanted by leaves and flowers, which seemed more appropriate for the women and children I was now painting. In *Hide Little Children,* two black children and one white child are hiding in the trees with only their little faces showing. This painting was inspired by my own children and the fears I had about their friendships with white children with whom they socialized in and out of school. New Lincoln School had a reputation for being ultra-liberal, but what about the parents? What kind of reputation did they have?

In 1966 I was invited to join the Spectrum Gallery on West 57th Street between Fifth and Sixth avenues. It was an early cooperative gallery run by Robert Newman, a poet and critic. It took some convincing on his part before the members of the gallery voted me in. There were about twenty artists in the gallery — all mainstream abstract painters and sculptors, five of whom were women, and the only black was me.

Mainstream art was the art of the sixties, despite the "revolution" going on in the street. The art was cool, unemotional, uninvolved, and not "about" anything. Issue-oriented art was dismissed as being naive, if not downright vulgar. Art was a conceptual or material process, a commodity and not a political platform. Most mainstream artists, black as well as white, agreed on that. To be emotionally involved in art was considered primitive.

Many artists painted large canvases as if to say, "To be big you have to paint big." My paintings, on the other hand, were small, three by four feet. I felt like a tiny fish in a big pond, although I realized that anybody could paint the same configuration of circles and squares and lines on a six-foot canvas as on a smaller one. The magic of painting had nothing to do with size. In most cases, people were just painting big to be in style. Mainstream art was tailor-made to satisfy the rich art collectors and patrons who did their art shopping in Madison Avenue galleries. Artists who wanted to get into a good gallery were the most conscious of the mainstream rules. They named their canvases *Untitled,* and did not sign them — people were supposed to know who you were and what the work was about. That was "art cool."

Robert Newman decided that Spectrum should host a panel. He invited Ivan Karp, the former curator at the Leo Castelli Gallery who had discovered Andy Warhol, together with the art critics Dore Ashton and John Ashbery and some others whose names escape me. Robert also invited The Black Mask, a group of dissident young art student radicals who had become popular for "jumping bad" at a lecture at Cooper Union some weeks before. There they had practically come to blows with Larry Rivers during his presentation.

I took Mother to the panel, not realizing what we were in for. We heard some loud talking in the stairwell leading up to the gallery, while inside the panelists were having a soft exchange of mainstream art talk. I remember Dore Ashton was announcing that "Art is dead," and Ivan Karp arguing that "Andy is a real star. He never talks because he has nothing to say. His art is a copy. He's just doing what anybody can do." (Karp was seen as very close to being God among many artists.) Audience members wanted to know how to become a big star like Andy, and how to get reviewed by important critics and represented by mainstream galleries like Castelli. At this point we heard fists pounding on the door. Robert and some of the male artists rushed out, closing the door behind them. Outside we could hear quiet scuffling and sudden outbreaks of loud talking laced with cursing and name calling. The Black Mask had arrived. Though they had been invited, for whatever reason now they were not being admitted. I thought of teenage Harlem house parties of the forties. Some boys would attempt to crash a party by demanding to see someone and the girls would be left safely inside while the boys went outside to "cool those cats." Sometimes somebody got hurt. It was the chance you took when attending or having a party in those days.

A member of The Black Mask yelled out, "Where is Ivan Karp?" Karp jumped up from the table, leaving Dore Ashton behind, and, with the other men on the panel, rushed to the door yelling, "Who wants me? Who wants me?" My mother was terrified. She cautioned me never to come down here alone again. "Why, these people are just terrible," she said, turning around to see if anyone agreed. They did. Martha Graham was in the audience at the gallery that night. But in the confusion I did not remember to notice how she responded. As for me, I found the event not so much a "happening" as a distraction.

My first one-person show at the Spectrum Gallery was scheduled for December 1967. Since the gallery would be closed during June, July, and August, Robert suggested that I use the gallery as my studio. I sent the girls to Europe with Mother for the summer. They studied French at the Alliance Française while mother visited the couturiers in their salons in Paris and in Rome. For the first time since the girls were born, I had two months to myself. Had it not been for Mother taking them to Europe, I would not have been able to complete the paintings for the show. Birdie and I had a falling out about what I should be doing with my summer. I didn't want to spend my time cleaning the house and cooking, so I moved into Mother's apartment and every day I painted well into the night in the gallery space. By the end of the summer, when the girls and Mother came home from Europe, Birdie had left me. Who could blame him?

Living alone was a new experience for me. All my life I had been either a daughter living with my parents, or a wife and mother living with a husband and children. Now I could get up whenever I wanted to and had only myself to cook for, to clean up after, to amuse, and to generally consider. It was lonely but pleasant because for two months there was nothing between myself and my work.

Now that I was on my own, what would I paint? Robert wanted me to depict everything that was happening in America — the sixties and the decade's tumultuous thrusts for freedom. Maybe I would have done this anyway, but it was very comforting to have someone suggest something that is exactly what you should be doing. I've always been grateful for the support and direction Robert gave me that summer. I have never regretted all that the summer of 1967 cost me. It was well worth it.

The climate of America was changing in the summer of 1967. We were moving out of the civil rights period and were at the start of the Black Revolution. In 1966 Adam Clayton Powell Jr. and Stokely Carmichael had sounded the battle cry for Black Power, and by 1967 everyone was taking sides. I was at a public meeting in Provincetown where white diehard liberals openly expressed their dismay over the words *Black Power*. One of them tearfully asked, "But why would blacks want power? I thought we were all going to be equal?"

I felt white people were very much aware of me on Madison Avenue when I went there to window-shop, and when I walked along 57th Street to and from the subway on my way home to Harlem. Black people were no longer invisible: our articulate spokesmen were getting airtime and their followers were taking actions in the street. Protest demonstrations had reached epidemic proportions.

My only friend that summer was Jeannine Petit, a white woman and another member of the Spectrum Gallery. She and I painted together in the gallery. Jeannine was working on a series encompassing over two hundred canvases, with all the colors of the spectrum. We worked in very different ways: she with pure color abstraction and I with people and messages. We talked art all summer long while we painted. Afterward, we often went walking or out to eat. We had more in common as artists and women than either of us would have expected. We became good friends as well.

Working in the large space at the Spectrum meant that I could for the first time in my life paint mural-sized works. At the time, I had just seen a large canvas exhibition at the Jewish Museum curated by Allen Schoerner and Kynaston McShine featuring the works of Larry Poons and Robert Goodenough. I came away with the idea that there was more to a big canvas than its size; that there had to be a good reason for taking up so much space if the painting was to be more than merely expensive wallpaper. I had also recently visited the Museum of Modern Art yet again to see my favorite Picasso — the huge *Guernica*. It is a canvas that one first "sees" as a whole flat image, and only later does one become aware of its parts. Everything happens up front. Perspective can be the enemy of a mural, creating holes in the composition instead of distance.

In the summer of 1963 I painted five paintings to begin the American People Series. Now I planned to make three paintings to end the series. With these last paintings I felt that I would finally have said all I had to say about the civil rights era. The three large paintings were *The Flag is Bleeding, U.S. Postage Stamp Commemorating the Advent of Black Power,* and *Die.* Their large sizes made it imperative to plan every phase of them, and I made several drawings for each on graph paper to get a feel for the content and composition. They were painted in thin oil glazes that I had learned to make from formulas I discovered while in college. A "lean" glaze, composed of sun-thickened linseed oil and turpentine for the underpainting, and a mixture of stand oil, damar varnish, and turpentine for the overpainting. Each layer of oil paint on a canvas has a life of its own. It is what gives oil painting its luminosity, and makes it appear as if it is constantly changing.

First I painted *The Flag is Bleeding.* It was eight feet wide and six feet high and appeared to be twice that size. What could I do if the painting was a failure? How could I discard such a large mistake? By the end of July I had completed the canvas. When a painting becomes a copy of the picture in my mind, I always know that it is finished. Now I wanted the world to see *The Flag is Bleeding.* This was actually a very strong image in my mind and the first flag painting in which I showed the complete flag image. The fragile white woman standing in the stripes is the peace-maker. The black man carries a knife, while the white man packs a gun on each hip, ready to draw, western style. In 1967 not many black men had access to guns. And why is there no black woman in this picture?

Let us just say that in 1967 she was reluctantly standing behind her man. The white woman was too, but somebody had to get between these two men, and since she was the daughter of the white power structure, she had inherited the role of peace-maker.

I was partially inspired by Jasper Johns's flag series for two reasons — I liked the regularity of the position of the forty-eight stars as opposed to the uneven position of the fifty stars (which our flag actually had in 1967), and also I felt that Johns's flag presented a beautiful, but incomplete, idea. To complete it I wanted to show some of the hell that had broken out in the States, and what better place to do that than in the stars and stripes?

I next painted *U.S. Postage Stamp Commemorating the Advent of Black Power,* another canvas that measured six by eight feet. This was probably the most difficult picture I have ever painted. I needed to resolve the problem of a composition of a hundred faces that could be read as both a single image and as separate ones. I wanted to give individuality to each face, but I didn't want to — if you know what I mean — because it was so much work. Yet I did it and it took forever. The only way you will ever know if a composition works is to try it. And, if you can't make it work, let it go. The good news is that the more work you do, the less chance you have of disliking what you do. I am relieved to state that after over thirty years of painting, I still love what I do.

U.S. *Postage Stamp Commemorating the Advent of Black Power* was a difficult work for me on two counts. It was difficult to paint the hundred faces, but equally it was difficult to visualize the subject itself because, in many ways, I had no idea what Black Power meant. My own need to feel a sense of personal as well as public power was in direct contrast to a world that ignored women of all races. For me the concept of Black Power carried with it a big question mark. Was it intended only for the black men or would black women have power, too? I expressed this idea by depicting the words "Black Power" in a diagonal line of letters descending across the canvas from left to right. The words "White Power" are shown in horizontal white letters and represent the white (racist) power whose challenge led to the creation of the Civil Rights Movement and its rallying cry for "Black Power." In his press release for the show, Newman described this painting as "an American classic."

The last painting was *Die,* the largest of the three canvases. Composed of two parts, it measured six by twelve feet. At the time of this painting Martin Luther King Jr. was still alive but Malcolm X and John and Robert Kennedy had been assassinated. I had to paint *Die* just as I had felt propelled to paint the other two murals in this series. I was also terrified because

I saw *Die* as a prophecy of our times. I saw it as a warning that violence would become the new "pornography." Newman had written about *Die,* too: "Faith Ringgold's . . . deep emotion about the terrible incommunication is unforgettably vivid in her stunning mural of the riot, *Die."*

Romare Bearden and me at 1967 opening at Spectrum Gallery

"American People," my first solo show, opened at the Spectrum Gallery on December 19, 1967. My three murals occupied the outer gallery, and the smaller works were in the other two spaces in the inner gallery. Most people were responsive to them, although some felt that *Die* was too bloody, or, as Robert put it, "You would not see that much blood in Vietnam." One woman got off the elevator, which faced the painting, only to lunge backward and shout to the elevator operator to take her down. She had been face to face with *Die* and she couldn't stand the blood. Today hardly anybody remarks about the blood, except to ask, "What blood?"

The opening party was a joy and celebration. I invited everybody and over five hundred people came. I had music for the kids, and my girls invited their classmates and friends from the New Lincoln School. The adults were delighted to be around young people: they stood in the door of the middle gallery where the children were occupied with the latest dances. The kids were oblivious to their stares. This was the youth generation, and kids were "in." Everybody was watching them. They were our future, our young hope, the answer to all our failures.

The "old men of black art" were there: Romare Bearden, Norman Lewis, and Richard Mayhew came together. Had they come to see why Robert argued in his provocative press release that "in her dramatic first major exhibition, [Ringgold] emerges as the major American Negro artist, an essential American artist." He had gone on to praise my murals as "unique and unforgettable."

My reviews were encouraging too. *Arts Magazine, Art News,* the *Amsterdam News,* and *The United Teacher* (the United Federation of Teachers' Union paper) carried pictures. I was delighted. In the review in *Arts Magazine* (February 1968), John Fischer wrote:

Faith Ringgold's "American People" exhibition is, as might be expected of a Negro, about the struggle for equality. Violent action is depicted in *Die,* a mural of rioting, knifing, shooting and bloody, screaming humanity. Painted against a background of grey squares, powerful figures cross, extend and overlap as they inflict mortal wounds. There is much blood depicted in bright, pure pigment. The faces are graphically powerful. Blackie is grim. Whitey has blond hair. At bottom a tiny interracial couple (a white child clutching a little Negro girl) strikes the viewer where it counts. Although self-consciously ambitious, these paintings show exceptional talent. The artist has a penetrating sense of irony which she graphically translates into pictorial emotion effectively.

In January 1968 the *Art News* reviewer, Ralph Pomeroy, praised my "big bold protests against the black white situation." He described *Die* as "a horror cartoon of bloody street fighting with two frightened children (colored and white) bundled in each other's arms." He saw *The Flag is Bleeding* as a "blond girl arm in arm with a knife-clutching Negro and an unarmed white man." For Pomeroy, "Formally, *Postage Stamp Commemorating the Advent of Black Power* is the best; rows of eyes and noses of many shades with various legends worked into and over them."

Every Saturday during the four weeks of my show, I went to sit in the gallery and talk to people. One Saturday a tall, distinguished-looking black man was waiting for me. It was Professor James Porter, the chairman of the Art Department at Howard University in Washington, D.C., and the author of *Modern Negro Art* (1943), one of the first books on African-American art to be published. Porter told me how much he liked my work, especially *Bridesmaid of Martha's Vineyard* (1966). This painting of a bridesmaid, carrying flowers and standing on a lawn next to a large oak tree, had been inspired by the old-fashioned though somewhat timely saying, "Always a bridesmaid, never a bride." I knew black women, friends of mine who were in their thirties, who were unmarried, but not by choice. These women would be, I thought, a great catch for a smart man. Why were there so many good women still unmarried, unappreciated, and overlooked by the men of their generation?

Professor Porter did not share my concerns. He wanted to rename the painting *Bride of Martha's Vineyard;* it reminded him of his own wedding, which had taken place a year before at Martha's Vineyard. I consented to the change in title but in my mind the bride was still a bridesmaid. The sale of this painting to James Porter was my first important one — not only because he paid me several hundred dollars, but because it was to be part of the collection of a famous black artist, art historian, writer, and educator. (James Porter has since died but his wife, Dorothy Porter, continues his art collection.)

By the end of 1967 I had had my first one-person show, had received positive reviews of my work in mainstream art publications, and had sold two paintings — *Bride of Martha's Vineyard* to Porter and *Hide Little Children* to Carol Bobkoff, a young art collector. The American People Series was complete, and I was excited about the new experiments in what I called "black light." But I was also apprehensive about painting more pictures when I had nowhere to show the ones I had already made. After all, despite the recognition I had received, I was still unconnected to the art world, black or white. I saw my lack of opportunity as an indication that being a black woman was a major drawback in my career and, therefore, needed to be addressed openly.

I was not yet ready to deal with women's issues. However, I felt that since black America was confronting racism in almost every area of American life, why not in art? In 1968 I got involved for the first

Soul Sister, *1967, Oil on canvas, 36 x 18 inches, Artist's collection*

time in art politics and participated in a demonstration, although I had already been deeply concerned with American race politics. In the early 1960s, for example, I had approached the SCLC (the Southern Christian Leadership Conference) with an offer to volunteer my help in their New York office in any way I could. They said that they needed money and so I invited them to send a speaker to one of Mother's fashion shows to make an appeal. They sent Fannie Lou Hamer and another woman. We were all horrified to hear their firsthand accounts of the beatings and attacks by southern police with dogs and fire hoses. The audience made a generous donation. Now, in 1968, I was even more determined to help make changes relevant to black people and to do it in the art world.

Come the summer of 1969, I found myself longing to paint. In 1967 I had begun to explore the idea of a new palette, a way of expressing on canvas the new "black is beautiful" sense of ourselves. In the painting of *Die*, I had depended upon the blood-splattered white clothing of the figures to create the contrast needed to express the movement and energy of the riot. I felt bound to its use, having been trained to paint in the Western tradition. But I was now committed to "black light" and subtle color nuances and compositions based on my new interest in African rhythm, pattern, and repetition. In 1971 I described these new works as experiments in toning the light to the blacks, browns, and grays that cover my skin and hair; and the shades of blues, greens, and reds that create my forms and textures. In years to come my colors have lightened, but I feel more comfortable with "black light" even now.

I was interested in Ad Reinhardt and Josef Albers since they, too, had created black paintings. Reinhardt's paintings are so hard to see; a guard at the Museum of Modern Art once told me that often people get frustrated looking at them because the canvases appear to have no images at all. Only after intense concentration do Reinhardt's images become visible. People got angry about his style of painting. Were they angry because it was black? Wasn't Ralph Ellison's *Invisible Man* black? And how much of the hatred directed at black people had to do with their lack of high visibility? Is black racism just another term for low "color" visibility?

The way we see color is influenced by the colors that surround us. Our own color, for instance, is indelibly etched in our mind and, unless someone tells us otherwise, it influences our overall sense of color. As an artist and woman of color, I had become particularly interested in this idea. I had noticed that black artists tended to use a darker palette. White and light colors are used sparingly and relegated to contrasting color in African-American, South African, and East African art — and used as a "mood" color in African supernatural and death masks. In Western art, however, white and light influence the entire palette, thereby creating a predominance of white, pastel colors, and light-and-shade, or chiaroscuro. Chiaroscuro and light, employed to suggest space and form, were first seen in the Italian painter Masaccio's *Expulsion from the Garden of Eden,*

Ego Painting, *1969, Oil on canvas, 40 x 40 inches, Artist's collection*

which is a classic "beginning" moment in European Renaissance art history. As a young art student, I tried feverishly to paint black portraits using light and shade. I became frustrated because dark-skinned images painted this way lose their luminosity and therefore look better painted in flat color. The South, West, and East Africans knew this and created their paintings accordingly.

I made my early black paintings in 1967 by very crudely mixing ivory black into other colors to darken them. Because ivory black has a high oil content, it dries slowly and produces an uneven glossy sheen. Continuing to perfect my new palette, I switched from ivory black to Mars black, which dries faster and has a beautiful matte finish. Then I decided to add burnt umber, which also has a beautiful surface quality and emulates dark flesh tones. I used flake white to create opacity and to lighten my colors a little. Against a white background, the color differences between red/black, blue/black, and brown/black, and so on are indistinguishable — all the blacks look alike. I began to realize that such dark colors must be placed next to other equally dark colors in order to see their true surface quality, color value, and depth of contrast.

I had begun the Black Light Series in 1967, but stopped working on them for much of 1968 and the early part of 1969. It was only in that summer of 1969 — suddenly realizing that I had only six months to produce new work for my second one-person show at Spectrum in January of 1970 — that I returned to painting the Black Light Series intensely. By the end of the year I had completed the twelve paintings of the series. They had a new serene subject matter strongly influenced by African design. The mask face, first introduced in the American People Series, reappears here in many forms. In *Soul Sister* (1967), the first painting of the series, and *Mommy and Daddy,* painted early in 1969, the mask face appears somewhat lifelike. In *Man* (1968) and *Big Black* (1967), the mask face is more abstract and superimposed on a background composition of multicolored rectangular shapes. In *The American Spectrum* (1969), six mask faces, each occupying its own rectangular space, are horizontally linked together, combining African design with modern serial art concepts. Another major change in this new series was my incorporation of words as posterlike elements of design as in *Love Black Life* (1969), *Ego Painting* (1969), *Red Black and White* (1969), and the *American Black Art Poster* (1969).

The most complex use of language in the series is found in *Flag for the Moon: Die Nigger* — made during the famous moon landing in the summer of 1969. Here I wrote the words *die* and *nigger* in such a way that they are at first difficult to read — just as I had in 1967 hidden the phrase *white power* in *U.S. Postage Stamp Commemorating the Advent of Black Power.* Now the word *die* is concealed among the flag's stars, and *nigger* is written horizontally in deliberately hard-to-decipher lettering. In *US America Black* (1969) and *Party Time* (1969), I placed mask faces and figures within triangular and rectangular spaces, echoing the piecework character of a quilt. At that time, however, making quilts was the farthest thing from my mind.

Chapter 8: The End of the 1960s: Out of the Studio and into the Streets

Me speaking against apartheid at press conference outside South African consulate in New York, 1985

The sixties were mean but intriguing, wonderful but alienating, inspiring and godawful, productive but self-destructive, enlightening and confusing, informative and contradictory. We were all together and all apart. Everybody was a leader and everybody else was to follow. Everybody felt threatened. Many people couldn't keep up with the changes, and they were frightened by the rhetoric: "Get your shit together," "Niggers, are you ready?" and "Black is beautiful." We had never been called beautiful before.

It was fashionable to be politically chic — "Have a Panther benefit at your cocktail party." This was a time when many people who thought their freedom was guaranteed found out that it just might depend on being able to afford the right lawyer and on how many people could be rallied in the street to make sure the media carried the story on the six o'clock news. "The Revolution will not be televised" was an early politically chic rap song, but even that was on television.

On November 15, 1968, the Whitney Museum of American Art opened an exhibition called "The 1930s: Painting and Sculpture in America." Not one black artist was in

*Judson 3: Jon Hendricks,
me, and Jean Toche at the
People's Flag Show, 1970*

the show, not even Jacob Lawrence, whose work was in the Whitney's permanent collection. The black art community was outraged, but they had been outraged before.
What would they do now that the public protest demonstration was the new means of
social expression in America? Just sit, or get off the pot?

A group of black artists asked the black art critic Henri Ghent, the newly appointed
director of the Brooklyn Museum's Community Gallery, to organize a show of black art of
the thirties in order to counter the Whitney's show. The Studio Museum in Harlem volunteered space for the show, and formally invited Ghent to be the show's guest curator. The
members of the board of trustees of the Studio Museum, however, felt that Henri's press
release, "Black Artists of the 1930's Snubbed," was too militant. They called a meeting of
the board at the office of Charlie Cowles, the publisher of *Artforum* magazine, to discuss
the matter. At the meeting were Wendell Wray, director of the North Manhattan Project;
Eleanor Holmes Norton, head of the NYC Commission on Human Rights; Betty Blayton
Taylor, artist and director of the Children's Art Carnival; Kynaston McShine, curator of
painting at the Museum of Modern Art; and Cowles. Henri also invited the painter Vivian
Browne and myself — for reasons that were never made clear. Certainly, I was not an
artist of the thirties, had no association with the Studio Museum, nor had I previously
met Mr. Ghent. I went out of curiosity and dedication to the cause of black artists.

Among the black artists left out of the Whitney show were some of the most
notable: Jacob Lawrence, Charles White, William Johnson, Lois Mailou Jones, Augusta
Savage, Ernest Crichlow, Norman Lewis, Aaron Douglass, and Eldzier Cortor among others.

No one disagreed that the Whitney's omission of black artists in the thirties in a major show of American art was a serious slap in the face of all black artists. If they, who had given a lifetime to art, were ignored, what could we coming up behind them expect? The problem was what to do about it: to have merely a countershow at the Studio Museum was not sufficient. That could be ignored, too. Someone wanted to know how far we should go. Was the word *snubbed* in Henri's press release too strong? The meeting was quickly at an impasse. "The word *snubbed* is not enough, no language could be strong enough to protest this obvious racism," I argued, expecting to be interrupted. Since no one did, I continued to speak. "A public demonstration at a major museum protesting the omission of black artists is long overdue in New York City. I don't think we have to worry about making the Whitney Museum angry with us because they don't even know we are alive. Why would they care what we're doing? There are enough black artists who feel that the Whitney Museum discriminates against blacks and who will want to do something about it." Henri liked my proposal and the others went along with the plan. It was Henri's job to get in touch with other black artists and to organize the making of picket signs, and so on. We set a date for the demonstration, and the meeting ended. There were people on the committee, however, who were less than enthusiastic about black artists picketing a powerful institution. They knew, and rightly, that this could be the start of something big.

The demonstration was held on Sunday, November 17, 1968. I volunteered the Spectrum Gallery as its demonstration headquarters, since the gallery was closed on Sundays and was located on Madison Avenue and 79th Street, four blocks up from the Whitney Museum. Barbara, Michele, and I arrived early to make picket signs. Henri brought signs that stressed the words "left out in the 30s and left out in the 60s." On others, assorted demands were made for a black art show at the Whitney, and one demanded a show for Romare Bearden. I made a sign for Romare Bearden and also some that read, "Black Art Is Beautiful." Henri left to go home and get dressed. I called to notify the media of the demonstration.

Approximately thirty people showed up that day outside the Whitney — mostly black artists in paint-weary but clean jeans and expensive jackets. The girls and I were dressed in our most presentable demonstration clothes — threadbare raincoats we usually wore on the Cape during the summers. Henri himself arrived dressed to the teeth in a polo coat with a Russian crown sable collar. He was a big man and I must say he looked very well turned out, more like the man inside than one on the outside.

On the picket line I met the artists Tom Lloyd, William T. Williams, and Benny Andrews for the first time. Camille Billops, the artist and filmmaker, arrived and was gone in less time than it took Henri to read her sign, which was inscribed with the words "Whitney Whitey Sucks." Needless to say, he thought it less than appropriate. Camille didn't agree, and so she left quickly without being introduced around. She had words only for Henri, but the rest of us sensed what she might be saying. Although disappointed with the size of the demonstration, Bearden was on the picket line, too. "Where are all the militants?" I heard him ask. "Here's something for them to get involved in."

Grace Glueck, art editor for the *New York Times,* covered the demonstration. She interviewed Henri, Romare, and some of the other men about why we were protesting and what we hoped to gain from the demonstration. The *New York Times* carried the story the next day. I was proud of myself, although my name was not mentioned. I knew, and many others also knew, that I was the originator of the first black demonstration against a major museum in New York City.

Tom Lloyd, the lights sculptor, called me late one night. We had met briefly on the picket line at the Whitney but not long enough for him to finish telling me about the Art Workers' Coalition and what they were doing at the Museum of Modern Art. This had always been my favorite museum; I'd spent so much time in its galleries that I knew them inside out. In my mind's eye I had seen my paintings hanging in choice spots throughout the space. Tom had an interesting relationship to the Art Workers' Coalition; as its only black artist, he functioned like a separate committee.

The Art Workers' Coalition (AWC) was an organization of white artists who were activists of the moment in the art world. They had started the organization in 1968 with demonstrations against the Museum of Modern Art for its callous treatment of artists and their work. They had been especially provoked by MOMA's treatment of Takis, a lights sculptor, whose work had been displayed upside down. They were concerned, too, with political issues like the war in Vietnam and other oppressive United States activities, at home and abroad. The most leftist factions felt that MOMA was a part of this same repressive structure, and wanted nothing to do with making art for profit. Other AWC members were strongly opposed to museums generally and made public proclamations that they would not accept a show at MOMA, even if offered one. Some people had contempt for the total art establishment but they, too, attended the AWC in large numbers every week. And Barbara, Michele, and I had to admit that the AWC, whatever else it was, was never boring.

Tom demanded that MOMA create a Martin Luther King Jr. wing for black and Puerto Rican art, and a black and Puerto Rican study center for research on art and culture of these peoples. The AWC backed Tom's proposal and included it in its package of demands that it regularly presented to MOMA. I was impressed by

Lucy Lippard and Jeannine Petit at Air Gallery, 1978

Lloyd, after having seen the sheepish manner in which other male artists were dealing with their exclusion as black artists in the art world. They seemed overwhelmed by the Museum of Modern Art, its wealth and power, and desperately afraid that if they dared speak out, they would be exclusively categorized as black artists — as if that wasn't already the case.

The black art grapevine heard that I was working with Tom. I was warned repeatedly that he would coopt me. "Don't trust Tom Lloyd," they said. "He's out for himself." "Well," I thought, "staying home to paint in isolation isn't doing much for me, either." Since my girls were giving me the business at home, the excitement of the street seemed peaceful by comparison. Besides, I'd have never forgiven myself for not getting involved.

Every Tuesday night the AWC provided an excellent platform for airing disputes between artists and the art world. We met at 8 P.M. at a place called "Museum," located at 549 West Broadway. No one was officially in charge, but since this was the sixties it worked because so many people did things out of passionate conviction. The agenda of the meetings depended upon the issues raised by the artists. "Museum" was a huge loft space and we sat in a big circle on folding chairs. If you wanted to raise an issue or make a proposal, you wrote it up and included it in the packet of flyers on the floor in the center of the circle. Before the meeting began, we all collected copies. People then had a chance to present their issues and invite others to rally to their cause.

The AWC had a way of dealing with the people at MOMA that must have been frustrating to them. The MOMA people were masters of self-composure — something in the bloodline I'm told — but we were not intimidated by their reserve. It was fun to watch

Tom Lloyd, unknown man, Ossie Davis, and me at the Museum of Modern Art 1970

Tom talk "bad" about what he would do if he had some power. "Talking bad" was one of the techniques of the militant — keep 'em so busy worrying about what you say you're going to do, that you won't have to do anything. In other words: "Whip 'em with words." Another technique we used was to be totally inflexible — our demands were nonnegotiable.

Chicanery aside, we discovered a "secret" that the museum officials and the members of the board of trustees of MOMA didn't know we knew. Forget about trying to engender a social or cultural responsibility toward blacks or anyone else. I had discovered, with the help of an accountant friend of mine, that a tax abatement might work. This would make it advantageous for collectors to donate works of art to the museum for the "public good." Since a large portion of museum collections come from donations by rich collectors, MOMA stood to benefit from this practice. The general public would also benefit if the work collected served the "public good" — but, if a museum only collected the art of one culture to the exclusion of all others, this could no longer be considered good for the segment of the public whose art was overlooked. Furthermore, we knew that the tax abatement given to donors of works of art was actually a drain on the public, since those taxes not paid by the rich collector and lost by the IRS were redistributed among the not-so-rich.

Armed with this information, Tom and I, with the support of the AWC, set out to wage an all-out attack on the Museum of Modern Art. The way to hit them hard was in the pocketbook. The tax exemption idea was right on target. Today, people are far more aware of the public responsibility of public and private institutions that receive or benefit from public money.

During the years from 1968 to 1970, I was caught up in a steady stream of activities protesting MOMA's exclusion of black artists. I stayed up many nights typing press releases. I spent many days at the museum distributing questionnaires to museumgoers in an attempt to expose the racist exclusion of black art from the MOMA exhibition schedule. Needless to say I did not produce much art during this time.

In the spring of 1970, John Hightower, the new director of the Museum of Modern Art, created an advisory board for the proposed Martin Luther King Jr. Study Center. He was more open and easy to talk to than his predecessor, Bates Lowery, who had recently been fired. There were six people on the board: John Hightower; Vinette Carroll, writer of the off-Broadway musical hit *Your Arm's Too Short to Box with God;* Tom Lloyd and me; and two MOMA trustees. Things were beginning to take shape as the Martin Luther King Jr. Study Center project was now presented as a proposal to the museum for funding. The qualifications and responsibilities of the director of the center were outlined, and the program's educational and cultural guidelines had been worked out. The demonstrations against MOMA, however, continued. A woman close to Nelson Rockefeller told me that he once asked her, "What's going on at 'my museum'?" "They want a wing for Martin Luther King Jr. to exhibit the work of black artists," she told him. "Oh," he said, "what's wrong with a Nelson Rockefeller wing for Martin Luther King Jr.?"

Tom Lloyd, John Hightower, and I had a meeting at my house. John wanted to fill us in informally with what was going on with the proposed study center. We talked for four hours and, since Tom and I kept tapes of all our meetings, we taped this one, too. We decided that Carroll Greene would curate a show of Romare Bearden for the Museum of Modern Art in 1971. Carroll would be hired as a consultant for the Bearden show. I had recommended Carroll and, since no one could think of anyone better, he got the job. Yet the whole thing seemed so tenuous. Was this all there was in return for so much time and energy? I wanted Carroll to be on salary to the museum and believed that he could sustain his position after the Bearden show. Maybe later he could move on to become the director of the Martin Luther King Jr. Study Center. The study center could then pave the way for the "wing."

People used to say jokingly, "Now you and Tom are asking for a wing at MOMA, but later you'll want the whole bird." Hightower visited the lofts of several black artists to assess support of the wing and the study center. They were not in favor because they were afraid that Tom and I would monopolize for ourselves any gains made for blacks at MOMA. The museum did not want to go ahead with plans for black artists that were not approved by the black community. They were afraid of another "Harlem on My Mind" controversy. (In 1968 the black art community was up in arms because the Metropolitan Museum had mounted a photo documentary show called "Harlem on My Mind," complete with catalogue, of the history of Harlem. It was curated by a white curator without any input from the black art community. Demonstrations had followed, led by Benny Andrews.)

John Hightower warned us that, without the support of the black community and the black artists, there would be no wing. I tried to reach Coretta King to solicit her support for the project. I sent her a letter with a packet of information, and asked her to endorse the program for the good of black artists and in the memory of our greatest leader, Martin Luther King Jr. I never did understand her reasons for ignoring our request. At any rate, I received a copy of the letter she sent to John Hightower at the museum, which was less than enthusiastic. It never mentioned anything about the wing for Martin Luther King Jr., or the study center. It only referred loosely to the hiring of Carroll Greene to curate the upcoming exhibition for Romare Bearden.

So the wing and study center were out. Yet all the men got something — a show, a sale, a grant for a community project. I got nothing, but that did not surprise me. And today, some twenty-five years later, nothing much has changed at the Modern except which white man gets the next show.

CHAPTER 9: THE 1970S: IS THERE A WOMAN'S ART?

Slave Rape, *Mother, and Me, 1973*

1970 was an extraordinary year. It hit me like a tidal wave: my second one-person show at the Spectrum Gallery in New York; Women Students and Artists for Black Art Liberation's art actions against the New York superstar male artists to liberate the "Liberated" Biennale with our demands for open shows and for fifty percent women; the Whitney Museum of American Art demonstrations; and the People's Flag Show at the Judson Church. All of this took place in my first year of becoming a feminist.

My second solo show opened on January 27, 1970, at Spectrum Gallery's new location on Madison Avenue and 79th Street. Robert Newman had named my first show "American People," but I named this second show myself — "America Black." Robert was displeased with the title: he felt it was too militant and separatist. For me, however, it was an expression of our new appreciation of blackness — we had never known until now that we could love our black selves. The show contained twelve canvases in my new "black light" style. The American People Series and the Black Light Series really said all I had to say about the civil rights period of the 1960s. The American People had been about the complicated interrelations of black and white people struggling with injustice, inequality, oppression, and fear. My Black Light Series was a celebration of our newly recognized beauty. Robert understood that, but his press release for "America Black" — unlike the one he had written for the "American People" — glimmered but didn't glow. He wrote: "This exhibition limits itself to the study of black values. . . . The most single element in these paintings is their resolved search for unique color and light. . . . [They] describe a creative direction in the search for the color-light of her race."

Birdie helped to hang the show, made me a gift of three cases of champagne from the local liquor store, and wished me luck. On the day of the opening, he went to work as was his custom when I was exhibiting or otherwise on center-stage. The show was reviewed by *Art News* and *Arts Magazine.* A good many critics and art world figures came to see the show, including Bill Rubin, the curator of painting and sculpture at the Museum of Modern Art.

One outcome to the show was that David Rockefeller wrote me about purchasing a painting for the Chase Manhattan Bank art collection. Two representatives from this collection came to make a selection. They almost bought *Flag for the Moon: Die Nigger* since, at first glance, it appeared to be an appropriate one for the collection. Unlike my other paintings, which had obvious political content and titles, this was a simple painting of the American flag. Upon closer scrutiny they discovered the word *die* superimposed on the stars, and the word *nigger* in the stripes. They left in a huff. I coaxed them back to see slides of other paintings. Finally they decided on a painting depicting six faces in varying shades of dark to light skin tones, a subtle statement of black people's multiethnic heritage. Since they didn't know it was titled *Six Shades of Black,* they likened it to the color spectrum of America, and suggested calling it *Untitled.* I renamed it *The American Spectrum* and received $3,000, my first formidable sale. However, after this everything slowed down and I found I could not paint because of the lack of an audience.

There was a time when belonging to a gallery and having a one-person show that was reviewed in *Art News* would have been enough. But now I'd had a second one-person show, had produced several major works, and received good critical attention, yet I was at a standstill. There was nothing coming up: no shows, no new associations or contacts, and, now, no gallery. The Spectrum Gallery was moving to SoHo, the new artists' digs downtown, without Robert as director. Spectrum would now be run by the artists themselves. On the surface the new arrangement had good prospects — the move to SoHo for one — but underneath there was the unmistakable rumbling of a sinking ship. After the move I never heard about Spectrum Gallery again.

In 1970, white women were on TV screaming about "male chauvinist pigs." The women's art movement in New York was just beginning. At the Art Workers'

Coalition, some women had created Women Artists in Revolution (WAR) and they asked me to join and come to meetings, but I didn't have the time. I was too busy with Tom Lloyd and MOMA trying to get a wing for black artists, money allocated to buy black artists' works, and black trustees on the museum's board. Trying to get the black man a place in the white art establishment left me no time to consider women's rights. I had thought that my rights came with the black man's. But I was mistaken. Now what was I to do?

I first found out about the Women's Liberation Movement in 1967 from Flo Kennedy, the civil rights lawyer. I had called her to get some names of people to invite to my solo exhibition and she gave me those of Betty Friedan and Ti Grace Atkinson. They were the founding members of the National Organization for Women (NOW). Betty Friedan was the author of a most provocative book entitled *The Feminine Mystique,* which some felt made her the founder of the movement; and Ti Grace Atkinson, a feminist theorist, had been an art director in a Philadelphia museum. Flo suggested that both could be helpful to me, and further that I should arrange to meet them, join NOW, and get involved with the women's movement. I sent them all invitations to my 1967 show and attempted halfheartedly to reach the two women by phone with no success. Flo came to my opening with some women from NOW. They were all women's liberationists and I admired them that night for looking the part. They carried with them propaganda about the movement: notices of meetings, plans for feminist actions — all of which later came to be called "bra burnings" by the media.

It was not until 1970, however, that I got involved in the women's movement. In this year I became a feminist because I wanted to help my daughters, other women, and myself aspire to something more than a place behind a good man. The "Liberated" Biennale, the Whitney demonstrations, and the Flag Show were my first out-from-behind-the-men actions. In the 1960s I had rationalized that we were all fighting for the same issues and why shouldn't the men be in charge? I would be just the brains and the big mouth.

In the 1970s, being black and a feminist was equivalent to being a traitor to the cause of black people. "You seek to divide us," I was told. "Women's Lib is for white women. The black woman is too strong now — she's already liberated." I was constantly challenged: "You want to be liberated — from whom?" But the brothers' rap that was the most double-dealing was the cry that "the black woman's place is behind her man," when frequently white women occupied that position.

In May of 1970, Art Strike was formed out of the AWC. Its purpose, though not stated in quite this way, was to give superstar white male artists a platform for their protests against the war in Cambodia. Robert Morris, then called the "Prince of Peace," had issued an appeal for American artists to withdraw their work from the 1970 Venice Biennale. The purpose of this international exhibition was to display the work of contemporary artists of the "free" (white) world. Each nation chose and sent its own exhibit. In 1970, the Americans selected were Claes Oldenburg, Andy Warhol, Frank Stella, Robert Rauschenberg, Roy Lichtenstein, Jim Dine, and Robert Morris among others — all superstar white male artists.

Organized by Morris, the "Liberated" Venice Biennale was a protest against the war in Cambodia, and more generally against the American government's policies of racism, repression, sexism, and war. This protest exhibition was scheduled to open July 6, 1970, at the School of Visual Arts on West 23rd Street in New York City. I began to fantasize that, since the United States government had not presented in its original Venice selection an unbiased representation of the "fine" art of American artists, then we would now have the chance to rectify their shortsightedness. And, since there was a stated commitment among these powerful superstar white male artists concerning racism and sexism, surely there would be support for a *truly* liberated Venice Biennale. In fact, we could create an "open show," although it soon became sadly clear that that was hardly the intent of the organizers.

When I made this suggestion to the women artists preparing to install the show at the School of Visual Arts, they were aghast. "But there were no women in the original group that withdrew from Venice, and no blacks," they explained to me condescendingly. I explained: "That's because the committee which selected the artists for the Venice Biennale was racist and sexist, and we are not." Well, these women, many of whom had spoken to me at length about feminism and the women's movement, could see nothing politically wrong with presenting the show "as is" — with no women and no blacks. Even though it was the racist and sexist policies of the United States that were being protested, the goverment's prejudices were still dictating the show.

Art Strike took over the AWC, with Morris and the artist Poppy Johnson in charge. Michele was living at home now, attending City College and going to AWC meetings with me. She and I speedily formed an ad hoc group called Women Students and Artists for Black Art Liberation (WSABAL). We were persistent about liberating the "Liberated" Venice Biennale. We made it clear that WSABAL would demonstrate if the show did not include blacks and women. The white women at the AWC, including most of the WAR women, were against us. They didn't seem to understand the real meaning of the feminism they were espousing. Some "girlfriends" of the superstars were verbally abusive and physically threatening to us. We stood toe-to-toe at meetings in open confrontations. One woman became so irate at the prospect of having women and blacks included in the superstars' show that she screamed, "Don't you understand, we can't have that shit in this show!"

"We will demonstrate and close it down if it is not opened to include women and blacks," we responded forcefully. WSABAL was a small group composed of Tom Lloyd, Michele, and myself together with a couple of students from the School of Visual Arts who regularly attended AWC meetings. (The students had had a longstanding battle at the school over special funding for black students and demands for programs and black teachers.)

When we started to prepare a press release on our position, we needed to decide on how many blacks, women, and students should be included in the show. We wanted to prevent them from merely selecting a few token black male artists. "What percentage of women do you think we should demand to be in the show?" I asked Michele. She looked up from her reading and said abruptly and matter-of-factly, "Fifty percent." I was stunned. I had never heard anyone suggest that much equality for women. She was so young, not yet eighteen, and we had been through so much recently with Mexico and Barbara's tumultuous last year at high school. Maybe she was under a strain, maybe she just hadn't heard me right, or I hadn't heard her right. I asked again, "What percentage for the show . . . I mean of women?" This time I listened more closely. Michele looked up and, raising her voice, looked me dead in the eye. She repeated herself, "Fifty percent women, and fifty percent of those women have to be black and twenty-five percent have to be students." Well, the numbers game began. There were now all kinds of jokes over our percentage demands. The point, however, was made. We were talking here about real equality. After all, this was the way racism had worked all these years with percentages and quotas. Maybe we could now work it to our advantage.

All hell broke loose just before the show was to open. Brenda Miller, one of the women artists against the revised show, kidnapped the original show and took it to her loft in New York's Westbeth. (There was a secret plan to take the show to Washington, D.C., to open at the Corcoran Gallery, and the arrangements had been made with Walter Hopps, the director of the Corcoran.) But Morris, again in his role as Prince of Peace, got the show back in time for our opening. The liberated Liberated Venice Biennale was open to all who wanted to participate. The exhibition began on July 22, 1970, in the newly painted loft space of "Museum," the meeting place of AWC and Art Strike. The show consisted of more than fifty percent women and included more black artists, students, and political poster artists than any other "Biennale" before or since. However, some of the superstar artists and their dealers felt that the show was fraught with too much confusion and decided to withdraw. They included Claes Oldenburg, Richard Anuszkiewicz, Ernest Trova, Nicholas Krushenick, and Adja Yunkers. The ones remaining were Andy Warhol, Carl Andre, Frank Stella, Robert Rauschenberg, Roy Lichtenstein, Vincent Longo, Leonard Baskin, Jim Dine, Sam Francis, Robert Birmelin, Michael Mazur, Deen Meeker, Sal Romano, and, of course, Bob Morris.

Within a few weeks' time the show ended abruptly. As the story goes, one of the women artists enticed Bobby, the night watchman at Museum, into the back room under the ruse that they were going to make passionate love together — which, if you had known Bobby, you would know how funny that was. After she detained Bobby long enough for her women accomplices to get four works by the show's superstars out of the gallery, she released Bobby, leaving him "high," which he was all the time anyway, and "dry." The paintings were retrieved, again by Morris with the assistance of Carl Andre. They took the works back to Castelli and to the other galleries that had loaned them. The show was over. Security had been broken. And Bobby split.

In the fall of 1970 Poppy Johnson and Lucy Lippard formed an ad hoc women's group to protest the small percentage of women in all past Whitney Annuals. I was asked to join and I agreed. I was excited about the prospect of black women artists being included in the Whitney Annual. Our goal for the 1970 Annual was fifty percent women: Michele's equality percentage for women in the art world had caught on.

The corridors and galleries of the Whitney Museum became the focus of our attention. We went there often to deposit eggs. Unsuspecting male curatorial staff would pick up the eggs and experience the shock of having raw eggs slide down the pants of their fine tailor-made suits. I made hard-boiled eggs, painted them black, and wrote "50 percent" on them in red paint. I didn't want to waste food. They could eat my black eggs. Sanitary napkins followed. These upset the female staff as well as the men. Generally, everywhere the staff went they found loud and clear messages that women artists were on the Whitney's "case."

The Whitney Annual that year was to be a sculpture show. I was not making sculpture yet, and there were only a few black women sculptors in the country who were known. Elizabeth Catlett and Selma Burke were well-known figurative sculptors. Elizabeth Catlett was my all-time favorite but, because of the Whitney's well-known preference for abstract art, Catlett's prospects waned. Selma Burke was eliminated by a false report by one of the curators that she was dead. Instead, Betye Saar and Barbara Chase-Riboud were cited, whose work was more in line with the Whitney's taste. So they were the ones I unconditionally demanded to be in the show. Saar and Chase-Riboud became the first black women to be in the Whitney Annual; more to the point, they were the first black women ever to be exhibited at the Whitney Museum of American Art. The total percentage of women in the Whitney Annual in 1970 was twenty-three percent — as opposed to the previous years' averages of five to ten percent. This was better than ten percent, but it still wasn't fifty.

We decided to demonstrate during the opening to make that point. We had to get our demonstrators inside, since the opening was by invitation only, so we printed fake tickets and distributed them outside the museum on the night of the opening to anyone who wanted to demonstrate. A guard with an ultraviolet detector confiscated over a hundred forged tickets; nevertheless, we got in a lot of people. Once inside, we mingled with the crowd. Museum officials knew something was afoot as rumors began to spread that there was to be a demonstration that night. One of the trustees of the museum who was on our side, for whatever reason, was concerned that we would not be able to round up the women demonstrators, since everyone was all over the place, drinks in hand (the Whitney had free booze in those days), chatting and locating the art of friends (Louise Bourgeois was in the show) or talking to the other exhibiting artists. I assured him that we would be fine, and that everybody would know when and where the demonstration was happening, even though the show was spread out on the museum's three floors. What I didn't tell him was that we planned to blow police whistles to signal the start of our actions.

Although they supplied us with tickets to enter the museum, the white men in the show did not join our demonstration. (There were no black men there I could approach.) However, the fashionable Whitney art-going crowd was eager to witness our action. They had heard of "sit-ins" and now they were going to see one for themselves. At a predetermined time, Lucy Lippard and I began to blow our whistles. The women came toward the center of the main gallery on the second floor. We continued to blow. The people gathered

God Bless America, *1964, Oil on canvas, 31 x 19 inches, Artist's collection*

around us and we formed a big circle sitting on the floor. Then we got up and walked around chanting, "Fifty percent women, fifty percent women." We pulled it off. The crowd was sympathetic, and the event satisfied our need to protest. The trustee I had spoken with seemed pleased that it happened.

Throughout the show we demonstrated every weekend, blowing our police whistles and singing off-key. Barbara and Michele, who were with me at these demonstrations, had suggested that we sing off-key intentionally. However astute their own ears (they are both musical, probably a talent inherited from Earl), intentional off-key singing was bearable to them, and natural to most of us. Barbara made up catchy tunes on the spot, and everybody joined in. "The Whitney is a helluva place, parlez-vous. The Whitney is a helluva place, parlez-vous. They're down on women and they're down on race, a honky donkey, parlez-vous." Flo Kennedy joined our line one Saturday and was quite at home, singing off-key and making music with police whistles.

The women artists' movement in New York was on its way. There was now a plethora of panels and statements being made concerning women's art and culture. Artists and other folk, both male and female, were beginning to demand explanations of the women's art movement. "Is there a women's art, and if so, what is it?" was the constant question posed to us. The concept of making female images as opposed to male, and black images as opposed to white or abstract, was the crux of the issue. "Who needs all this talk about black art and women's art?" some artists would say. "I'm just an artist who happens to be black or a woman." It was a real challenge to try to define oneself and one's art outside the narrow parameters of the mainstream art world. But we were doing this and it felt good.

The People's Flag Show at the Judson Memorial Church in Greenwich Village was the culmination of the year for me. The show opened on November 9, 1970, and was scheduled to last two weeks. It had been organized by the People's Flag Show Committee, a group of independent artists interested in having a show of flag art to protest against American oppression and repression at home and abroad. This was a time of massive protests about the war in Vietnam, and Richard Nixon was our president; but still I did not see the danger of being arrested that some people spoke of. I had been using the American flag as a form of protest in my paintings since 1964 and I had exhibited my flag paintings at both of my solo shows without incident — *God Bless America,* (1964), *The Flag is Bleeding* (1967), and *Flag for the Moon: Die Nigger* (1969). However, Stephen Radich, the art dealer, had been arrested in 1967 for showing art made of American flags; surprisingly, his case had garnered little or no support in the artist community. It was thought that our show, organized by artists, would give real strength to the artists' right for free "speech." What was wrong with that? If our show could help Stephen Radich, why not? But not if it called for my arrest. As events developed, however, I had no other choice.

There were over two hundred artists in the show. Unlike Radich's one-person exhibition of Marc Morrell's flag pieces, this was an open show, a concept borrowed from WSABAL and the hectic events of the summer's liberated Liberated Venice Biennale. An open show meant anyone who wanted to participate in the show could put in any piece they chose. There was no selection committee and no jurying of pieces. Everyone in the show had to sign a statement that they would assume full responsibility for their work and "release the independent Artist Flag Show Committee from all responsibilities." Kate Millett, Jasper Johns, and Carl Andre were among the artists in the show.

On opening night, Yvonne Rainer and her dancers did a dance in the nude with flags loosely tied around their necks. At the beginning of the performance I was talking with Yvonne about all the obvious plainclothesmen who were there. (The Nixon administration had us all placed under close scrutiny, just how close was yet to be determined.) Yvonne suddenly said, "Well, I'm going to dance," and began to undress right there, letting her clothes drop around her feet. I moved back as a hush spread over the entire place. People began to separate themselves from the performance as they noticed Yvonne's dancers stepping out of their clothes and tying the flags loosely around their necks. The floor was now clear and the dancers, all nude except for the flags they wore, began to move in the way Yvonne's dancers knew so well — convincingly, strong, free, and fresh. CBS taped the entire evening.

After Yvonne Rainer's performance, there was a speak-out against all the injustices of our time. Abbie Hoffman, Gerald Lefcourt, the attorney for the Panther 21, several Panthers, and artists, including myself, made statements. Jon Hendricks and Jean Toche did a pre-opening performance outside the church in the courtyard. They burned a flag with a mess of old bones and rotten meat. I thought that surely if there was going to be an arrest, that was the moment. But their flag action went off unprotested, though "the man" (police) was there.

During the course of the exhibition, people came to do mini-performances. Some took off their clothes and viewed the exhibit in the nude, others sat quietly in the sanctuary of the church as if at a funeral and appeared to meditate. My *Flag for the Moon: Die Nigge*r painting paled in comparison to all this. The Judson Church had been famous for its association with artists since the early sixties; the only difference now was the inflammatory theme and the presence of the TV cameras and the "law."

On November 13, 1970, I was arrested, along with two white male artists, Jean Toche and Jon Hendricks. We were charged with desecrating the flag and arrested for being members of the People's Flag Show Committee, the ad hoc group of over two hundred artists who had organized the show. Our arrest was on a Friday night and it was raining slightly. We usually closed the church and went home at 8 P.M. Michele was with me that night, but Barbara was at home waiting for us to have dinner. Birdie and I were separated again since the summer. We had one of those arguments that men have when they want to move out. I was too busy with all my activities to finish the arguments with him, and I kept forgetting what they were about.

At just the time we were preparing to lock up the church and go home, four people knocked on the door. They said they were friends of the pastor of the church, had come from New Jersey, and could not return another day, but were eager to see the show. I was against this, but Jon Hendricks and Jean Toche were determined to show them the exhibition. "Don't let them in," I cautioned, but they were admitted anyway. They were three white men and a woman. The men looked like Greenwich Village types with their blue jeans, short jackets, and longish hair. But the woman was out of place; she definitely looked like a cop. They were escorted upstairs to the sanctuary of the old Baptist church where the flag art pieces were on display. I remained downstairs, trying not to have all the answers — I decided the woman didn't have to be a cop just because she looked like one. I waited by the entrance desk for them to come down; since Michele was with them upstairs, I could not leave.

Finally, I went to see what was keeping Michele and the others. As I entered the sanctuary of the church, I saw everyone standing in the center of the room in a reluctant circle as if waiting for me. Nonchalantly, I approached them, saying, "Come on, Michele, let's go. Barbara is waiting for us at home."

"She can't go anywhere," one of the men proclaimed, flashing his badge. It was as serious as armed robbery.

"Why?" I demanded to know.

"She's under arrest, " he blurted out.

"For what?" I yelled, looking at the sheer terror on Michele's face.

"For being a member of the Independent Flag Show Committee," answered the woman officer.

"She's a minor and I'm her mother," I retorted. They looked at me as if to say, "So what?"

I paused to size up the situation. Clearly they had been sent there to arrest two or three men and a woman, and that's what they had. They were not likely to release Michele for that reason. An arrest of my daughter was not something, however, I could tolerate. Let them take me instead. "She's not a member of anything, but I am," I announced, stepping out in front of Michele. It was ransom — me for Michele, a mother for a daughter — and I had no choice. "Well, then you're under arrest," one of them said. It had worked. They proceeded to inform us of our rights: anything we said could be used against us. It turned out that Jon, Jean, and Michele had been arrested illegally since the officers had asked them if they were members of the Independent Flag Show Committee without first identifying themselves as officers of the law. I was arrested legally, however, although under duress. I knew they were officers of the law and that I was admitting something that would cause my arrest.

We left the church in two unmarked cars. I rode with the lady officer in the back of her car and all the men were in the other car. I had expected a whole lot in the way of abuse. For instance, I was waiting to hear my lady officer say, "Lean over, put your hands against the wall and spread your cheeks." She got a chance to look in my pocketbook when I emptied out the valuables to give to Michele, along with my rings and my brief-case, which I had been carrying since school that morning. To my surprise, however, she and the male officers took our arrest rather lightly, maybe because it was an "art arrest." Evidently we were considered predictably nonviolent and safe, and the event provided something different to their workaday lives.

Our officers were plainclothes detectives from the New York County District Attorney's Office. Would you believe that they had to ask where the local police precinct was? Jon told them, and we were taken there to be booked. We went upstairs to the office where there was a cage, and a godawful filthy bathroom with a toilet that had no seat. The sight of it was enough to turn a bad case of diarrhea into chronic con-stipation at one glance. The cage in the office enabled the officers to "mind" the pris-oners while attending to office details. The whole thing was most depressing, not only for the prisoners, but for the officers who were, you might say, "trapped in the same cell." We only spent a few minutes in the police station, just long enough to get booked and get the hell out of there.

Our next stop was night court at the infamous Tombs (the city prison) on Center Street. We went in a side door and were stopped by a police officer who wanted to know which of us were the officers and which of us were the defendants — maybe that will give you an idea of the kind of picture we made. Jon and Jean were dressed in "high sixties" attire: rumpled jeans with unmatched shabby jackets, and unkempt, unstyled hair — the national uniform artists and others of the white middle class wore in order to distinguish themselves from the suit-and-tie crowd of the same class. The irony was that the male cops were similarly attired, although the woman officer wore a standard, working-class, conservative dress straight off the racks of the local depart-ment store. I was wearing a knee-length dress made of African print with a matching cloth around my head — one of my mother's designs that was definitely never sup-posed to see the inside of a jail. I must say I was decidedly overdressed for the occa-sion. However, at such times there is no chance for going home to change. An invita-tion to the Tombs is strictly come as you are.

The officer at the entrance to the Tombs told us no one could be admitted after 9:30 P.M. "We're to meet the district attorney in night court so we have to get these people in tonight," the police said. "Well," responded the officer in the Tombs, "I guess you'll have to sneak them in. I'll just turn my back." He opened the gate, keeping his back turned, while the seven of us sneaked into the Tombs on a Friday night. Now, if that's not something unusual, what is? Once in the Tombs, we went up a long narrow staircase to a row of offices. We talked to a citizens counsellor about our rights. He said we didn't need any money, and that our lawyers were waiting for us in the courtroom. He also told us we would not be fingerprinted and that we would be going home right after night court. He was most congenial and, in a few minutes, was gone. This was the last time I saw Jon or Jean for a while. My officer then took me on what seemed like a walking tour of the Tombs. I saw columns of men, mostly black and Latino, being moved along by corrections officers. Everywhere I looked was barren, ugly, and reminiscent of that bathroom at the Charles Street police station — life at its lowest ebb.

I was brought to the section of the Tombs for women. Two black female officers asked my officer, "What's she in for?"

"Desecration of the flag," she informed them briskly. As I followed her down the hall, I could see the two other women out of the corner of my eye muffling spurts of laughter with their hands over their mouths. I could appreciate their need to laugh, if even at me, but frankly it wasn't funny to me.

At the end of the corridor, I saw a cage with three women in it. "This is it, Faith," I told myself. "Now you're going to get your ass kicked for the first time in your life in a godforsaken cage in the Tombs on a Friday night." But we passed right on by. Next we came to a large cage with several men, including Jon and Jean. They looked very white as they sat among an assortment of black and Latino drug addicts and other sordid types, although their attire made them otherwise indistinguishable from their cellmates. They seemed pleased to be so close to the people, a dream of many middle-class white radicals at this time. They assured me that they were fine, and that they would see me later in the courtroom.

Reverend Moody, the minister of the Judson Church, was inside the courtroom, and so was a lawyer to represent us. He was a nice man and I wish I could remember his name. I never saw him again because later on we got three fancy lawyers: Flo Kennedy, Bob Projansky, and Gerald Lefcourt. But that night we had the nice man whose name I cannot remember. Michele had called everybody to tell them we had been arrested. Reverend Moody called Barbara to assure her that I was fine and would be home shortly. Barbara never remembered what Reverend Moody told her and, unworried, slept through it all.

After our arraignment at night court, we were released on our own recognizance. With our arrest the People's Flag Show became famous, but I felt like a scapegoat.

Being arrested and facing a trial, even though the charge was a misdemeanor, was extremely disturbing to me.

We were now known in the art community as "The Judson Three." Many events were organized to raise money for our defense; people sent letters; and there were petitions of support from art communities all over the world. On April 8, 1971, a jury trial was waived for a preliminary hearing. The New York Civil Liberties Union joined the defense (Burt Neuborne was the attorney), and the trial date was set for April 15, 1971. Our courtroom supporters were so numerous that we had to move to a larger courtroom. Lucy Lippard, John Hightower, Allen Schoerner, the visual arts director of the New York State Council on the Arts, and Sam Wiener, an artist, were the witnesses for the defense. The testimonies of Schoerner and Hightower were denied but read into the court record.

Never mind the Constitution and the Bill of Rights, my mother considered my arrest a family disgrace. I am not sure that Michele did not feel the same way, despite the fact that I had had myself arrested to save her. I often felt alone at court although there were many supportive people there including the black artists Art Coppedge and Iris Crump. On a few occasions as the case dragged on, I had to make Michele go to court with me. Barbara was not living at home by then, although she came to court once or twice on her own. Birdie and I were still apart. On May 14, 1971, we were found guilty. On May 24, we were sentenced to one month in jail or a hundred-dollar fine. We paid the fine. The New York Civil Liberties Union said they would accept the full burden of the appeal to the Supreme Court. Yet, despite the sixty thousand dollars raised at a 1972 Leo Castelli art lottery, on June 17, 1976, the day the appeal was to be made by the New York Civil Liberties Union, they failed to appear in court.

In New York I found it difficult to exhibit my work because of my figurative style, the political content, the lack of social connections in the art world, and, also, because being black and a woman was not as fashionable as the Civil Rights Movement and the Women's Liberation Movement might suggest.

When I first thought of being an artist, I thought I had too normal and simple a life. How could I be a suffering artist when my life of bringing up my children and teaching art was so steady and secure? Except for Earl and Andrew, I had never really experienced emotional pain. That was how I felt in my twenties and early thirties before I had actually begun to be an artist. Now I was about to find out what it really meant to survive as an artist: that feeling of creation for which I would have suffered almost anything.

In the 1970s I searched for and found an audience. To be successful you must find a market as well, but in those days making money from art was not nearly as important to me as making art. As long as I could produce, it didn't matter where the money came from. I had started touring colleges and universities in 1972, and the following year I quit my teaching job at Brandeis High School.

I accompanied traveling shows of my work and lectured on black and feminist art. The black men on campus avoided me because they believed I had come to preach. Some black women did, too: they had been warned that I was one of those feminists from New York who had come to separate them from black men. In the North I talked mostly to small white audiences. In the South, however, my audience had a large percentage of blacks, especially black women. Blacks in the South seemed to appreciate me for my cultural achievements. They knew how hard things were for us — they would tolerate my feminism. Yet, at Fort Valley State College in Georgia, I was warned: "You're in the South now. Our women don't want to hear nothing about Women's Lib — we men are king down here."

Language had become increasingly important to me in my art since 1967, when I first incorporated words into *U.S. Postage Stamp Commemorating the Advent of Black Power*. I needed to speak with more than images and I began to explore words and texts more and more. *Flag for the Moon: Die Nigger* (1969) was my way of saying that too many American people go to bed hungry, while the government spent billions to place their flag on the moon. In *Love Black Life, The Black Art Poster*, and *Ego Painting* (in which the word "Ringgold" is repeated four times), the meaning of the words was fairly literal as on a poster or a picket sign.

Today, posters are included in many museum and private art collections. But at this time the poster was a political quasi-art form that many artists and activists used solely to communicate important messages to the masses; it soon became a cheap or giveaway form of art. I began making posters in 1970. I did my first poster, dated July 1970, for the Committee to Defend the Panthers, a radical-chic New York group whose purpose was to raise money for the Panthers' legal defense. I remember being rather shocked that rich white people like Leonard Bernstein would associate themselves with such a controversial cause. The day I took them the poster, their office had been fire-bombed

The United States
of Attica, *1971, Offset,
22 x 28 inches.
Private collection*

and there was water everywhere. They seemed paranoid that day and rightly so. They rejected the poster; perhaps because they had just been bombed, or maybe not. My poster had a central image of a red-eyed, black-faced, snarling panther-looking man, flanked on both sides by profiles of two raging white panther heads. The text read "Committee to Defend the Panthers, Free all political prisoners, All Power to the People" with the committee's address and phone number: 11 East 13th Street NYC, 243 2260. How was I to know the committee was operating undercover, especially since they had originally tried to talk me into making the high Panther rhetoric — "Off the Pigs" and "Kill Whitey" — the central theme of my poster. This is the only poster I've ever done that was never reproduced.

The People's Flag Show was my next poster. I did it in November of 1970 and it was not only reproduced but sold at the opening for one or two dollars; later it became one of the "people's" exhibits in our trial. This poster was an image of the American flag. On the stars was an announcement of the show, and on the stripes was a statement by Michele, which said in essence that the American flag belonged to the American people to do with as they saw fit. I followed this in 1971 with two posters I made for Angela Davis — *Angela Free Women Free Angela* and *America free Angela free America*. (Davis was in prison at the time following the Marin County shootout.) The words of these posters were set into a Kuba design. This design of eight triangular spaces in a rectangle is an ancient one often seen on African textiles and attributed to the Kuba tribe of the Congo region of Central Africa. At this time I was trying to use these Kuba triangular spaces and words to form a kind of rhythmic repetition similiar to the polyrhythms used in African drumming. These posters were reproduced on heavy cardboard and sold at women's conferences and other events for three dollars or so. The money from all of these posters went to support various student and community causes.

The United States of Attica (1971) was my most widely distributed poster of the 1970s (about two thousand were made and I sold them for a dollar or so each), and I dedicated it to the men who died in 1971 at Attica prison in Upper New York State demonstrating against the deplorable conditions of the prison system. This red-black-and-green poster depicts a map of the United States. Within each state I recorded the dates and other details of infamous acts of violence that occurred there, such as race riots, witch hunts, presidential assassinations, lynchings, and Indian wars. Around the periphery of the map I included a statistical history of the dead, wounded, and missing in American wars — starting with the 1776 Revolutionary War through to the Vietnam, Laos, and Cambodian wars, which by 1971 had resulted in an estimated 45,564 dead. The most infamous of all the statistics recorded here are from the Indian Wars where the dead numbered in the millions, leaving a current Native American population of approximately 900,000; and the Middle Passage, in which an estimated 4,000,000 African slaves died en route to the U.S. New acts of violence were increasing at such an alarming rate that I had no space to include all of them. And so, realizing I would not be able to revise annually, I wrote an appeal for people to add their own updated information as they saw fit. There was an interesting time in the mid-seventies when this particular poster fell into disfavor: political apathy was nationally on the increase, and students felt the poster's information was too depressing. They didn't want to be reminded of how many American Indians, black slaves, and others had died in the making of this country. I gave the poster away then. Now it is in short supply, and I only release it for benefits, exhibitions, or occasionally for gifts.

In 1971, I received my first award from the Creative Arts Public Service Program. This allowed me an opportunity to create a work and give it to an institution as a permanent installation. This is not as easy as it sounds, especially if you are relatively unknown. Initially I wanted to make a feminist mural painting and install it on a college campus — I thought of my alma mater, City College — but then decided that a women's prison might

Me and For the Women's House, *1971, Oil on canvas, 96 x 96 inches, The Women's House of Detention, Rikers Island*

be more receptive to me, simply because probably no one else would suggest installing a mural there. I was right. The superintendent of the Women's House of Detention on Rikers Island in New York was very receptive, and gave me an opportunity to talk with some of the women inmates about what they would like to see depicted in a mural. One woman said she would like to see "a long road leading out of there"; and another spoke about "women of all races holding hands and having a better life."

The mural was entitled *For the Women's House* and was the first painting in which I portrayed a large number of women. Here again I based my composition on the Kuba design; it seemed a good way to combine several ideas in one composition. I had invented this first in *US America Black* in which I presented eight portraits to depict the mood of black America. In *For the Women's House,* each of its segments showed a different role for women. Some were new roles as yet to be achieved: the president of the United States, a basketball player on the Knicks team, a bus driver, a police officer, and so on.

The Department of Correction sent two uniformed prison guards and a truck — the same truck that was used to transport prisoners — to pick up the painting. The truck drew a crowd. No doubt it was a familiar means of transportation for some of the young brothers in the neighborhood. They knew the guards and came up to speak to them and tell them how they were faring on the outside. *For the Women's House* was painted in oil and measured in total eight by eight feet, although it was done in two parts of eight by four feet each. Its size was a hassle when we tried to get it down the fourteen flights of stairs to the truck. Since it was too large to put in the elevator, I had to bargain with Barbara and Michele to get them to carry the painting down the stairs. This would be the last time that I would paint a large stretched canvas for a long time.

The mural was installed in the corridor of the Women's House of Detention in January of 1972 in an impressive ceremony sponsored by the Department of Correction. Present were female and male inmates — the men were invited from the nearby men's facilities. It was a happy day for them and the beginning of mixed events on Rikers Island. A prison band from the men's facility played and, as you might imagine, the music was great. I invited over two hundred of my artists friends and colleagues to the installation. My guests wanted to see the facilities. The Department of Correction reluctantly agreed to conduct a limited tour of a few public spaces — the cafeteria, library, and so on — but Mother, not realizing it was forbidden, broke from the guide and led a group to see the living conditions under which the women were being held. They were visibly shaken by the appeal of a young man they saw. He'd had a sex-change operation and desperately needed his hormone medicine or his male sex characteristics would reappear. He appealed to Mother's renegade tour group to contact his doctor and make him aware of his condition — and they did.

Michele and I went to Europe in the summer of 1972. Our relationship was not particularly good at that time but Michele had friends in Spain and wanted to visit Paris, and I was always fearful about going to Europe — since 1961, when Andrew died while we were there. For that reason, I took Michele with me, and would have taken Barbara, too, but she was not living at home and chose not to go with us. After a few weeks in Paris, Michele went on to visit her friends in Spain and I traveled to Kassel, Germany, where the famous international Documenta art exhibitions are held. I had already been in Hamburg in April of 1972 for the opening of the first European showing of the new American feminist art. The show, "American Women Artists, Gedok," had been curated by Lil Picard, the performance artist and critic, and Gedok, a German group of women which had originally been formed before the Nazi regime. This time around I had not been invited, although the organizers of Documenta IV boasted that they had a political theme — yet they included no political art by blacks or women. This needed to be addressed.

I must say I was not prepared to be the only black person in this tiny German town. I tried to appear inconspicuous in my Afro-American-styled clothes, but there was simply no one in Kassel who looked anything like me. With that in mind, I strategically deposited my posters, women's newspapers, and journals throughout the exhibition. I searched for the curator, but since he was out of town I went to the post office and mailed him an extra package of what I had put in the show, wrapping it in my red-black-and-green poster *The United States of Attica*. Then I headed for Copenhagen, where I was due to meet Michele in a few days. Later I received a letter from the curator of the show acknowledging receipt of the package.

In Europe I planned to continue working on my new series in watercolors called Political Landscapes. I have always loved watercolor painting, and trees and landscapes were a favorite subject for me at the time. In the early 1970s Richard Nixon's visit to China was in the news, and books on Chinese art were prominently displayed in bookstores. I began noticing Chinese landscapes and the messages written on them — often merely descriptions of who did the painting and who bought it, with the purchase date and place.

I wanted to make landscape paintings that had writing on them, like the Chinese, but that said something about people. From this concept I came up with the title Political Landscapes. That's what they were: delicate landscape images with short "political" texts written vertically on them so that, at first glance, they looked as if they were in Chinese. I started in the spring of 1972, working in watercolors on colored sheets of rag paper. I divided the series — which eventually consisted of fifty-seven small paintings — into seven parts, and did the first three parts before I left for Europe. The subjects of these texts were U.S. racism and the relationships between black men and black women. I wrote the texts for the first two parts: I, "A Tribute to All the Black Women," and II, "War and Other Truths." However, Michele contributed the eight texts that form part III, entitled "Listen Brothers." These texts by Michele are my favorite ones in the entire series. She really socked it to the brothers, beginning with "He's leaving her. Says he's got to do his own thing. How come she don't?" (#19). The rest of Michele's texts continue with this wonderful, terse, sharp tone of address.

Michele was only twenty when she wrote these messages for my paintings. Twenty-three years later her words still sound fresh and vital. Michele was such a good writer that I would have been so pleased if she had written all the messages on the Political Landscape Series. After writing these eight, however, she had her own writing to do and I was left to continue on my own.

While traveling through Europe I carried a large portfolio of colored papers (18 by 24 inches) and several tiny tubes of watercolors and brushes. It was easy to paint in the water medium since clean-up required only soap and water, and the paper, paint, and brushes were fairly light to carry. Michele would watch me intently as I spread my paint and watercolor paper on the floor of our hotel room and then taped the finished paintings on the hotel wall. I knew she thought it a little bit odd, but I was driven to complete these paintings before I returned to the United States.

In Europe I painted and wrote the texts for the remainder of the series: parts IV–VII: (#4) "Sisters Don't Fall in Love," Paris, France; (#5) "No Black Art at Documenta," Kassel, Germany; (#6) "Peace and Freedom," Copenhagen, Denmark; and (#7) "Summer Games," Amsterdam, Holland.

In the texts for these watercolors, which were done "on the move," so to speak, I explored European racism, including the exclusion of black art in the "political" Documenta exhibition, and a tragic event that had horrified all Europe — the Palestinian terrorists' assassination of the Israeli team at the Olympic Games in Munich. I had just returned to Amsterdam and was about to take off for the U.S. when the news broke that eleven members of the Israeli team had been murdered. I responded with a Political Landscape text: "There are certain things you are really not supposed to put up with — even if you are used to it — one of them is inequality and the other is war" (part VII, #7).

Today when I read the texts of the Political Landscape Series with their emotional messages about racism, sexism, war, and violence, I'm turned off by the writing. I'm embarrassed by its lack of originality and wit, and also its heavy-handed 1960s rhetoric. Yet it was the first time that I had really tried my hand at writing prose. Images alone were insufficient. Despite my passionate desire to write, however, I simply wasn't able to find my voice. It was so frustrating. Michele could not continue to write for me but I couldn't write in the way I wanted to. Yet I wanted very much to be heard. I was looking for alternatives. When I came back from Europe I found a temporary solution — I turned to statements by famous black women for the texts of the Feminist Landscape Series.

Had Michele continued to write the Political Landscape Series texts for me, I might never have gotten any better as a writer. That experience of writing had thwarted me, but it had also whetted my appetite. A few years later I started to write again when I produced the first draft of my autobiography. But it was only in the early 1980s that I returned to incorporating text into my art — beginning with my very first story quilt, *Who's Afraid of Aunt Jemima?* Since then I have not only written thirty stories for my story quilts, but I have also written five children's books and this autobiography: my first adult book.

Another major event in this European summer of 1972 was my encounter with Tibetan tankas. I met a black Japanese museum guard at the Rijks Museum in Amsterdam, Holland. He had lived in Harlem and was eager to touch base with someone from the "ticker tape." "You're from Harlem?" he asked. I smiled, and nodded yes. "Oh, goddamn, oh shit, goddamn. I used to live in Harlem on 125th Street. Me and my boy had a loft there. He was an artist. I know that fuckin' place. . . ." He went on and on, as if he remembered the words but had forgotten what they meant. "You're an artist, too?" I nodded again. "Oh wow, goddamn, I show you some art, not this shit. This is that honky shit," he announced, waving his hands at the rooms of Rembrandts and other Dutch painters I had come to see. "Nina Simone was here last week. You missed her. She's beautiful. And Odetta and her baby too. Goddamn, I miss that place. Ain't nothing here now. We're all just waiting for the next colored act," he continued. He turned, motioning for me to follow. We arrived in a gallery of Tibetan and Nepalan paintings of the fourteenth and fifteenth centuries. I had never paid too much attention to these paintings on silk cloth before. Now I began to inspect the ancient brocaded cloth frames around them, so old that they were literally in threads. I thanked the guard for showing me the art — without him, I would have never seen this hidden-away exhibit which was to have such an impact on my art-making in the near future. I could do this, I thought to myself; I could get rid of my frames, the glass and the cumbersome heavy stretchers and frame my paintings in cloth. That way I could roll up my paintings and put them in a trunk and ship them in the same way I used to ship the girls' clothes to camp.

When I returned home I was due to begin a traveling exhibition and lecture tour of college campuses with the Political Landscape Series. During this tour, sixteen of the watercolors were stolen from a truck on their way to New York City from the University of Louisiana in Baton Rouge. This was my first experience with an art theft and it discouraged me from continuing in this art form — watercolors were expensive to transport and their glass frames made them susceptible to breakage.

In the fall of 1972 I painted my first cloth-framed paintings. Like the watercolors done earlier in Europe, these, too, were "Political Landscapes." They were inspired by the tankas I had seen at the Rijks Museum in Amsterdam. (It wasn't until I began to show these that I discovered from Camille Billops that the name for them was "tankas.") I glued on the cloth frames meticulously and hung them with gold tassels and red, black, and green braided cords.

I named them The Feminist Series and they were also my first acrylic paintings. On these painted landscapes I printed in gold paint statements made by black women, dating from slavery times until the present. I found these statements in Gerda Lerner's *Black Women in White America,* a book published in 1972. Lerner's book came at a time in my life when I really needed to know about the past feminist history of black women. I felt renewed when I discovered that, along with Harriet Tubman and Sojourner Truth, there were many other black women who were in the vanguard of the feminist movement.

I inscribed several of Sojourner Truth's statements onto my new series. One was from a speech she gave in New York City in 1853: "I wanted to tell you a mite about women's rights and so I came out and said so. I am sitting among you to watch and every once and a while I will come out and tell you what time of day it is." I found another powerful Sojourner Truth text, which I also put into the Feminist Landscape Series. In 1867 in New York City she announced defiantly: "I used to work in the fields and bind grain keeping up with the cradler, but men doing no more got twice as much pay. . . . We do as much, we eat as much, we want as much. I suppose I'm about the only colored woman that goes about to speak for the rights of the colored woman." I was also fascinated with Maria Stewart, credited with being the first American woman public speaker. In a speech in 1833 in Boston, Stewart proclaimed: "Men of eminence have mostly risen from obscurity; nor will I, although female of a darker hue and far more obscure than they, bend my head or hang my harp upon willows for though poor I will virtuous prove." Amy Jacques-Garvey, the wife of Marcus Garvey, the leader of the Back to Africa Movement, said in 1925: "Be not discouraged, black women of the world, but push forward regardless of the lack of appreciation shown you." She continued with "Mr Black man, watch your step! Ethiopia's queens will reign again and her amazons protect her shores and people. Strengthen your shaking knees and move forward or we will displace you and lead on to victory and to glory."

Shirley Chisholm, one of the few contemporary women included in Lerner's book, is the only living woman in my Feminist Series. Chisholm was the first African-American woman to run for the presidency of the United States. She told an audience in a speech in 1970 in Washington, D.C: "I don't want you to go home and talk about integrated schools, churchs or marriages if the kind of integration you're talking about is black and white. I want you to go home and work to fight for the integration of male and female, human and human." Chisholm also made the famous statement that: "Of my two handicaps, being female put more obstacles in my path than being black." Chisholm had really been the woman who first inspired the Political Landscape Series. In the spring of 1972 I had been invited to a benefit (at Flo Kennedy's house) to raise money for Chisholm's presidential candidacy. For this event I made the first Political Landscape paintings on which I inscribed supporting messages for Chisholm. Don't ask me to quote any of the texts because I don't remember them. I sold them, however, and contributed the money to her campaign fund.

Back in the early seventies black women were in denial of their oppression in order to be in support of their men. This made it very important for me to put the words of these valiant black feminists in my art so that people could read them and be as inspired as I had been. At one exhibition, however, a college student was moved to destroy one of the Feminist Landscapes. Its text was from a speech by Harriet Tubman, made in Auburn, New York, in 1869. "There was one of two things I had a right to liberty or death; if I could not have one, I would have the other; for no man would take me alive" (#6). The wooden dowel on which the tanka was hung was broken in half, but the picture, painted on finely woven linen canvas, was unharmed, as were Tubman's powerful words.

Painting is the ultimate magic act in which you transform a flat surface into a three-dimensional illusion of form and space. Time and place disappear as you begin to see your ideas materialize. Yes, painting is a throughly self-absorbed activity, but still you need someone to look with you, to see what you see. I tried to draw my family — my mother and the girls — into my work to help make up for the fact that I had no one else. Mother always thought that art was too tenuous an occupation for me, not good for the family, my children, or my marriage. She thought I should spend more time with people, go back to get a Ph.D., and do college teaching. Yet Mother, despite her negative feelings about my being an artist, was one herself. Fashion design was her art, and her skills with fabrics were to become the basis for our collaboration. We began to work together in the summer of 1972.

I was preparing for a ten-year retrospective at the Voorhees Gallery at Rutgers University in 1973. The Feminist Series, my first tanka paintings, was not going to be included in the show and so I wanted to do a new series to indicate the future directions my work would be taking. The Slave Rape Series was a narrative in which I placed myself in the time of my female ancestors, those brave African women who survived the horror of being uprooted and carried off to slavery in America.

Mother made the tankas for the Slave Rape Series after I had taken her downtown to a gallery that sold Tibetan tankas. Mother was fascinated. There were several tankas laid out on the floor in the back space of the tiny gallery; before I knew it, Mother was back there inspecting the fabric and the workmanship of the tankas for minute details. The gallery dealer was less than pleased that we had discovered his workroom where he was restoring old tankas to look like new. But Mother placated him by telling him how beautiful they were, and he could see that she appreciated the exquisite fabric and fine craftsmanship. After this we were out of there in a flash. Mother took me to one of her favorite places to buy brocaded fabrics and we bought several. Mother made the tankas for all my paintings and they were beautiful, though at the time I was horrified by the asymetrical liberties she took with the design. Later I realized how skillfully she had translated the Tibetan tankas (which she had seen at this Tibetan art gallery) into a unique African-American expression. My first experiments with all this were three single canvases: *Fear: Will Make You Weak, Run: You Might Get Away,* and *Fight: To Save Your Life.* They were large, close-up figures of idealized African women struggling against capture and enslavement. I discovered only too late that having painted these in oil on unstretched canvas made their paint surfaces susceptible to cracking and, therefore, unsuitable for framing in cloth. Despite this they made a beautiful contribution to my ten-year retrospective exhibition at the Voorhees Gallery. And, now, twenty years later, although they have some cracks, they are still some of my most prized pieces, primarily because of the work Mother did on the tankas.

I decided to continue with the Slave Rape theme, but this time I used acrylic paint on unstretched canvas, which made them easy to roll with no surface cracking. Mother made the tankas for these, too, in a style much simpler and appropriate to the tiny fleeing figures in various stages of pursuit. In some of the tankas, however, the tiny figures are armed with hatchets and defend themselves. The captor then retreats and is depicted as a fragment of a man, clothed in white pants and boots, running from the scene. The Slave Rape Series has sixteen paintings depicting three different themes. *Help: Your Sister* shows two women fighting off their captor. *Fight: To Save Your Life* depicts one woman standing alone wielding a ceremonial hatchet in defense of herself. In *Run: You Might Get*

Weeping Woman #2, 1973, Mixed
media, 46 x 4 x 6 inches, Collection of
Moira Roth

Away a lone woman flees in a desperate attempt to avoid capture. All of the tiny nude figures are set against an African landscape of flowers and trees. (On a trip to Nigeria and Ghana in 1976, I was amazed at how much my imagined scenes resembled real African people and places.) After more than twenty years these tankas have been restored by my assistant, Denise Mumm. I know Mother would be proud of the liberties we took with her original tanka designs.

Still there were people who were confused by these tankas; they called them weavings, banners, textiles, fibers. They didn't seem to realize they were looking at paintings on canvas — there were no wooden frames and no stretchers. I didn't like being accused of doing crafts. Being black and a woman were enough. Did I need to be further eliminated on the grounds that I was doing crafts instead of "fine art"? At a meeting of artists at Howard University in the early seventies, I was on a panel with Sam Gilliam, who is known for his huge color-field draped paintings. I began to tell the audience that I was unsure as to how to describe my new works. Gilliam cut me off by inquiring, "Have you ever heard the word *banner*?" My first inclination was to counterattack with, "Have you ever heard the word *drapery*?" But I am proud to say I suppressed the urge to respond then — but not now.

If my audience, and the other artists couldn't understand that a tanka was a painting framed in cloth, what chance did I have of explaining that a mask was a sculpture? Especially if it was made of soft materials. Well, I felt compelled to make them, just as I had the tankas. This kind of sculpture drew me like a magnet.

At this time my students were making wonderful masks based on the African art I was teaching them. Several of them were surprised that my own art did not include mask-making. In 1973, I began to make masks of intricate beading, using raffia for hair.

198

The first ones had no bodies; later, I added a width of cloth to make a dress. I embroidered the dress with raffia thread and hung two gold-painted gourds on it to suggest breasts. These were my Witch Mask Series, and I made eleven of them. The very first one was woven with red, black, green, and gold beads, and I named it *African Design Face Mask.* The next in the series was called *Women's Liberation Talking Mask;* it, too, was woven with gold and multicolored beads. The others were called *Weeping Woman* and *Kissing Witch* and there were several in each of the series. My first male mask, *Male Face Mask #1,* was also a part of the Witch Mask Series. These mask faces were made of a combination of macramé, appliquéd fabrics, and sewn beads. The Weeping Woman masks had beads hung on cords for tears, and the Kissing Witch masks had puckered lips. All of these masks were hooded so that they could be worn, although a masked performance piece had not yet entered my mind.

Women's Liberation Talking Mask, 1973, Mixed media, 59 x 29½ inches, Artist's collection

I must tell you that when I first conceived of these masks, I was reluctant to include costumes. I planned to show two of the masks along with the three large Slave Rape tankas in my ten-year retrospective exhibition that year. This would represent a new direction my work would be taking in the future. But wouldn't it be too "way out" to have costumes on the masks? I decided to exclude the costumes for the exhibit and add them later. I had seen African masks adorned in wonderful costumes at the Museum of Natural History and other museums. From these exhibits and the books on African art I had read, I knew that the costume was an integral part of the mask: it made the mask a more complete spiritual and sculptural identity, and stressed the fact that masks are not just objects to hang on a wall but are also to be worn. I wanted my masks to be like that. Once I made one costume, I could not turn back — now all my masks had costumes. I made the ones for the Witch Mask Series; after that, Mother made costumes for the rest.

Mrs. Brown and and Catherine, *1973, Mixed media 61 x 19 x 10 inches; 27 x 11½ x 6 inches, Artist's collection*

In the summer of 1973 I had taken a short trip to Vermont to visit the artist Pat Mainardi and her husband. During that visit I created *Mrs. Brown and Catherine,* the first of the Family of Woman Mask Series. Mrs. Brown was my mother's best friend, and Catherine Brown was mine, so it might be expected that they would be first since this was to be a commemoration series of women and children I had known as a child. Mrs. Brown's face mask was made of elaborately stitched needlepoint and took forever to do. I have never done another like it. When I completed the face, I attached some fabric for the dress and propped the mask in a chair by the window. I loved it, but I don't think my hosts did.

I returned home bursting with ideas for this new series. The remainder of its thirty-one masks would require costumes as only Mother could make. I explained the project to her and we selected the fabrics and trimmings. She created the most wonderful dresses and I padded their shoulders, breasts, and bellies to create the illusion of a body. Even when the masks were worn, the body of the mask kept its original identity; a man wearing the mask would have the breasts and belly of a woman. In traditional African masked rituals, all of the masks have female features although the wearers are almost always men. Mother knew the people the Family of Woman Series masks commemorated — powerful women who never had had a chance to be all they could be. They were women who lived their lives fully making a lot out of the little they had, and sharing some, too. Among the masks I created were *Mrs. Curry and Charles,* who lived next door to us on

Edgecombe Avenue; *Aunt Edith and Aunt Bessie,* my mother's older sisters; and our own family portrait, *Mrs. Jones, Andrew, Barbara and Faith.*

These masks took me back to painting. The Family of Woman Mask Series was inspired by the Dan masks of Liberia. The Dan mask is carved out of wood, but my masks were made of finely woven linen canvas which was painted, embroidered, and beaded. The face featured a gaping screaming mouth and large round eyeholes through which the mask's wearer could see. The brightly colored yarn hair was in long skinny braids that hung free on the hooded mask head. Because she made the costume, Mother determined how tall a mask would be; when the mask was hung, its height was the length of its dress. The more stately older women, like Mrs. Curry, were the tallest. I gave her and her grandson Charles white faces in the manner of African masks, because both were dead.

In the winter of 1973, I was invited to give a series of lectures and exhibitions for the Syracuse public schools. To prepare for this week-long engagement, I made my first dolls, and the children loved them. The dolls were really puppets with heads made of painted gourds with raffia hair. Like my first masks, the bodies came later. Mother made a kind of dress to attach to the gourd head. I also made hat masks. These had intricately embroidered and beaded masked faces of painted canvas with wigs of brightly colored yarn hair which peeped out from under-

Wilt, Willa,and Wiltina, *1974, Mixed media.*
7 feet 3 inches high, Artist's collection

neath the hat. Many of the hats were from my hat-wearing days; one was a hand-made French original of pale green chiffon, trimmed with tiny pearls around the brim. Some of the hat masks were made from Birdie's hat collection. The kids donned the hat masks

201

Zora and Fish, 1975, Mixed media, 5 feet 4 inches high, Artist's collection

and immediately went into character, producing a mini-performance.

The dolls led me to soft sculpture figures. I made one of Wilt Chamberlain, the famous basketball player. *Wilt,* who was seven feet three inches tall, was my first. Later, I made so many of these figures that I named them The Dude Series. They were lanky male figures dressed in bright clothes with colored yarn for hair. I hollowed out coconut shells for their heads (I baked the shells to harden them) and painted them with enamel paint. The bodies were shaped out of cloth on a knotted rope armature to suggest a structure. The sculptures hung from the ceiling by invisible fish line cords. Some people called the masks and the sculptures "puppets" or "dolls."

The *Wilt* sculptures were intended as a comment on the negative statements he had made about black women in his autobiography. I don't recall exactly what he said, but it had every black woman I knew up in arms and mad as hell. My sculptures of *Wilt* included *Willa* and *Wiltina,* a (white) wife and child he didn't have. Men enjoyed *Wilt* as much as women. They liked seeing their own image anatomically correct. People were dissatisfied, however, when they felt Wilt's legs and discovered that he had no body — only rope which connected his pants to his high-heeled platform shoes. In May of 1974, after my tour was over for the summer, I developed foam rubber bodies for the *Wilt* sculptures and Mother made their clothes.

Mother had heard that I was making male sculptures anatomically correct. "Make that man a pair of underpants before you bring him to my house," she told me firmly on the telephone. "I've heard all about what you are doing over there and I don't want to see it," Mother warned me. She meant it. I made underpants for Wilt and after that I just covered his torso so she wouldn't have to see his bare flesh, so to speak.

In 1974 I did not only the *Wilt* pieces but also a series of couples which were my fantasy weddings for my daughters. I made sculptures of Barbara and Michele and their idealized young men. I gave them each a perfect child to start off their new families. I sewed all their hands together so that they could not easily be separated. These Couples Series represented ideal relationships and perfect weddings for my two daughters. Mother made both the clothes for the wedding party and the tanka frames for twenty paintings, which acted as backdrops for the figures. I called these the Windows of the Wedding Series and they were my first completely abstract paintings. They represent a visual language I was trying to invent based on Kuba designs. Each was intended to be a kind of hanging prayer rug for the couples to meditate with every morning and evening, giving them magic protection — and, above all, happiness.

The Windows of the Wedding Series had names that invoked the theme of the "family": *Mother, Fathers, Children, No Children, Equals, No Equals, Patience and Understanding, Family Love, Love, Peace,* and others. In these wedding environments I also placed the Family of Woman Mask Series and the Witch Mask Series, which I had done in 1973. The exhibitions traveled to many colleges where the "weddings" were celebrated. All the while, in real life, my daughters were unmarried and unaware that this was going on. Barbara was at the University of London for her senior year abroad, and Michele was finishing her bachelor's degree at City College and beginning a career as a writer. I don't think I ever fully explained this series to Barbara and Michele; and, if they ever saw any of the couples, they never mentioned how they felt about them. How could they understand what this was about?

Zora and Fish (1975) were the first stuffed figures I did. All the other soft sculptures were made from my original patterns of flat pieces of foam, which I had cut so that they could be rolled and sewn together. *Zora and Fish* were made, however, of tiny pieces of irregularly cut foam or scraps from the other sculptures. I stuffed these scraps into the cloth body to create the form of the body. I made the heads out of coconut, and painted them with enamel paint and gave them a crown of wig hair. Their clothes were made of bits and pieces of fabric that I sewed onto their bodies. Zora's dress is elaborately pieced together with many colorful fabrics; and Fish's otherwise drab garb is adorned with a variety of campaign buttons with political slogans including "Shirley Chisholm for President." I named them Zora and Fish because Zora seemed a good name for a free spirit and Fish seemed a good name for her man. In the mid-seventies these two figures represented a familiar couple in our urban environment — the shopping bag lady and

Martin Luther King Jr., *1975, Mixed Media, Life size, Artist's collection*

the street man. They might have lived in Harlem but they would ride the subway downtown to work like anybody else. He carried her chair so that she could sit and beg while he'd sprawl out on the ground with his wine bottle. When exhibited, this sculpture piece was always accompanied by a bottle of Richard's Wild Irish Rose in Zora's shopping bag. I remember at the SoHo 20 Gallery in New York City, people would take a drink and put some money in Zora's cup. At the end of the exhibition, Zora had a nearly empty bottle of wine in her bag and about seven dollars in change and bills in her begging cup. Zora and Fish have made money at every exhibit.

In 1975 for the first time my beloved Harlem became an important subject in my art. I approached it through a series of bigger-than-life masks that I called "portrait masks." They were given this name by an admiring student at the University of Wisconsin at Whitewater. The name seemed appropriate since two of the masks, for example, realistically portrayed Adam Clayton Powell Jr. and Martin Luther King Jr. The others in the series were *Moma, Joanna,* and *Leroy.* These were the first life-like faces in my soft sculpture. I made the masks from foam rubber, which I cut to create a super-realistic likeness of a human face. I then sprayed the white foam with different shades of enamel paint to represent skin coloring. But don't try it — even though it looked great at the time, fifteen years later I had to restore all of the pieces because they were deteriorating badly. Restoration in this case meant that I had to cover the masks with cloth while still trying to retain the likeness of the portrait. This was hard to do and I lost some of the freshness in the process.

These masks had what in African sculpture is called a "superstructure." This means that they are worn on top of the head and not over the face. A helmet is sewn inside the body of the mask so that the wearer looks out through the two holes in his/her chest instead of a regular face mask's eyes. The part of the mask that is above the actual head of the wearer is called the "superstructure." These masks make the wearers appear two feet taller than their actual height — that nicely fitted the characters of both King and

Powell. It gave their masks the illusion of profound visibility which is naturally inherent in great people.

I involved the girls in my first performance pieces, which were acted out for the camera and not a live audience. The girls wore masks and the sculptures were the other "actors" in the series; I took color slides of these "performances" and included them in my slide shows at college lectures. All this was fun, but too limiting. I increasingly wanted the spontaneity of a live performance with real people, audience participation, and music.

Barbara and Michele in performance, 1973

My first multimedia masked performance piece was *The Wake and Resurrection of the Bicentennial Negro.* In *From the Center,* her classic book on feminist art, Lucy Lippard described it as a "funereal tableau." It was my response to the American Bicentennial celebrations of 1976. I certainly agreed with many black people at the time that we had no reason to celebrate two hundred years of American independence: for almost half of that time we had been in slavery, and for most of the following years we had still been struggling to become fully free. (In the year 2076, however, we must turn things around so that all Americans can join the celebration.) So, this was a wake not a celebration. I wanted to create a visual narrative of the dynamics of racism, including the self-imposed oppression of drug addiction. As the story goes — Buba, the hero of *The Wake,* died because of drug addiction and Bena, the heroine, died of grief.

The Wake began originally with two masks made of black satin fabric. They were part of a new mask concept I developed in a workshop I conducted at the University of Wisconsin at Whitewater. The idea of the workshop was to produce a completed mask at the end of the four-hour session. Deadlines for me are usually self-imposed. I love 'em and they give me a challenge that I enjoy meeting. For obvious reasons the process

The Wake and Resurrection of the Bicentennial
Negro, *1976, Mixed media, Life size, Artist's collection*

and the materials had to be simple. The mouth and the nose could be made three-dimensional by rolling and sewing together foam rubber pieces and covering them with fabric for color and durability. We used feathers, sequins, and beads to decorate and embellish the mask face, and raffia, yarn, or unraveled rope for the hair. The completed masks are light and extremely comfortable to wear. This was the way I made the masks for *The Wake* performance. Because a cloth mask is so light and comfortable, it is a good mask for dancers. In fact, many African dance troupes wear such masks today. I was to see these for the first time in 1977, when I was at the Festival of Black and African Art and Culture in Lagos, Nigeria.

All the while I was conducting the Wisconsin mask-making workshop, I was thinking about how wonderful many of the masks would be in a performance. It was a natural progression that I would next do a masked performance piece myself. *The Wake and Resurrection of the Bicentennial Negro* was an expression of all the different aspects of the art I had already done — the mask, painting, figures, and installations — combined with new media: music, story, and live performance. I particularly liked the idea of audience response. Paintings, no matter how skillfully done, rarely get applause.

There were, however, a number of things that had to be taken into consideration in planning a performance workshop. The most important was that the host university had to identify the students interested in performing. Then I would meet with them briefly on the evening I arrived, knowing that *The Wake*'s installation of masks, tankas, and soft sculptures of Bena, Buba, Moma, and Nana (Grandma) had already been on exhibition on the campus. The next morning we would have a quick runthrough of the music and the "I Have a Dream" sermon. Spontaneity, improvisation, and an understanding of "the black experience" were necessary to play the characters in this production. Those students who had that understanding knew it, and those who didn't soon passed. Students were always surprised by the ease with which they were able to play a character when wearing a mask.

The masked characters of the piece are Bena, Buba, and their Moma, Popa, and Auntie. Nana is part of the installation but not part of the performance. She is replaced by Auntie. It is written to be performed mainly in mime and lasts only thirty minutes. I made recordings of my favorite hymns, spirituals, and rhythm and blues songs as the musical background; I could think of no better sermon for *The Wake* than Martin Luther King Jr.'s speech "I Have a Dream."

The performance is set in a church, and I used *The Windows of the Wedding* tankas, which look somewhat like stained-glass windows, as backdrops for the church scene. A recording of the Abyssinian Baptist Church Choir singing the hymn "Amazing Grace" opens the first act. The audience is silent as they listen to the church choir and see the stage with its two masked figures of Bena and Buba lying on a red-black-and-green flag with floral wreaths all around them. At some point Moma in the back of the audience begins to weep audibly and sinks to the ground crying out, "my poor baby." The audience is now aware that Moma, Popa, and Auntie are ascending the aisle to the stage to mourn the deaths of Bena and Buba.

This is a very special moment for Moma's character and she must be able to display grief openly. I found, after seven years of directing this performance at a number of colleges across the country, that one needs to have a black experience in order to play this character. I tried out some white women students who were eager to play this role, but they never felt really comfortable screaming out in grief, and their knees were never quite able to collapse in the way that some sisters' could.

The performance proceeds with Martin Luther King Jr.'s speech "I Have a Dream," during which Auntie and Popa are seated onstage consoling and fanning Moma. Throughout the performance there are masked mourners and signifiers who speak out, informing the audience of what is going on. For instance, they might call out: "Look at Moma . . . she ain' gonna never get over Buba's death. . . . She sure loved that boy of hers. . . . Yeah, but he was on that stuff wasn't he? Yeah, he was. Just worried his poor wife Bena to death. . . . Well, they both gone now ain't nobody but the Lord can bring 'em back." These characters could be played by anybody who had a feel for the part and could improvise and speak well. Often these parts were played by white students or others who were not suitable to play the main characters.

The Wake and
Resurrection of the
Bicentennial Negro
performance, 1977

After the sermon Moma performs an impassioned dance to the old spiritual "Mary, Mary, Don't You Weep, Don't You Moan," wringing her hands and collapsing to the floor in grief. During the course of her powerful mother's-love dance, Moma literally brings Bena and Buba back to life. They begin slowly to come out of their prone positions as the exhausted Moma is helped back to her seat by Auntie and Popa.

Once resurrected, Bena and Buba relive their transgressions. Bena does a slow and melancholy dance to "My Man" while Buba turns his back on her, openly displaying his disregard for her love. Bena becomes disillusioned with Buba, who now goes through the motions of taking drugs. "Why Don't You Do Right?" is the music played as Bena and Buba have a fistfight in which they appear to exchange blows. During this heated exchange, all the other characters respond, and indeed Moma has to be held back from attempting to stop the fight. The signifiers and mourners keep up a running commentary on the action: "Buba ain't gonna change. . . . Yeah, but Bena ain't gonna take it no more . . . she gonna leave him this time for sure." Buba is moved by Bena's newly liberated spirit: the threat that she will leave him forces him to straighten up. Some of the men playing Buba remarked that they had never hit a woman and felt bad even pretending to do so. However, many of the women playing Bena seemed to enjoy the freedom the fight scene gave them. Next, Buba performs a new-man dance to "Pressure Cooking," a fast-tempo rhythm piece. (Bena may join him in the dance.) Bena, now liberated from fear and grief, performs her new-woman dance to "Sunshine," an up-tempo lyric about waking up to a new day. Buba and Bena embrace and kiss. Everyone loves this part. Moma, Popa, and Auntie, and the mourners and signifiers, all rejoice in a "hallelujah dance," shouting "praise God, them children back together."

In the closing scene, Moma, overcome with joy but weakened from the experience, is supported by Bena and Buba as Popa and Auntie — followed by the mourners and signifiers -- proceed down the aisle to the accompaniment of a tape of Harlem's Abyssinian Baptist Church Choir singing the hymn "He Arose." The players return to the stage with their masks off and talk with the audience about their performance experience and answer questions.

Most of the performers of *The Wake* were dancers. Right from the start it was apparent that students performing *The Wake* had to be able to move well onstage. Even if they weren't dancers, they had to be able to move like dancers because the masked performer's movements created the mood of the piece. Yet, some of the very best performances were by actors who, in the heat of the performance, yell out words they had never planned to say. As one young woman, who played Bena, expressed it: "I didn't even know what I was saying. It was the mask talking, not me. I've never been in love. I don't know why I would tell Buba that I love him." But she had.

I went to Africa for the first time in the summer of 1976. Since the 1960s I had wanted to visit West Africa to see the textiles, tribal masks, and sculpture of Nigeria and Ghana that had so informed my art. When I saw the African landscape and people I realized that I had already been there "in my mind's eye" when creating the Slave Rape Series. But the opportunity did not present itself until 1976, when I won a travel award from the American Association of University Professors. Mother had gone a year or so before and came back with so many stories of African hospitality that I was eager to go — and, since Mother had already been there, I felt quite comfortable going alone. For eight weeks I visited Nigeria and Ghana, traveling from the south to the north in both countries by plane, bus, and "struggle buggy" or public transportation. I must say their slogan of "there is always room for one more" describes the seating arrangements exactly. I have never been so completely accepted, nor had I felt so much a part of the majority as I was in Nigeria and Ghana. What it must feel like to be white in America is how I felt as a black woman in Africa.

I came back from Africa with ideas for a new mask face, more primitive than any I had ever done before. *Primitive* is a word I use in a positive way to explain the completeness of a concept in art. I like to layer and pattern and embellish my art in the manner

The Widows Masks,
*1976, Mixed media, Life
size, Artist's collection*

of tribal art, and then, like a blues singer, I like to repeat and repeat it again. Fragmented, understated, or minimalist art forms frustrate me. I want to finish them. In the 1960s there was a minimalist aesthetic advocating "less is more." To me, less is even less and more is still not quite enough. I was now using feathers and beads as never before. I had been to the African source of my own "classical" art forms and now I was set free. The new mask shed its clothes and body — just the face was the power of the whole thing. The African Series could be worn, but also they could hang triumphantly on the wall. This was a very productive time for me. I spent hour after hour working and collaborating on art projects. I was alone and loving it.

The Second World Black and African Festival of Arts and Culture in Nigeria took place in January of 1977. I went over with two hundred and fifty black American artists, dancers, musicians, and writers (selected by a committee of black curators) to celebrate our culture. We stayed in Festac Village, a government project erected for the festival in a suburb fifteen miles from Lagos. (After the festival the village was to be used as a model housing plan for the Nigerians.) The site accommodated the festival participants from fifty-eight nations representing Africa, the Caribbean, Europe, South America, and North America. These nations sent their most renowned black artists as their delegates. Can you imagine a better black cultural explosion? None of us will ever forget it.

The opening ceremony of the show of nations around the National Stadium in Lagos was a highly professional and obviously well-rehearsed performance by all the participating nations except the U.S. delegates. For us it was an unrehearsed, spontaneous outpouring of raw energy. Unlike the others, we had not prepared for a performance: we had no banners, no music, no costumes, no cultural display. Our (African) American leaders had failed to prepare us for what was to occur. Still, we were terrific. Just our being there caused the audience around the stadium to go wild. The two hundred and fifty American artists were the biggest single hit at the entire festival opening. As we circled the stadium grounds, everyone cheered us. We made the Black Power salute and sang "Amen" over and over, capturing the hearts of the black people of the world. As we approached, each section of the stadium stood with raised clenched fists and thundered "Black Power!" The sound was deafening — and not a word about it appeared in the American press, although they were all there. Where else had our press seen America cheered abroad?

But the real excitement was yet to come. When we left the stadium at the close of the opening ceremonies, we were joined by hundreds of people who left their stadium seats and tried to cut us off from the waiting buses. They were chanting while running in time. It sounded like a million drums playing to an African beat, "om ba gom, om ba gom, om ba gom. . . . " I didn't know what the people were chanting, or exactly what was happening, but I was careful not to miss a step. We arrived at our buses exhausted. I later found out they were saying, "Come back home, come back home, come back home. . . . " They thought we were leaving them again as we had four hundred years before. This time they would make an effort to keep us there.

I had trouble at the festival art exhibition. A young brother hanging the show thought my work unworthy of including with the so-called fine art. He chose an out-of-the-way spot for it with some other items labeled "crafts," high up on a wall under a balcony overlooking the exhibition. Chauvinist tendencies among the black male participants at the festival ran high, and the black women were strangely quiet, maybe due to the fact that many of them were in Africa for the first time. At any rate, this man who hung the show seized the opportunity to exert his authority — who knows, perhaps for the first time in his life. (I heard later that this artist had never been in an exhibition before. If that was true, I guess he was excited and took it out on me.) I refused to be manipulated in this way and withdrew my work from the exhibition, taking it back to the village with me. A young African-American woman working for a Lagos television station heard about this and asked me to be on her program to explain what had happened. I appeared in mask, and held up the two other masks as I was interviewed; thus I was able to show my masks to the television audience and talk about them. These masks were a homecoming tribute after four hundred years of being in America. The

Widows Masks Series were made of black velvet, heavily decorated with black-and-white glass beads. Of the three masks the central figure was *Moma,* wearing a mourner's veil of black chantilly lace. On either side of her were Bena and Buba, her son and daughter, the two characters from *The Wake and Resurrection of the Bicentennial Negro.* I was approached by several African art collectors who wished to purchase my masks but I wanted to keep them to bring back to America. I had made them especially to take to Africa, but I found it difficult to leave them there. In 1990 they mysteriously disappeared while on consignment at a New York gallery. If anyone knows of their whereabouts, I would appreciate hearing.

When I returned home, I made masks using even more feathers, beads, and other details. The work became more layered and bolder. I myself was shocked by it. I used authentic African brocades that I had bought in the marketplace in Lagos. I was obsessed with making these new African Mask Series. They were the first of my sculptures to sell; indeed, I sold so many of them that I could not keep up with the demand. Now, when I look back at the low prices I sold them for, I realize that I had a need to share this work — more so than anything else I had ever done. It may have been my way of sharing my African experience.

Since 1974 I had talked about writing a book on my life and experiences. But I never wrote a line until Michele left in 1976. I began writing the first draft of this autobiography when I returned from Africa in February of 1977. I wrote every morning from six until three in the afternoon. By the summer I had finished the text on the 1960s; it was the first chapter I wrote. There was so much happening in the 1960s that I thought it best to start there and work backward. During the summer months, I spent time interviewing my mother about events of the thirties and forties. I was pretty well entrenched in the manuscript by the end of July. Especially since I was living alone, I had time to write as much as I cared, without any interference or interruptions. But late in the summer I began to feel the need to see Birdie again. Without him, life would have been very different. We had similar values and that was so important to me. Without him, maybe eventually there would have been someone else. But who?

I saw Birdie one summer day in 1977 as I was walking down the street not far from my house. He was on his way to the doctor for a checkup after a cold. He was surprised to see me, and I to see him. He embraced me, trying to pretend that it had not been three years since we had seen each other. He was no longer just roughing it until we

The Purple Doll Series, *1986, Mixed media, 18 x 6 x 6 inches, Private collection*

could get back together again. Now he had an apartment in 409 Edgecombe Avenue, the landmark apartment building he had grown up in. Even when we were together, Birdie had always kept a tiny place with access to the roof so he could raise his birds. As a kid, he raised Flights (pigeons) on the roof. He no longer raised Flights, but he did own several prize-winning homing pigeons and he ran them on weekends in races from Washington, D.C., to New York City.

Birdie gave me a key to his apartment, and asked me to stay there until he came home from work. I told him that I preferred to see him on the weekend, that I was busy and needed to spend time at my own apartment since I was writing a book and he had no typewriter. I didn't see him for the rest of the week. On Saturday, after a full day of writing, I got dressed about ten o'clock in the evening and went to see Birdie. I had decided that since I had the key, if he was not home, I would let myself in and wait for him.

The doorman at Birdie's building just stood there at the intercom pretending to ring his apartment. "I have the key. I'm his wife," I told the now-stammering doorman. "He he he he he . . . is is is is . . . " I walked away impatiently and rang for the elevator. As the elevator door closed, the doorman stared at me, his eyes as big as saucers. Now he could reach Birdie and alert him that I was coming up. Birdie's door was open before I could insert the key. As I had thought, Birdie was home, but not alone. There was a young woman there with two babies, and I saw them instantly when I walked in. There was no time for introductions. Birdie rushed me right out and onto the elevator — as if we had a date and I was just arriving to keep it. "Who is that young woman and the

Cherie, 1977, from the Woman on a Pedestal Series, Mixed media, 17 inches, Artist's collection

babies and what the hell are they doing up here on a Saturday night?" I demanded, not caring who heard me. "Now, don't get excited, Mommy." (Birdie and I have a fondness for calling each other Mommy and Daddy.) "She's just a friend, the children belong to her and her sister. I have been very lonely without you. I have had friends while we were apart and I can't just get rid of them now that you're back," he explained, as if he had rehearsed what he would say.

Birdie had changed. He was older, more vulnerable. He needed me, and he was not ashamed to admit it. I needed him too. The girls were now grown. It was time for us. "I spoiled you," he told me, trying to explain why he had failed to contact me before now. "I had you on a pedestal. Nobody else could ever love you like I do. We belong together," he confessed. But could we stay together? That was the question. Birdie was very independent. I never felt that he needed me. Yet maybe things were different now. But what about his mother, who had always been so hostile toward me? "No one will ever come between us again," Birdie volunteered. Now that was new. Birdie was beginning to sound like he had learned something over the three years that we were apart.

Over the years I had learned that not many men wanted an equal partner; and, with advancing age, the numbers decline even more dramatically. I was comfortable with Birdie. We were two independent people doing our own thing. Maybe this time we could eliminate a lot of old problems by maintaining separate apartments. If we each had a place of our own, maybe we'd feel less trapped when we were together. So Birdie kept his apartment and I kept mine. Our new arrangement was like dating instead of being stuck in a tired old marriage. Birdie could spend whatever time he wanted seeing his family and friends, provided my need to see him was first and vice versa. Now we had to plan our days together, not just take each other for granted. Every night we ate dinner together and slept in the same bed together at his place or mine. But we had the option to get away from each other in order to have our private moments in our own space. And my art, which completely dominated my space, was not to be found in his. Birdie had assembled his own art collection. Most of it was godawful, but it was his.

The Woman on a Pedestal Series were my first freestanding sculptures. Birdie had said he always placed me on a pedestal. Was that really part of our problem? In any case, I think pedestals are for fragile, inanimate objects that are nice to look at and own but are otherwise useless. They are placed on pedestals to prevent them from being lost, damaged, or broken. Some people may see women like that, but I don't see myself that way and I told Birdie so.

In 1977 and 1978 I produced the Woman on a Pedestal Series. I was inspired by a dream in which I saw a woman with carrot-red hair and pink skin, wearing a yellow dress. In my dream she was about twelve inches tall and running all around my house. I tried to get Birdie to catch her because I was afraid she would run behind something and get hurt. Birdie said, "Leave her alone, she is not bothering anything." I tried to catch her myself, but she ran into the bathroom, disappearing behind the bathtub. I woke up. At this time, I was taping my dreams while still in a semiconscious dream state. This one is still as clear in my memory as the day I dreamed it. Cherie, as the tiny person in my dream was named, became the subject for the first sculpture in my Woman on a Pedestal Series. I tried to copy Cherie as accurately as I remembered her in my dream. The other women in the series represent types of women who, like Cherie, have come down from the pedestal either by choice or circumstance. They are shopping bag ladies, ladies of the evening, old women, or liberated women who are having second thoughts about the pedestal.

The Carters, 1979, Mixed media, 19 inches, Collection of Lucinda Bunnen

In 1978 I created another Harlem Series, a group of sculptures to be shown as an installation. These new Harlem sculptures were almost life-size and all had supports so that they could stand alone — their legs looked quite real. In this series, I tried again to capture the spirit of Harlem. *Moma* and *Daddy,* by now favorite subjects of mine, are two of the main characters in this series. *Little Joe,* the young "diddy bop," and his girl *Tina* are the young people on the block. *Reverend Ives* is the church minister, and *Nat* is the local hustler, with *Sugar*, his woman. *Lena* is the shopping bag lady and *Miss Martha* is the traditional church matron. A backdrop for the installation was a large piece of canvas on which I encouraged people to write messages. Now it is so crowded with words from all its exhibitions that they are no longer easily legible.

In 1979, determined to find a stable market for my art, I decided to go into making dolls as a business. I called them Sew Real Soft Sculpture — I used this name because I had created a lifelikeness in my sculpture that caused people to say, "Why, they look so real." Some of these dolls were made to represent harmless 1960s stereotypes of sharp-looking black dudes dressed in gold lamé coats with hats to match, and beautiful black women with braided and beaded hair. The women were dressed in sequined coats and slinky black satin dresses. I made a hippie with long blond hair who wore a wide hat with a feather, and a lamé coat of ice blue to match his sequined-blue eyes. I made Asian dolls and Latino dolls and African ones. Mother designed and made all the dolls' clothes. I even created an Iranian couple and had trouble finding out what they wore under their chadors. (There were no books or magazines with fashion pictures from Iran.) Fortunately, Mother made a chador before the hostages were taken because, after that, Mother didn't want to hear anything about whom she now referred to as "those people." Mother made a huge box of clothes for the dolls, many more than I requested, and I worked on the bodies, which took a long time to create. I sold a lot of these dolls for a couple of hundred dollars each. They were impractical to sell at that price since they took weeks to make. And many people who liked them could still not afford to buy them. I now had a sizable audience but the market was a challenge I still had to conquer.

Mother tried to help me, but I could feel her getting tired. She was, after all, now in her late seventies. I hated being such a drain on her, but I was having a serious problem keeping up my spirits. This was a time to look at my life as an artist and try to see where I was going. The seventies began with a bang but ended with a whimper. I must say I was very glad to see the decade go.

CHAPTER 10: TEACHING ART: THOSE WHO CAN SHOULD

My maternal grandfather, Professor B. B. Posey, 1880s

I grew up with family role models who were teachers. The most notable was my mother's father, Professor B. B. Posey, whose portrait hangs in my studio as a proud reminder of my family history. As I was the youngest child in my family, everybody taught me and they were never too busy to answer my questions. Daddy taught me to read from billboards and street signs; however, Daddy's main "course of study" had more to do with facts and figures — "Who was the first man to die in the Revolutionary War?" The answer is Crispus Attucks, a black man, and I'll never forget that. Mother was a specialist in morality lessons and family history. Andrew's lessons were made-up stories. For example, if you wore a fur coat in the house during summer, you would surely drop dead. My sister, Barbara, taught me to sing "La Marseillaise," the French national anthem. She and I played teacher/pupil-in-the-classroom like some kids played house and I loved it. Thus I was brought up to have a great deal of respect for the profession, and my family could not have been more pleased when Barbara and I both became teachers. And I am proud to say, my two daughters maintain the family tradition as they, too, became teachers. I came to teaching with the goal of learning to "paint like a child" — I taught them and they taught me. After forty years of teaching, I'm still learning. Teaching art has brought a richness to my life and my art that could never have occurred otherwise. I couldn't be more pleased to describe myself as both an artist and teacher.

Me with UCSD art students, 1993

I began teaching at the junior high school level in 1955 and resigned from my last position as a teacher in the New York public school system in 1973 — all in all, eighteen and a half difficult but not-to-be-missed years of service. I went back and forth from teaching in Harlem to teaching in Brooklyn, the Bronx, and Manhattan. In 1970, I began to teach college-level courses at the Pratt Institute in Brooklyn, and in the same year at Wagner College on Staten Island, and the Bank Street College of Education, then located in Greenwich Village. For a number of years, after leaving Pratt, Wagner, and Bank Street, I didn't have a regular teaching job but I did numerous artist-in-residencies, conducted workshops and seminars, and lectured in colleges and universities around the country. Then in 1985 I was offered a position as a full professor in the Visual Arts Department at the University of California at San Diego (UCSD), teaching studio courses in drawing and painting. I have been teaching there ever since — usually two quarters of each year. My good friend Moira Roth was then chair of the department and my advocate for the position. (She now holds the Trefethan Chair of Art History at Mills College.) In 1986 I developed a course I am particularly fond of — Collaboration in Sewn and Fabric Art — that reminds me of the course I had taught earlier at Bank Street College, although the subject of this UCSD course is the quilt. However West Coast the location, the classroom atmosphere is similar and, like Bank Street, the students and their work are thoroughly delightful. Now I live bi-coastally in La Jolla, California, and Englewood, New Jersey.

Me with John Jay High School students, 1957

My very first teaching assignment was in Harlem at the Harriet Beecher Stowe Junior High School (136 in Manhattan), an all-girls school. In my marvelous seventh-grade class was Paula Baldwin, a lovely, bright, and talented girl. She was the first to introduce me to the work of James Baldwin, her brother. This school, however, had some "hard little knots" (children with "hard heads" who never listen to a word you say) in it as well as girls like Paula. On one occasion I almost had to fight a classroom full of them. Would you believe they threatened to "kick my ass." I responded with a well-stocked vocabulary of four-letter words spoken in fluent "ghettoese," promising to counter any attack against my person with immediate and forceful retaliation. The "hard little knots" fell for it, which meant my days were numbered. I left not unhappily after one year there. I wanted to learn how to teach but I could not learn in an environment that had a weak principal and where many of the teachers were apathetic.

I searched for a high school that would hire a black teacher. You may not be able to imagine the degree of racism involved in acquiring a teaching position in a high school in the fifties and even in the sixties in New York City. Finally I found Max Greenberg, who was the art chairman at what is now called John Jay High School in Brooklyn (previously the Manual Training High School). Max hired me, and he was a joy to work with as well as a good friend. When I left in 1960 to teach at Junior High School 113, it was because my children's school, Our Savior Lutheran School, was also in the Bronx.

By 1960 I had already been teaching for five years and loving it, each year developing innovative teaching methods. Fortunately for me, I had the very best in supervisors. Principals were able to teach and supervise, and that meant that new teachers could learn from an expert, someone they could respect as a teacher as well as an administrator.

Mr. Leibson, the principal of Junior High School 113, was such a man and I taught in his school for four good years. Mr. Leibson had a slogan we used to joke about. "Every teacher is a teacher of reading." In order to enforce the principle of reading in each subject area, he often went from class to class and demonstrated effective teaching of reading within the context of the subject being taught. He was as proficient in teaching language studies and math as he was in science, geography, and history.

Mr. Leibson, balding with scanty mixed-gray fuzz for hair, almost always wore a serious expression on his face; his round metal-rimmed eyeglasses magnified his bright blue eyes. Although he was not even as tall as many of our students, his commanding voice and take-charge manner made him appear to be ten feet tall. I can still hear him now: "Every lesson starts with a problem, proceeds by a statement of aims and solutions, and concludes with an evaluation." All of this was to be skillfully solicited from the students through a process of questions and answers. To test this, Mr. Leibson would unexpectedly enter a classroom and address the class, asking them, "What is the problem today?" Because our kids were so bright, they would know the response to this, and also to his next question: "What are the aims of this lesson?" Mr. Leibson would then go on to teach a masterful lesson, using his slogan: "Every teacher is a teacher of reading."

There was one class Mr. Leibson did not teach, however, and that was the talk of the school. One Monday morning during the first period he had come into the kitchen in the home economics department, where the students were preparing to bake biscuits. This class was composed of a small group of girls who were slow learners and had some problems working in large groups. The girls were working quietly when Mr. Leibson came into the room. "What's the problem today, girls?" he enquired, drawing himself up to his full 5'6" height, as he stood poised in front of the room, chalk in hand. The girls stopped, rolling pins suspended in the air, and looked around to see who had asked the question. Then the spokesgirl for the group (there is always one in every class) blurted out, "We ain't got no problem, and, if we did, we wouldn't tell you."

I remember another episode at the school when I included three students, all classified as "chronic retarded mental defectives," into a "gifted" art class. One of them did wonderful, minute-detailed drawings of spaceships and launching pads. He either had a photographic memory or an unusual imagination. None of the teachers in the science department was able to refute the accuracy of his renderings. He had not copied these drawings either; I could vouch for that since I was with him all the time he was making them. What an artist he was. I wonder about the nature of his so-called retardation and what ever became of him.

In 1964 I received a permanent teaching license and was appointed to Walton High School in the Bronx. After a year I applied for a waiver to teach at P.S. 100, an elementary school in Harlem. At the time the principal at Walton warned me that my "sacrifice" of leaving Walton (an all-white high school) to teach in an all-black elementary school in Harlem would not be rewarded. She was wrong, of course. My motives were twofold: I wanted to teach in my own community and to gain experience teaching art to little children. But I knew that elementary school teachers and high school teachers were all paid on the same salary scale.

My job now involved not only teaching art but coordinating an annual art festival, a special event designed to bring our talented students in closer contact with some of the role models in the community. The children painted postcards, inviting prominent and community people in education, politics, the arts, and other areas of public life to attend our events. The children's work was displayed alongside that of artists, craftspeople, and collectors from the community. The children were able to meet and talk to many people with whom they would not normally have contact. Roy Wilkins, Judge Constance Baker Motley, Dorothy Maynor, Norman Lewis, James Meredith, and Judge Livingston Wingate were among some of the people who came and spoke at the festivals. Other celebrities responded with letters and signed photographs, including Jacqueline Kennedy Onassis, Pearl Bailey, Sammy Davis Jr., Ossie Davis and Ruby Dee, Arthur Mitchell, Duke Ellington, Jackie Robinson, Marian Anderson, and Leontyne Price. They sent their RSVPs directly to the child who had sent them the invitation. Some people who could not attend sent gifts of money for prizes to deserving art students. For example, George Meany sent a representative from his union who spoke and presented a gift of twenty-five dollars from the A.F.L./C.I.O.

By the late 1960s teaching, however, had become a profession that involved not only education but community activism and politics. There were no black principals and few black teachers in (or outside) Harlem at this time; and black children were receiving a grossly unequal education. In response, black parents and teachers began to demand community control of public schools and a curriculum that was relevant to the needs of black children.

During the school year of 1967, our school was constantly being picketed by members of the Harlem Parents Committee. They were trying to counteract a decision made by the Board of Education to fire a teacher who was greatly admired in the Harlem community for her militant stand against the school establishment and her commitment to teaching black history. Mrs. Timpson, our principal at P.S. 100 and the only black acting principal in the city at the time, was involved in this teacher's dismissal. She was also opposed to the community's demand for decentralization of the public schools, which would give the community the power to hire and fire teachers and principals.

The demonstrators who picketed the school daily were characterized by resplendent African attire, an aura of righteousness and total commitment, and very, very angry faces. One day to my surprise and delight I met "Queen Mother" Moore while talking to the demonstrators outside the school. She came to add her expertise, uncommon wit, and political flair to the demonstration. She was an older woman whose political activism went back to the Marcus Garvey period of the 1920s. In the 1960s she became famous on picket lines and at public meetings as a charismatic speaker for the black community. Many of the people involved in this demonstration moved on to occupy positions that black people never held before. Roy Innis, now president of the Congress on Racial Equality (CORE), was then working for the Board of Education as an arbiter in the conflicts between the community and the school. And Dorothy Gordon, a Harlem politician, at that time was the teacher in charge of community outreach at P.S. 100. She represented Mrs. Timpson with the demonstrators. Isaiah Robinson, president of the Harlem Parents Committee, served on the Board of Education from 1969 to 1977 (he was president of the board for two terms, from 1969 to 1973). As Flo Kennedy would have said, he went "out of the streets and into the suites."

The Flag is Bleeding, U. S. Postage Stamp Commemorating the Advent of Black Power, and *Die* — the last works in the American People Series — were inspired by the mood and events of this year. It was in 1967 that for the first time I heard the chant "Black Power every hour, Black Power every hour . . . " I could hear it in my classroom like background music while the children painted. It came to mind that this was more than a chant — it could mean a new way of life for black people in America. But what about me as a black woman? If black people got power, would that include me? Would I, too, have power? Would I be able to stand toe-to-toe with my contemporaries and work out the problems of our time? Would my accomplishments be recognized and rewarded in kind? Or would I still be in the kitchen making coffee and serving up the leftovers?

Me, students, and Mr. Pride at Art Festival at P.S. 100, 1960s

From 1964 to 1968 I taught at P.S. 100, which was part of the More Effective Schools (MES) Program — some people thought it was a MESS, but the program basically was a good one. It was designed to upgrade the reading scores and general educational level of ghetto elementary school children. Its special features included teaching specialists in reading, mathematics, science, social studies, art, and music, and small class sizes with a maximum twenty-two kids in a room, each class conducted by two teachers. We also had even smaller classes for problem children, and special funds for books, supplies, educational aides, and equipment. The MES program was an ideal plan on paper. There were problems that were insurmountable, however, and "being set up to fail" was not the least of them. Yet for the first time in my teaching career, I had an abundance of space, art supplies, equipment, and teaching assistants. I could freely design my own art curriculum for grades one through five, which included oil and acrylic painting on stretched canvas as well as tempera painting and drawing, ceramic and clay sculpture, and silk screen printing. This was an amazing teaching opportunity, so I tried not to waste any time implementing it.

As often as I was allowed to, I worked with the four- and five-year-olds in the kindergarten and pre-kindergarten classes. This was a privilege not to be taken lightly, since the principal felt that these classes were the gems of her program and did not want the children in them to be overstimulated by too many different experiences. She didn't seem to understand how natural art is to the development of a young child. It was fascinating to watch these children's random scribbles develop into pictorial compositions over just a few weeks. By that time they would be fabricating long, involved, highly imaginative tales about their drawings that seemed to have no end.

My students at P.S. 100 were very gifted, hardworking, and fabulous little people. These days when I walk five blocks in Harlem, before I reach the sixth I am stopped by a former student. "Do you remember me?" I can count on them saying. "My name is Daryle [or Mildred or Karen or Kevin] . . . " Whether I do or not, the rest of the conversation is the same. "I was in your art class at P.S. 100 . . . ," and then they recount stories about our many exhibitions and art events and the ones that I took them to see. They often remember things that I have long forgotten, like Hale Woodruff's show at New York University's Loeb Student Center in 1967, and the fact that he came and spoke to us. So Walton's principal was wrong; my reward for a grueling four years of teaching art in an elementary school in Harlem was that I got a chance to teach art to little children, and nobody does art better than they do. And now, years later and middle-aged, they still haven't forgotten me.

In 1968 the MES program at P.S. 100 was phased out. As we teachers used to say about the school system: "If it works, change it" and "All good things must come an end." Now, I had to either go back to Walton High School in the Bronx or find another high school.

I'd always wanted to teach at the famous Music and Art High School, which was located in Harlem on the campus of City College, just ten blocks away from where I lived. In 1968 Music and Art had about a hundred black students out of a total student body of twenty-five hundred. Among the art faculty of forty teachers there was not one black; indeed, there had never been a black teacher appointed to teach art at Music and Art High School at that time. To be the first black person to teach there would have been like stepping into shoes two sizes too small. I felt I had a lot to offer the kids, but getting reassigned to a school required a vacancy in that school. Vacancies could be and often were created to fill the educational need of the school or community. In those days the principal had the absolute power to hire someone of his own choosing. One would think that in 1968 the need to appoint at least one black art teacher at the Music and Art High School would have been all too apparent. Yet the district superintendent concurred with the principal that there were no vacancies in art at that time. By June of 1968, I had still not been reassigned. The arts supervisors, other educators, politicians, and assorted community persons who had promised to help me were doing the community/school system shuffle and my problem got lost in the politics.

In the summer of 1968, while the girls enrolled in Music and Art Summer High School (Michele took dance and Barbara painting), I took a summer job teaching

*P.S. 100 students at
Spectrum Gallery
opening, 1969*

African art at Intermediate School 201 (grades six through eight), the most controversial school in Harlem. I had actually wanted to teach there earlier on and applied for a
job but didn't get that one, either. I.S. 201 was the first school to demand its own local
school board and community control. It was the school without windows — an archi-
tectural statement that, along with everything else, had the community up in arms.

Jim Campbell, the black artist, had been newly appointed as the school's assistant
principal, and he brought his skills and connections as a pioneer in the black literary
art movement. He had worked with Leroi Jones in his Black Art Theater in 1966, and,
as before, now he was trying out new ways of teaching black children by coordinating
African and Puerto Rican art history and culture. Each morning we began with a greeting in Swahili and Spanish, and there were courses in both languages. This was a crucial period in my artistic development. In both my teaching and my art, I was increasingly influenced by African art. As I searched for a way to voice my new awareness as
an African-American woman, teaching African art to little children turned out to be a
useful vehicle for me: I could watch the little masters work, and they always gave me
inspiration and ideas.

Things in the black community were getting "blacker" and "blacker," and there was a
real guilt trip laid on anyone who was not black enough. All the women at I.S. 201 wore
Afros except me; I had my hair straightened. They often looked at me as if they wanted to
say something, but thought better of it. One young woman told me that she was going to

225

braid her hair as soon as summer school closed. Nobody, but nobody, wore braids — corn-row or any other kind — to work in 1968, even at the radical I.S. 201. I upset people by wearing short dresses made of brightly patterned African-style prints. (At the time Mother was designing African dashikis and African-styled women's dresses.) "That ain't no African dress," I heard one of the teaching assistants say. "She need to get her head [meaning hair] together too," she continued blithely, referring to me. She didn't know I'd heard her. She was in the stall; and by the time she had flushed the toilet, I was gone.

In a teacher's meeting one day, the men were talking and the women were listening. Suddenly a man mentioned hearing John Henrick Clarke, the renowned African historian, state: "The black woman should wear long dresses to the floor or nothing at all." My dresses were just above knee-length, worn with matching short pants, a kind of fashionable semi-mini dress and pants outfit. When I sat down or walked, you could see just a peak of what was underneath my dress. "And you men," I said before I knew it. "What will you wear, a loin cloth? Or nothing at all?" They went on with the meeting as if nothing had been said. But, like the young woman who wanted to wear braids, I waited until summer school closed to get my first Afro. By the time I went back to teach in the fall, I was quite comfortable with my own hair worn naturally.

In the fall of 1968 I was assigned to Brandeis High School Annex on West 66th Street in mid-Manhattan. It was to be my last public school job. Situated across the street from Lincoln Center on West 66th Street and next door to Juilliard School of Music, we were in good company, but it had little or no effect on what went on in our building. We were housed in the old Commerce High School, which had been cut in half to make room for the ultra-modern Juilliard next door. Consequently, our half of the building had no auditorium, so we could never have assemblies. There were only two functioning public toilets for the kids on the first floor of the five-story building. I was not too surprised the day I saw human excrement in the stairwell.

Ninety-nine percent of the students were black and Latino and many were from Harlem. They called Brandeis "The Drugstore" because it was said you could get any kind of drug there. Students on heroin came to school infrequently. I always knew who they were and my heart went out to them. When they didn't show up anymore, I'd get the word, "He's on smack." Pot smokers were more regular about their attendance but more apathetic about doing their work. The only white students in the school were potheads who had been thrown out of private or "better" public schools and were just "cooling out" at Brandeis.

We also had alcoholic kids. They were already drunk at nine in the morning with their daily bottle of chilled Richard's Wild Irish Rose. One young man came regularly drunk to my class. I talked to him about it, realizing that to ignore him was not the best thing for him or the other students. Everyone could see and smell that he was drunk. He was only fifteen or sixteen years old and already an alcoholic, and I had to ask myself what I could do for him. The school administrators were not ready to accept the possibility that a student so young could have a drinking problem. So, I was not able to help him although he was obviously asking me for guidance. Situations like this were making my job, which was enjoyable for the most part, intolerably frustrating. In a sense, I felt responsible because I could do nothing to help these young people with many of the problems they were facing.

As you can see, Brandeis was no prep school unless it was for the Rikers Island prison complex. Most of our kids were undereducated, coming from the elementary and junior high schools that had just passed them on without requiring them to complete successfully the requisite work. But we had some fabulous kids at Brandeis Annex, too. They were what made my four and a half years there so worthwhile — they had character and a real willingness to achieve. I tried to give all of them the best that I had, and in a surprising number of cases they gave their best right back to me.

Parents, teachers, and other interested adults can be role models and mentors, but the burden to become educated lies with the kid himself (or herself). When high school kids in the ghetto understand that, they'll demand teachers who can teach them and they'll maintain a classroom environment so they can be taught. Only then will they learn — in spite of the movies, television, the streets, the school system, the community, and even their parents. But admittedly that kind of mature leadership is hard for a child to come by. Today, with AIDS, guns, drugs, crime, violence, and babies having babies, children have had a lot thrust on them.

I taught the kids at Brandeis some of the same material I was teaching my college classes, and they ate it up. They learned to recognize the work of many contemporary and historically significant black artists, and to appreciate the beauty of traditional African masks. The Educational Program at the Museum of Modern Art loaned me slides of contemporary white artists so my students had a well-rounded survey of modern art.

The lack of supplies at Brandeis (for example, one year we had no blue paint and I was told to mix it) forced me to be both creative and resourceful in choosing projects. To get paint, paper, and brushes, I had to wait for an order to come from the main building. The main building was over a mile away, but Woolworth's was across the street. Most teachers didn't know what to do with the big roll of tapestry mesh in the supply room, but I did. I realized, too, that I could buy tapestry needles and wool at Woolworth's.

In the more advanced art classes I taught them to make needlepoint masks of their own original designs based on traditional African masks. My honors art classes learned their needlepoint stitches in no time, and the boys were as good as the girls. Some made political emblems, too, to be sewn on their sweaters, and many of them made their names in some original logo. In addition to face masks they created red-black-and-green (African-American) and red-white-and-blue (Puerto Rican) flags. In my regular art classes, I taught macramé and bead stitching as well as needlepoint. We made belts, jewelry, and headbands. (Most of the boys already knew how to do macramé from the key chains they had learned to make in camp.) Some kids took their bead jewelry and headbands to sell on 125th Street. That was their excuse for an occasional cut from art class.

My classes were usually small, especially after lunch period. Some students forgot they had an afternoon class and took to the streets to enjoy the sun or snow . . . whatever the weather. After waiting in the long line outside the bathroom, they were often in no mood to climb the four flights of stairs to get to the art rooms; they were already "high" enough. However, most of the boys as well as girls loved the art classes. Even though many of the kids at Brandeis Annex were considered difficult, art held their attention and so I had very few discipline problems. Each term, however, I had one or two students who were put in art against their will and wasted no time letting me know it. I encouraged such students to drop my class and take something that might prove more beneficial to them. Young people who do not enjoy art class are the rarity in my experience. Some may be frustrated performers who can't stand to create in isolation. Their need for an audience can wreak havoc in an art room, upsetting the quiet decorum necessary for visual creativity. Where art classes were concerned, my motto was "love it or leave it." I tried to make them love it, but if they didn't I showed them the door.

One young woman, who obviously hated art and me, refused to drop my class. She stayed on, making both her life and mine miserable. She failed to answer even one question on a slide examination, and I had to give her a zero. "You could have answered at least the question about a contemporary black artist. Why didn't you use me for that one?" I asked her. "You?" she responded incredulously. "Oh, you mean I could just put down anybody's name? If that's the case, I'd just as well put my own name down," she continued curtly, cutting her eyes at me. "Your name is here right next to your grade," I responded equally curtly, pointing to the big red zero. The class looked back and forth from me to her. Someone yelled, "Oh sweat! I know what your grade is." They began shaking their hands as if this was something too hot to handle. "You think you're so cute, 'cause you give us all this black work," the girl sneered as she settled herself in a sprinting position in her seat. Accommodatingly the bell rang, and like a racehorse through the starting gate, she was gone. A group of sympathetic students gathered around my desk to assure me that she was not worth listening to. "Some kids are like that, Mrs. Ringgold," they said. "They always want to cause trouble. We like the work you give us. She just doesn't want to do any work, that's all." Kids are often unpredictably sensitive: they can stroke as well as strike.

I stopped showing students my art after this episode. Subsequent students did not know that I was an artist unless they were told by someone else. I felt in some ways I had caused this young black woman to feel competitive with me. She was probably having enough trouble just keeping up her academic grades in school. I didn't need to add to her burden.

In January of 1973, I decided to resign from Brandeis at the end of the fall term. It was time to leave teaching in the public schools. I felt trapped on a sinking ship. I was being asked to lecture at feminist art conferences all over the country, and I was developing an audience for my art and ideas. Flo Kennedy had recommended me to Lordly and Dame, her speaker's bureau; and two young women agents there were interested in me, and helped me put together a package of lectures and traveling shows of my art to tour college campuses. Surely this was the time to get out of teaching in the public schools and try being an artist full time?

In 1970 while still teaching full-time at Brandeis, I also began to lecture part-time at both Wagner College and Bank Street College of Education. These colleges hired me in response to the students' demands for black instructors to teach black history and culture. At Wagner, I taught a black art course that traced the history of black art from Africa through to contemporary African-American art, and dealt with slave artisans, the early black painters and craftsmen of the nineteenth century, and the marvelous achievements of the Harlem Renaissance period. I researched my lectures from a meager collection of books, filmstrips, and slide sets on black artists. Among the artists I included were (the women first) Elizabeth Catlett, Meta Warrick Fuller, Lois Mailou Jones, Augusta Savage, Laura Wheeler Waring, Edmonia Lewis and Alma Thomas, Betty Blayton Taylor, Betye Saar, Vivian Browne, Camille Billops, Emma Amos, and Barbara Chase Riboud. There were many more male artists, and some that I discovered have inspired my work ever since: among them, Robert Duncanson, Horace Pippin, William H. Johnson, Sargeant Johnson, Archibald Motley, Aaron Douglass, Romare Bearden, and Jacob Lawrence.

In my course I gave lectures, showed filmstrips, and ran discussions about a wide range of art. We went to museums and to New York gallery openings — Wagner College was on Staten Island, but only a ferryboat ride away from Manhattan and the art world in the city. We visited the studios of many black artists to discuss with them issues pertinent to their art and their life. Though most of my students were black, they had not known of a single black artist before the class began. By the time the semester was over, however, they were calling many of them by their first names — Benny, Romie, Vivian, Camille, Howardena, Art, Nigel, and so on.

As a result of campus unrest in the late 1960s and early 1970s, it became acceptable to be lenient with attendance and course requirements. My students were committed to community-based free breakfast programs for ghetto youth, after-school study, and Black Heritage programs. Many of the young men actively protested against the war in Vietnam and were involved in draft counseling. When the student protesters were shot at Kent State and Jackson State Colleges, we were cautioned by the administration not to add more fuel to the fire by making demands on students that could not, or would not, be met. Faculty all over the country were frustrated. College presidents for the first time in America were out of work and receiving unemployment insurance. Although many professors were right out there with the students — protesting the war in Vietnam, going on Freedom Rides in the South, sitting down at segregated lunch counters, and confronting other injustices in America — many young students of this tumultuous period paid the supreme penalty. They may have gained their souls, but they lost their education. Some lost their lives as well.

I tried to be fair to the students. To make it easier for them, I suggested that they present audiotapes instead of written papers. A taped interview and discussion of an artist was a valuable record. It would also take less time to do, would not necessarily have to be edited, could be entertaining as well as informative, and could be reviewed by the entire class. As a result of this program, I developed a library of tapes — and I still have them — over the seven years that I taught at Wagner College: an oral history of New York black artists in the 1970s.

Despite the positive experiences of the students in my class, there was cause for deep concern over the plight of the black women students. A group of them approached me one evening after class and asked me to speak to their black student organization about a most serious problem — the brothers and their white girlfriends.

Wagner College was a conservative white middle-class private Lutheran College perched on top of a hill in one of the most affluent sections of Staten Island. There were only thirty-five or forty black students on campus, out of a total student body of twenty-five hundred. Most of the black students were part of Wagner's minority program to bring black and "disadvantaged" white students from poor sections of Staten Island into an otherwise affluent all-white campus. Many of the middle-class white students were from the suburbs of New York, New Jersey, and Pennsylvania. They were new to black people and black/white dating, and some were eager to get started.

I had thought the young black men and women on campus were surprisingly close and obviously committed to the cause of black unity. Like a family they ate breakfast and supper together at a nest of tables in the cafeteria, but rarely saw one another otherwise. Too often, sisters noticed brothers strolling on campus hand-in-hand with white women students, although the brothers had just announced that they were "off to study." The black women students complained that the brothers would not make social commitments to them for weekends and holidays for fear it would conflict with their ongoing relationships with white girlfriends on campus.

My role was to confront the brothers with this story so that the sisters could open up a dialogue and try to clear up a bad situation before it got worse. On the night of the meeting, I came in with the black women students, sat down and was introduced. "Faith Ringgold, our new and very together instructor of black art. . . . If you're not already signed up to take her courses, make sure you do it next semester . . . all the black students should." Finally I had the floor. The men students were seated across the room and the women students were seated around me. I decided to start by rambling on enthusiastically about how I had become aware of their black student organization, and that many of the brothers and sisters present were responsible for the administration's increased commitment to black students on campus, and to outreach programs of relevance to the surrounding black community. I went on to mention that the sisters, who had been arrested and gone to jail in support of the black male leadership, were being rejected for white women.

Nobody spoke, so I continued. "These sisters want to know where your white girl-friends were when you needed support to take over the building. And why didn't they go to jail with you?" The brothers looked sheepishly at one another. They recognized that this was a family dispute, potentially volatile but not terminal. They had to proceed with caution to make sure that nobody gave any ground or made any promises he couldn't keep. "They have money and they can afford to give us some of the things we need," came a voice from the brothers' corner. The other young men made a protective circle around the speaker. He was a very tall, good-looking young man who wore a school sweater and was probably a freshman on the basketball team. They all knew him. "Are you for sale?" yelled out a sister, who had stopped braiding her hair and stood facing the brothers' side of the room. (Half of her hair was standing straight up with the Afro comb sticking up in the part, separating that hair from the fresh cornrows already done. She was obviously preparing for bed. Tomorrow her combed-out Afro would be full with tiny crimps.) "You sound like you're for sale," she repeated, now focusing on the young man in the circle. "Like you're hungry and you think these white people gonna feed you for nothing."

"Uummmh, Ummmh," testified the other young women in the way that black women speak, their voices trapped down deep in their throats as if to disguise where the sound was coming from.

This sister reminded me of a young woman from the University of Milwaukee, who told me that her boyfriend was dating white on campus. When she finally confronted him, he told her, "Well, she gives me money."

"Money?" quipped the young woman. "You want money? Why don't you go with the white man? He's the one who's got all the money."

It was time for the brothers to speak, to say something — anything to get off the hook. Another brother spoke up this time; he was much shorter than the basketball play-er and slight of build. The minute he rose to speak, the young women went back to their throat-talking chorus of "Uummmh, Ummmh," as if they already knew what he was going to say. He faced the brothers and spoke directly to them. "You know, it's hard out there, and they're attracted to us. What's wrong with it as long as it's on our terms?" The rest of the brothers gave in to embarrassed laughter as they engaged in a slapping of hands. They had made their point: This was the sisters' problem not theirs.

It was my time to speak again. "And what about the sisters?" I asked, facing the brothers in their victory circle. "Can they go out with whomever they want on campus?"

"Sisters better not be seen on campus with no white dudes," said the little guy who had spoken earlier. He was obviously speaking for the brothers. The sisters weren't talking, but their silence was convincing. They would be faithful no matter what — at least that's what they wanted the brothers to think.

I tried to get the young women to understand that they didn't have to depend on male leadership for their organization. They were doing all the work. Why couldn't they give each other the same support they were giving to the brothers? "You don't have to wait for the brothers on campus to pay attention to you. You can be with each other too," I told them. "You might be surprised to know how often men are just hanging out together when you think they're with other women." The young black women tearfully assured me that they could not stand up to an all-white male administration for the things they needed to keep black student organizations

Aunt Edith and Aunt Bessie Masks, *1974, Mixed media, Life size, Artist's collection*

going. The brothers had clout. Many of them were on sports scholarships and, therefore, had an "in" with the deans and other college administrators.

I was reminded this time of a football player I had met from the University of Nebraska. He told a group just like this one that he was going with a white girl on campus because he was receiving tutoring from her. His coach had assigned her to help him with some subjects he was behind in. "This is a practical matter," the young man

Bank Street student displaying art she made, 1973

disclosed. "The sisters want to be too possessive of us. After all, we're all just here for an
education. We're around when it's important," he said, looking at the other football
players, who nodded back at him in anticipation of what he would say. "We know the
sisters can't fight the man alone."

And so the Wagner College black students
continued to be together during class, mealtimes, and at special events. In class, they sat
in a block on one side of the room, and the
white students on the other. I often wondered
whether these were the students who ignored
each other so completely during class, and
who would afterward stroll arm in arm?

By the late 1970s things had changed,
and students were less concerned about
black issues. They no longer expected so
much of each other. The "revolutionaries"
from the late 1960s were all gone and the
"new breed" didn't know anything about
what had happened before they came.

I taught at Bank Street College of Education
in the graduate program at the same
time I was at Wagner. As far as teaching
was concerned, Bank Street was the icing
on the cake. My Bank Street students were older and already teaching themselves. If
I loved teaching at Wagner College where I interacted with the young about art and
life, being at Bank Street — where I could teach making art as well — was a job I'd
have done for free. The first semester was rough, however. The students wanted me
to prove that I was black enough. The ones who were responsible for getting me
hired were the most outspoken in my class; they wanted control over the speakers I
invited and the materials I taught. On the surface this was not out of line, but in

reality it was all too often a power play on the part of the students and could reduce a professor's course to an ongoing rap session on "Whitey." Some white students got so used to the attention that when I refused to rap on "Whitey," they felt left out, ignored, if you will.

I refused to have the study of African art reduced to a discussion of something else. I was more concerned with the creative powers of black people as expressed in African art and how I could teach my students about it so they could take the information back to the children in their own classrooms.

That first semester was a standoff. They were not ready for art; instead, they wanted conflict. The black students assumed that because they were black they knew the work of the course, so they gave it a minimum effort. Finally I called a meeting in my office. Like the kids at Harriet Beecher Stowe Junior High School who had threatened to kick my ass some fifteen years earlier, we now needed to "communicate." With that in mind I spoke to them in ghettoese, the four-letter-word Black English that speaks for itself. They were surprised that we spoke the same language. We communicated well after that, and the semester passed uneventfully.

From then on most of the students who enrolled in my courses were women who were interested in learning about African art. Occasionally a man enrolled who didn't resent being in what was unofficially a course in African women's art. As time passed, however, the African art course had little or no audience among black students at Bank Street, and there were not enough interested white students either. Enrollment dropped. It was time for a change.

By the mid-1970s I had invented a new course which was cross-cultural. I taught textile design and included African as well as other techniques of tie-dye, batik, and textile hand-printing, using design motifs and stenciling patterns from all over the world. It was well attended but not by black students. There was a problem with "us" and art as educated adults: we didn't seem to see the value in it. Yet, if you'd asked the black kids I taught in the public schools, they would disagree — they loved art. It never fails to amaze me that black scholars, intellectuals, teachers, heads of Black Studies programs, historians, and so-called black cultural critics — who write articles and books on the cultural history and achievement of black people — invariably fail to give credit to the glorious contribution of black artists. Black art history dates back to the first millennium before Christ with the Nok tribe in Ancient Nigeria — although this is rarely acknowledged in print or public forum. No wonder black students don't want to study art. I can count, on one hand, the number of serious black students I have taught at UCSD. As far as the black community is concerned, being an artist is thought to be an unrewarding experience.

I developed my own soft sculpture while teaching at Bank Street College in the early 1970s. My first needlepoint and beaded mask faces, dolls, and soft sculptures were developed at this time. However, I simplified the techniques to make it easy for the teachers to share these concepts with their young students. The teachers often brought examples of beautiful masks, beadwork, dolls, and other projects the children made to show in our class.

In my early classes on mask-making I introduced them to papier-mâché, but rather quickly we advanced to making tapestry-stitched faces for our masks on needlepoint canvases. The students used their own original designs for the mask faces, which were inspired by traditional African masks. In 1975, I taught them how to make appliqué face masks out of scraps of colored fabric sewn together. The dolls we made were constructed of stuffed and covered-over paper towel rollers glued into empty tin cans weighted down with rocks. Their heads and bodies were made of foam rubber pieces sewn together and covered with fabric, painted gourds, or self-hardening clay painted in flesh tones. I had an idea for a course in puppet-making, staging, and ventriloquism, but I never did get around to it before leaving Bank Street.

Each semester Mother used to come for two sessions to teach the students how to make African-styled dresses and dashikis from the tie-dye fabric we made. She had gone to Nigeria and Ghana in 1972 and after that trip she kept in close contact with current African fashion through business contacts she had made there. She showed the students how to make patterns for sewn as well as wrapped dresses and skirts. Mother also demonstrated sewing techniques she used to make clothes commercially. Many of the women could sew, and often someone would volunteer to bring her portable sewing machine to class.

At the close of each semester, we had a class potluck dinner. Each student dressed up in the clothes and jewelry she had made in the class; and we had an exhibition of the beadwork and dolls, which were also a part of the course. I photographed them and have an album of the proud and smiling faces of those wonderful people I taught at Bank Street College and the beautiful work they did.

Chapter 11: We Flew over the Bridge: Performance Art, Story Quilts, and Tar Beach

Being My Own Woman *performance, 1980*

I n 1980 my career as an artist was in limbo and I was so preoccupied at the time that I hardly noticed I had turned fifty. I desperately needed a major New York exhibition to show the work I had made over the past twenty years. Although I had quite a large national audience from my many exhibitions in college museums and galleries around the country, I hadn't had an exhibition in New York in ten years. I was eager to document my experience of being a black woman artist — that seemed as important to me then as breathing. I had also just written my autobiography but could find no one interested in publishing it. Since I couldn't "tell" my story in either of these traditional ways, I looked for an alternative.

It occurred to me that performance art was a good way to have an oral publication of my autobiography. I had a lively schedule ahead of me of lecture dates at colleges and universities in all parts of the country and I was already familiar with the performance genre. After all, my first performance piece, *The Wake and Resurrection of the Bicentennial Negro,* was still enjoying a good audience on college campuses where students were eager to experience performance art. Why not now create an autobiographical performance? So in 1980 I designed *Being My Own Woman: An Autobiographical Masked Performance Piece.*

Unlike *The Wake and Resurrection of the Bicentennial Negro,* in which I was the director and student participants played all of the major roles, in my new one-hour performance, I appeared alone wearing a mask. I distributed a program at the beginning that documented

237

No Name Mask Performance #2 *(Michele and me), 1982*

my artistic development and gave a chronology and description of the slides to be shown. The text was excerpted from the introduction to my autobiography manuscript. As I read the text reflecting on the struggles and events of the various periods of my life, slides of the art I had done at these times were projected on the screen in six-second intervals. The slides were repeated several times during the performance. People often remarked that the art appeared just at the time I would be saying something relevant to it, but in fact that probably happened less often than they imagined.

My performance mode was not inspired by the unfathomable art performances of the 1970s or the avant-garde happenings of the 1960s (I found what was going on in the streets of New York City far more "happening" than any performance I had ever seen in an art gallery) but rather by the African tradition of combining storytelling, dance, music, costumes, and masks into a single production. I'd seen this done when I visited Africa in the late 1970s. Performance for me was simply another way to tell my story, rather than to shock, confuse, or irritate my audience.

I did this performance, which I varyingly entitled *No Name Mask Performance #1* and *#2,* from 1980 until 1985, when things began to change professionally for the better, and I no longer needed to tell my story in this way. During the course of these five years I made several different masks and costumes for these performances. The first masks were made of tie-dyed cloth, elaborately sequined, and had colored raffia for hair. With them I wore flowing white robes of painted and decorated cloth.

Within a few years I had developed the performance from that of a simple masked reading to a dramatically staged one with lights, more elaborately masked costumes, music, and taped texts. I would place the mask on top of my head and a hanging collar of raffia would hide my face. (They were made on the same principle as the Portrait Mask Series of the 1970s.) I could see through the raffia although no one could see me. Around my ankles I wore African shells to make clanging noises as I stomped my feet at dramatic intervals in the performance. I had seen this done in Africa in a performance with one hundred dancers from Swaziland, all wearing several rows of shells on their legs and stomping their feet to a thunderously magnificent polyrhythm — several different rhythms playing concurrently. I remember once hearing a group of Nigerians sitting behind me in the theater yelling out "They try! They try!" — the highest form of praise a Nigerian can give. I also had taped music playing throughout the performance. In the finale I would invite the audience to come up onstage and dance with me. Others were given music sticks, which I had made from wooden dowels adorned with shells and raffia, to beat together to keep the rhythm.

Performance at University of California, San Diego, 1984

In August of 1982 my sister Barbara died, less than a year after Mother's death. Barbara had been drinking rather heavily for a number of years and there was nothing any of us could do to help her. Mother and I had gone to Alanon, an organization for friends and relatives of alcoholics, and they had told Mother to stop picking Barbara up and coddling her with chicken soup; but Mother had a hard time "letting go" of Barbara. However, we did convince Barbara to go to Alcoholics Anonymous, although she found it difficult to identify with the group. Finally, she admitted to being an alcoholic, but always she was the "Princess" and, therefore, simply not like "those people." It was Mother's worst fear that Barbara would die alone in her apartment and no one would know. Since Barbara and I lived in the same building, Birdie and I tried to keep in touch with her on a daily basis, but Barbara rejected our attempts to be close. After Mother died, she dropped out of AA and began drinking heavily in the evenings after school and on weekends. It was the summer and the school was closed when we discovered her one Monday morning. The neighbors on her floor complained of a suspicious odor: Barbara had died of a massive heart attack after a weekend of drinking. Birdie, Michele, and I had spent that weekend at Birdie's apartment at 409 up the street, so we had not heard from Barbara since Thursday. She must have died late Thursday night or Friday morning. I could have killed myself for not seeing her that weekend. Now not only had I lost my fabulous sister but I felt I had let

Me performing at Sushi Gallery, 1984

Mother down, too, by not being with her Barbara at the end.

The week after Barbara died, I had an exhibition and a performance to do at the Kenkelaba House Gallery on the Lower East Side. I was grieving so much at the time that I was afraid to cancel for fear that I would never start again. I created *No Name Mask Performance #2* as a mourning performance for the deaths of both my sister and my mother. Michele joined me in that performance at Kenkelaba House. We were both elaborately robed and she wore the *No Face Mask #1* and I wore *No Face Mask #2*. These masks had no distinct facial design and were painted to look like the Emanon Series of paintings I had done when Mother died. I hung these paintings on the walls of the gallery as a backdrop to our performance. Michele attempted to set the audience on its ears, confusing them with meaningless repetitions of words and demanding that they leave the room: "Get out! Go!" However confused they were, no one left. Baby Faith, my daughter Barbara's first child who was no more than six months old at the time, had a front-row seat in her stroller at our performance that night and was attentive throughout. The performance medium was by now not only a storytelling medium but a healing one for me.

The Bitter Nest, my next masked performance piece, was written in 1985 at a time when Michele, Barbara, and I were having some serious mother-daughter problems. I had grown weary of hearing how my daughters felt about me, so I conceived this performance piece to give "Mother" a voice. Oddly enough, I created a mother who was both deaf and dumb. The story takes place in the 1920s during the Harlem Renaissance. Ce Ce, the mother, became pregnant by Dr. Prince, a prominent Harlem dentist who was twenty years her senior. They married and Ce Ce moved into the doctor's house on Harlem's fashionable Striver's Row. Ce Ce was a fabulous homemaker, wife, and mother and gave wonderful parties. Among the frequent dinner guests were W. E. B. Du Bois, Langston Hughes, Aaron Douglass, Zora Neale Hurston, Florence Mills, and other prominent figures of the Harlem Renaissance period. To make up for her inability to hear or to speak, Ce Ce communicated with her guests by performing for them in elaborate costumes and

240

wearing a mask. Celia, her daughter, was embarrassed by her mother's eccentric ways and generally alienated by Ce Ce's being deaf and dumb. Celia became a doctor like her father, but much to Dr. Prince's horror had a child out of wedlock. Over Ce Ce's objections, the doctor forced Celia to give up her child so as not to disgrace the family name; the boy was raised by a family friend. However, when the doctor died, Ce Ce and Celia became reunited with Celia's son (who had followed the family tradition of medicine and became a dentist like his grandfather, Dr. Prince). Magically, Ce Ce was now able to speak and the story has a happy ending. This performance piece is not autobiographical, but it does dramatize a happy conclusion to a family's lifelong struggle over irreconcilable differences. I performed this piece against a backdrop of

The Bitter Nest *performance at Newark Museum, 1985*

paintings (created as a stage setting) entitled *California Dah.* At the end of the performance the audience was invited to come onstage and tell their own family story. In 1987 I designed a five-part story quilt with the same name — *The Bitter Nest.*

In 1986 I lost a hundred pounds over a span of a year. To celebrate this, I created a performance piece, *Change: Faith Ringgold's Over 100 Pound Weight Loss Performance Story Quilt.* I was using my art as a way of making a public commitment not only to lose the weight but to keep it off. This was the first performance in which — significantly — I appeared without a mask. The story I told had to do with the eating patterns that had led me to gain weight. I began by making a photomontage of pictures of me beginning with the 1930s through to the 1980s. A plate was made of them and I had these etched on canvas and pieced into a quilt along with the text for each of the six decades. Looking at these pictures of each decade, I discovered that it was only in the 1960s (when I married Burdette and my girls were approaching their teenage years) that I began to gain the weight. During the performance I wore a quilted coat that had the same photo etchings and written texts that appeared on the quilt. In 1989 the coat disappeared from the director's office of a South Carolina museum. I would have never thought anyone would take it, but they did. Thank God it was insured, but no amount of money can replace this precious documentation of my life.

Dah #1, *1983, Acrylic on canvas, 74 x 58 inches,*
Collection of Michele and Eugene Nesmith

The performance was divided into six acts, one for each decade, and for each act I recited anecdotes that related to my eating habits over the years. To dramatize the weight I had lost, I duplicated it in pounds of water for the performance. Each venue I performed at was asked to collect twenty empty two-liter soda bottles and fill them with water weighing collectively approximately a hundred pounds. The bottles were then divided into two bundles of ten bottles each and placed in two black garbage bags, tied securely with heavy cord, leaving a long cord for me to pull the bundles during the performance.

In 1988, two years after the *Change I* performance, I created *Change 2: Faith Ringgold's Over 100 Pound Weight Loss Performance Story Quilt,* for which I was scheduled to lose an additional thirty pounds in order to arrive at a goal weight of a hundred and thirty pounds. I must admit I failed to do that, but still I was fortunate because I didn't gain back the weight I had lost. For this performance I created another quilted coat pieced with recently photographed portraits that had been lithographed onto canvas. In the center I placed a painted self-portrait showing a miraculous (though fictitous) weight loss of the proposed thirty pounds.

For the *Change 2* performance, I sang songs I had written to express both the frustration and joy of losing weight and keeping it off. Joan Ashley, a fabulous drummer with the Women of the Calabash group, accompanied me with a mélange of percussion instruments. In *Change 2* the performance had become a lighthearted account of my history of eating and was also intended to function as a document of my attempts to change. It consisted of the following texts and rap songs:

In 1986 I lost 100 pounds. In 1988 I gained it all back. No! In 1988 I continue to pursue my goal to lose an additional 30 pounds. Change 2 is about trying to lose 30 pounds. The songs and raps I will perform for you are written on the Change 2 quilt and this performance costume. I can't sing or dance and 30 pounds might just as well be 300, but I am still trying. That's what it takes to change.

The Change Song:
Because I think you are so very nice
I want to offer you some good advice
You may be rich, you may be poor
Livin' high on the hog
Or stretched out on the floor
You may be a professor
With knowledge to burn
Or just a young kid with a lot to learn
You may be black, white, red, yellow
Or inbetween
You may be kind or a little mean
But if you remember this simple phrase
You'll be a winner for the rest of your days
First stand up everyone in this place
Now put a great big smile on your face
Everybody ready? Let's go!
This is the phrase you need to know
I can change, I can do it
I can change, I can do it
I can change, I can do it
Now!

Faith Ringgold's Over 100 Pound Weight Loss Performance Story Quilt *performance, 1987*

The 1930s

My mother brought us up to eat three meals a day, without eating between meals. When I got old enough to run my own kitchen I ate three square meals a day. And then three or more at night. My Mama made me do it.

Mama Made Me Do it
Mama made me do it [repeat 2 times]
Told me clean my plate [repeat 2 times]
That's how I gained this weight

Mama made me do it [repeat 2 times]
Told me eat to grow strong [repeat 2 times]
My mother was never wrong

Mama made me do it [repeat 2 times]
Said there were children starving [repeat 2 times]
As she just went on carving

Mama made me do it [repeat 2 times]
Piled my plate up high [repeat 2 times]
Right up to my eye

Mama made me do it [repeat 2 times]
Mama taught me to be good [repeat 2 times]
Said shut up girl and eat your food.

Mama made me do it [repeat 3 times]
Yea!

The 1940s

We walked everywhere when we were kids so we could spend our carfare on chocolate candy bars and ice cream cones. They were both five cents then and bigger than the ones you pay a dollar for today. Though I no longer spend my carfare on candy bars, I still love to eat them but I hate to exercise.

I Hate to Exercise

I hate to exercise [repeat 2 times]
Sometime I fall from grace
Fast foodin' all over the place
Weighty gains on hips and thighs
Trays of Danish flash before my eyes
Listen to what I say
I struggle every day

I really hate to exercise [repeat 2 times]
It doesn't matter how big my size
I just hate to exercise [repeat 2 times]
Can't do it
Can't stand it
Early to bed and late to rise
Makes a woman unhealthy and oversize

Oh baby, I hate to exercise [repeat 3 times]
Yea!

The 1950s

We had something called dates in the 1950s. Not the ones you eat, but I ate on all of mine. I was in my twenties, and it was a very romantic time. When young men came to call on me instead of bringing me flowers they brought me pork chop sandwiches. They were fried, cost seventy-five cents and were better than steak. That was romance in the 1950s — greasy food.

Greasy Food
Greasy food. Tastes good
Make you big like a pig
All fat like that
Starts a crave. An early grave.

Greasy food. Tastes good
Creamy dips. Pad your hips.
Burgers and fries line your thighs
Sweet treats, fatty meats
Are unkind behind
Make your belly shake like jelly

Greasy food. [repeat 3 times]
Tastes good

Faith Ringgold's Over 100 Pound Weight Loss Performance Story Quilt *coat, 1986*

The 1960s
The 1960s was a fabulous decade. I discovered French wine and cheese in Paris, and learned to be an activist in the streets of New York. At home my teenaged daughters drove me to drink wine with my pork chops, bread and cheese with my ribs and trouble.

Trouble
Trouble will make you eat [repeat 4 times]
Run out in the street
Lookin' for a treat

A treat to eat. To eat a treat. [repeat 2 times]
Trouble [repeat 6 times]
A treat to eat, to eat a treat
Trouble [repeat 3 times]

The 1970s
In the 1970s food was a feminist issue and I was a fat feminist. Always looking for a quasi-politically correct excuse to eat. In the 1960s it was being a wife and mother, the rejection of

being a black artist and other oppressions. In the 1970s it was all that and being a woman too. The 1970s kept me wondering when I'd get enough pain.

Pain
Pain, pain pa-a-a-ain
I feel a pain in my knee
So bad I can't see
Make me hobble around
And twist my hip
I'm sorry I ate those chips

I feel a pain in my back
Feel like it could crack
Make me holler and scream
Stay away from that ice cream.

I feel a pain in my leg
Like I'm pullin' a keg
Can't get up those stairs
Stop eatin' chocolate eclairs

Will this end? [Joan Ashley asks me]
Yes [I respond]
When? [Joan Ashley asks me]
Now [I respond]
How? [Joan Ashley asks me]

Move around shake your body
Make a sound make it hearty
Walk a mile and you'll smile
You'll feel good, you'll feel great
You'll lose that weight [repeat 3 times]
Oh yea!

The 1980s
By the 1980s there was no diet I hadn't tried. I gained weight on all of them. I didn't know you couldn't, so I combined them. If one worked good, two or three would work better. I finally broke the scale at 258. God knows what I weighed after that. Tomorrow I'll change.

Tomorrow
Tomorrow [repeat 2 times]
I'll lose it tomorrow
Tomorrow I'll lose it
I'll lose it tomorrow
Tomorrow [repeat 3 times]

No today!
I can change I can do it [repeat 3 times]

Now!
The worst thing about being fat was squeezing through the subway turnstile sideways; hobbling down the stairs panting and blowing while some bewildered passenger holds the door open for me. And then to have two people get up to give me one seat. I just got to change.

I Just Got to Change
I just got to change [repeat 2 times]
I can't stand the pain
It's like a fire in my brain
Everyday it's the same
Never mind who's to blame
It's me that's got to change
Eatin' all that food is so insane
I just got to change [repeat 2 times]

In the performance's finale, the "Change Song," from the opening, is repeated and the audience is invited to come up on the stage and dance with Joan and me. This performance piece was by far my most successful. I performed it approximately twenty-five times from 1988 until 1991. I had wonderful and informed audiences who always seemed to have something in their own lives that needed to be changed — not the least of which was overeating. Among the places I performed the Change performance were the Woman's Building in Los Angeles; Three Rivers Arts Festival in Pittsburgh; the Baltimore Museum; the High Museum of Art in Atlanta; and the Albright Knox Museum in Buffalo.

In 1989 I created my last performance up until now, *Change 3*. By now I had begun to gain a little of the weight back, but the scheduled performances kept me in shape and helped me to take the weight off. In August of 1990, however, I went to the South of France to paint the French Collection Series and remained there until the end of the year

— during which time I canceled all performances, gained twenty-five pounds, and experienced a recurrence of osteoarthritic pain in my knees. I couldn't exercise — in fact, I could hardly walk. (I have since had bilateral total knee replacement surgery and I must say I am exercising, walking, and planning to enter the New York Marathon next year.)

In 1991 I made the *Change 3: Faith Ringgold's Over 100 Pound Weight Loss Performance Story Quilt,* which contained no photographs but rather a painted "group" self-portrait in the nude, showing me at my various different weights over the years — a testament to the continuing struggle I have had with food. The text for this quilt is about the eating habits of the different "women" (all of them, of course, are just me) who are portrayed on this quilt.

Change 3: Faith Ringgold's Over 100 Pound Weight Loss Performance Story Quilt
Can you imagine a party where everyone invited is a manifestation of yourself? I am having such a party, and finding it is fun and a great way to get to know myself. It's been a long time since I learned anything new about myself. I talk to myself and I understand and accept my point of view. But what I don't know is who am I — really?

At my party everyone invited is actually me and therefore knows me so there is no need to posture and pretend. Even our disagreements and rejections are stimulating and enlightening. The extreme manifestations of me showed up at the party uninvited, and were snubbed. One was eating a fried pork chop sandwich from a greasy bag. When she left in a huff, she got stuck in the door.

But can you imagine a party such as the one I suggest, with only me there or you there; in every possible expression of myself or rather of yourself? Wouldn't you find that intriguing? Wouldn't you like to be surrounded by yourself: the You who are your repressed dreams and fantasies; your second helpings, midnight binges and lackluster, lazy, barefoot TV-watching cookie-monster demons? Can you imagine what you would look like, be like in every color, shape, form and combination of your being? You could answer some very pertinent questions like "Why do you eat so much?"

Because you already know the person you are talking to is really you, you could ask anything. But ask only a thin you about over-eating; otherwise the answer could lead to a second helping.

I am often so demanding. I want everything I fantasize to be good and come true. If I fantasize something bad like eating a chocolate cake, I change it quickly to salad, or I deny the whole thing. But who can deny over-eating?

All of my guests came to the party in the nude. They were every degree of weight loss and gain I've had over the past 40 years. I was shocked though delighted to meet them all face to face. Among them was a best friend, though we have fallen out lately, who sometime eats only one low-fat meal a day. She caught me eating her food once, when she came late for a lunch date. This woman exercises and works out, has facials and dress fittings and is a very together person. I love being around her even though I consider her diet of only low-fat, low-calorie food compulsive and far too rigid. I have not seen her lately.

There is another woman who likes only to look at food. She is a culinary voyeur. I admire that. She will prepare delicious food and never eat it. I am very fond of her, though I rarely see her.

There is another woman who always wants to "do lunch." I don't do lunch, I eat lunch. The only thing I like to do when I eat lunch is order more. When I crave a piece of chocolate cake and ice cream it is she who supplies me with a fix. "I'm here for you any hour of the day or night," she says. But, I don't want to know her. I have told her that, "although I think you are basically a nice person, I find your presence very threatening. You are simply not my type." But still she sticks to me like glue.

I prefer the woman who is often too busy to eat; and picks over her dessert until her ice cream melts, and makes her cake soggy. You might know I never ever see her. We once had breakfast together to plan a trip to Paris. I happen to know that she hates French food — all that bread and butter and patisserie. But she was as usual too busy to eat breakfast — or go to Paris.

This is one woman who is my greatest fantasy, though she will never be invited to my party again. I identify with her too closely. She eats nonstop and never gains weight.

There were two very large women who had eaten three trays of hors d'oeuvres each before dinner. They invited me out for coffee-cake and ice cream after dinner. Really!

Currently I am in the planning stages for yet another *Change* quilt and performance entitled *Change 4,* which will appear at the same time as the publication of this book. The content of the quilt and performance is slowly evolving from a daily documenting of the following: food intake, exercise, work, play or entertainment, feelings either pleasant or traumatic, happenings, which includes good things as well as bad. The first six months of this personal research will shape the form and content of the quilt and performance. My premise is that if I make a public document of my behavioral patterns, then I will be forced to transform them in order to make myself more acceptable. This public self-therapy will reveal not only the food I eat but what else is going on in my life at the same time. Although I have been in therapy, I have never kept a journal or recorded my daily behavior. This time I am doing it and it feels good. Along with the anticipated change in behavior that I am documenting in the text, I am also each day drawing a self-portrait to see if there is an accompanying change in my self-image.

Just recently I was mentioning to some friends that it had taken me fourteen years to find a publisher for my autobiography. Baby Faith, now no baby at all at twelve years of

The Wedding, *1986, Acrylic on canvas; printed, tie-dyed, and pieced fabric, 77½ x 58 inches, Collection of Marilyn Lanfear*

age, blurted out in surprise: "But, Grandma, how could you expect to be published before you did your story quilts?"

The story quilt idea was inspired by growing up listening to my family talk and tell stories about their lives. By the 1980s I was the only member of my immediate family still alive. The need to write became more and more of an issue. It was as if I, with all my story-tellers gone, was now authorized to be one.

In April of 1984 I had a twenty-year retrospective at the Studio Museum in Harlem, the major museum of African-American art in this country. This was my first exhibition in New York since 1970 and my very first solo exhibition in a major museum. I wanted it to be memorable. Mother would have been so delighted to be there to see my dream of recognition as an artist beginning to come true. I decided to create a special work for this occasion to show a future direction in my art. The idea of a painted quilt was uppermost in my mind. I had already made *Echoes of Harlem* with Mother in 1980 and, after her death, *Mother's Quilt* in July of 1983. However, it was in January of 1984 that I began to conceive *Who's Afraid of Aunt Jemima?*, which was to be not only my third quilt but my very first story quilt. It took about a year to complete; I made *Mother's Quilt* in a single weekend.

The story of Jemima Blakey, the name I gave to my radical revision of the character and story of Aunt Jemima, flowed from me like blood running from a deeply cut wound. I didn't want to write it — I had to. I was tired of hearing black people speak negatively about the image of Aunt Jemima. I knew they were referring to a big black woman and I took it personally. White people had Betty Crocker but I had never heard any of them say hateful things about her. I couldn't really understand the black artists of the 1960s, who portrayed Aunt Jemima as a gun-toting revolutionary, or the white people's stereotyped portraits of her as a despicable human being.

If you asked me, I'd say the Aunt Jemimas are the world's "supermoms." I've admired women like Aunt Jemima for their tireless devotion to nurturing. Personally, I was a reluctant supermom; I've always feared that a supermom could spend a lot of time in the kitchen feeding others, but never really feel fed herself.

My Aunt Jemima text and the other story quilts might never have been written had it not been for the fact that Michele refused in 1983 to write the story of Aunt Jemima for me. When Mother died in 1981, Michele had come back home after being out of the house for many years. She had been at Yale working on

Burdette and me and Baby Faith on roof, 1986

a doctorate when she became ill and needed to come home to recuperate. It was an uncomfortable yet necessary arrangement for both of us. With Mother and my sister, Barbara, both dead within a year, I guess we needed to feel close. Now that Michele was living with me, I thought it would be a great idea if we could collaborate on a story quilt. The text would actually be hand-written on the quilt together with painted pictures to illustrate some aspects of its story. I had never written a story and I was, frankly speaking, afraid to write one and put it on my art. What if I made a fool of myself? What would the director of the Studio Museum think about this? Better to get Michele to write it for me, but Michele was not interested.

"Aunt Jemima is our feminist issue," I argued. "One that all women should be concerned with."

"She's from your generation not mine," Michele answered back. "I run seven miles a day to keep from looking like that."

I continued to plead my case. "Aunt Jemima is more than a big black woman with a rag on her head. I want to make a story quilt about who she really is," I said. "Let's do it together. You write the story and I'll paint the images." After all, Michele had written *Black Macho and the Myth of the Superwoman,* the first treatment of this black feminist issue. Surely in no time at all she could knock out some words on the oppression of the Aunt Jemima stereotype? I rambled on trying to convince her, but Michele remained disenchanted. "Michele, just think of her strength. No one ever raped Aunt Jemima. They hate her because she is not vulnerable. Isn't she the one who takes care of the children — her own and everyone else's — and yet is able to make something of her life? Isn't she the ultimate female survivor, the one mainly responsible for keeping us together — as necessary to the family as she is to the race? Don't you think she's the sacrificial lamb who loves those who often don't love her? A woman to whom food is her lover? Should we hate her for that?"

My ramblings fell on deaf ears. Michele stated decisively at the end of a long exchange that "Aunt Jemima is not my concern. She is your generation. You write about her." And that was that.

For the next several months I became a "closet writer," out of fear that I was doing the wrong thing. When Moira Roth (the editor of this book) came to New York to stay with me (she was writing an essay for my Studio Museum exhibition catalogue, which Michele was editing), I hid my story under the guest bed, which was in my studio. Then, feeling guilty about the deception, I told her that I was concealing a story about Aunt Jemima. Moira was fascinated and asked me to read it to her. That was all I needed to hear. I yanked out the vertical canvas strips of pieced texts and painted images and read the following story out loud.

> Jemima Blakey didn't come from no ordinary people. Her Granma and Granpa bought they freedom out a slavery in New Orleans. Granma Jemima Blakey — they called her Aunt Jemima too — made cakes and catered fine parties for them plantation owners in Louisiana. And Granpa Blakey was a first class tailor too. From memory he could make a suit of clothes fit like a glove. They was sure smart people, them Blakeys. And Jemima was just like 'em, hard working, and God-fearing till the day she died.
>
> Jemima could do anything she set her mind to. When Ma Tillie and Pa Blakey, Jemima's Ma and Pa, forbid her to marry Big Rufus Cook on account a they wanted her to marry a preacher, Jemima up and marry Big Rufus anyway, and they run off to Tampa, Florida to work for Ole Man and Ole Lady Prophet cookin', cleanin' and taking care a they chirrun, somethin' Jemima never had to do livin' in her Ma and Pa's comfortable home in New Orleans.
>
> Ole Man Prophet used to joke that Jemima was his heir. "Jemima keep my house and family like they hers. I reckon I'll leave 'em to her when I die," he used to tell Ole

Lady Prophet. "Over my dead body," she used to say. Well as God would have it, lightning struck they house one night whilst the servants was away and burnt it to the ground. Ain' nar' a one of them Prophets survive. And sho nuff Jemima was in Ole Man Prophet's will as "the last to survive." And, praise God, she was.

Jemima and Big Rufus was rich now. They come to New York with they chirrun, Georgia and Lil Rufus, and opened a restaurant and catering business in Harlem.

Big Rufus was a fine chef too, and could tailor clothes out this world just like Granpa Blakey. He looked like white, and couldn't see nobody but Jemima, black as she was. No — never did. "Where you get that fine lookin' man from, Jemima?" folks used to ask her. "Where I get you from asking me that question?" she'd say, laughing.

Now Lil Rufus, Jemima's baby, handsome as a Greek God, took color after Jemima's side a the family. Jemima likena died when he married a white gal, name a Margo he picked up in Germany, of all places, during that Korean war. Brought her home too, to live in Jemima's house in Harlem. They had three girls: Jemmie, JoAnn and Julia. They look just like Jemima. They ain' look nothin' like they ma, Margo, she a scrawny little ole white gal. Love the ground Lil Rufus walk on.

Georgia, Jemima's daughter, was high yaller likena her pa, Big Rufus, and had green eyes and long straight hair she could sit on. Only thing she take after Jemima was her shape. Georgia was real big up top and had skinny legs and big feet.

Jemima'd blow up like a balloon when folks say'd she was Georgia's maid. Georgia'd laugh and call her ma Aunt Jemima. Jemima'd take that piss-tail gal over her knee and whoop her till she quit. "You ain' no more'n your ma," Jemima'd tell her, and Georgia'd screw up her lil horse face an holler.

Jemima was some proud at Georgia's wedding to Dr. Jones. But Ma Tillie said, "Jemima, that's a evil ole ugly black man, you'll see."

Tillie Blakey, Jemima's ma, was half Indian. A real beauty in her youth, she was coal black with long braids and keen features. They say she ran a bad house for white men in New Orleans. All's I know she was a good church going woman, owned a fine house and left plenty money to the church when she died. Pa Blakey called it penance money from the devil. He swore he'd never touch it. Much as he loved Georgia and her struggling doctor husband, and they two chirrun Peter and Annabelle he never give 'em a cent of Ma Tillie's money.

After Pa Blakey died, Jemima an Big Rufus give they restaurant business in Harlem to Lil Rufus and his German wife, Margo, and moved to New Orleans. There they opened another restaurant near Georgia's house.

But Jemima ain' never see her grandchirrun, Peter and Annabelle. "My pa don't want you in our house," they told her one day. And then Peter kicked Jemima in her bad knee and he and Annabelle ran off. The next day before Dr. Jones could leave for his office, Lil Rufus was there, and he was mad as hell. When Dr. Jones saw him, he jumped in the pool fully dressed, doctor bag and all.

That same morning Jemima and Big Rufus had a fatal car accident on the way to open they restaurant. God rest they souls. Lil Rufus brought they bodies back to Harlem, and give 'em an African funeral — praise God! Dressed Jemima in an African gown and braided her hair with cowery shells. Put Big Rufus in a gold dashiki. They looked nice though, peaceful, like they was home.

Georgia, her doctor husband and them two worthless chirrun a hers got Jemima's restaurant business and Ma Tillie's big fine house in New Orleans. Now, who's afraid of Aunt Jemima?

Much to my surprise Moira liked my story of *Who's Afraid of Aunt Jemima?* and encouraged me to complete the quilt and show it to Terrie Rouse, the curator of my exhibition at the Studio Museum. I am pleased to say that both she and Dr. Mary Schmidt Campbell, then the director of the Studio Museum, also enjoyed the story quilt so much that Dr. Campbell decided to put it on my catalogue cover, and also to do a poster of it. (This was actually the first work of mine from which a poster was made.) Ten years later it is still selling in the Studio Museum's gift shop in Harlem and is featured in its catalogue.

Since 1980 I have made eighty-five quilts. Almost half of them are story quilts; most of them are painted, but some incorporate printing media such as etching, lithography, and silk screen, and a few have appliqué as well.

People often ask me if my stories are autobiographical. After reading the *Slave Rape Story Quilt,* a black woman at the Newark Museum rushed up to me to inquire if that story had been about my life.

"Well," I said, "slavery is not something I can forget about."

"All that happened to you?" she exclaimed in amazement.

I was about to do a performance of *The Bitter Nest* so I didn't have time to tell her that slavery ended over a hundred years ago. I just reassured her with "No, not yet," and began my performance. But this woman was not convinced: throughout the performance I could see her staring at me with a perplexed look on her face, and, at the end, I glimpsed her shaking her head in disbelief. I wondered if she thought I was also Ce Ce, the main character in *The Bitter Nest* performance, but I didn't dare ask. So maybe I should tell you right here and now that my stories are fantasized adaptations of real life — based on issues and historical events in the lives of people. My stories may include actual real-life experiences that I have had — that I know about or can imagine happening to me or to other people — but they are almost always also imaginary. None of them can be read literally.

For instance, the *Flag Story Quilt* (1985) is about Memphis Cooley, an armless, paraplegic Vietnam veteran from Harlem, who is accused of an unlikely crime. This story is based on the premise that the black man's guilt, whether likely or unlikely, is almost always taken for granted long before it is actually proven. Although *Flag Story Quilt* was written nine years ago, it seems to bear a resemblance to the recent Rodney King case in which we were asked to disbelieve the classic video we all saw on television of the brutal police beating of Rodney King that would seem to suggest that the police applied undue force to an unarmed man.

The *Flag Story Quilt* is the last text I'm including in this book. Here it is:

Memphis Cooley's Ma and Pa ain' never been no fools, they know'd they son ain' commit no murder and raping. How he gonna slash some girl's throat and throw her in the Harlem River, and he ain' got no arms? How he gonna rape her sitting in a wheel chair paralyzed from the waist down? You reckon Memphis scared that girl into slashing her own throat, and raping herself? Well, Memphis wadn't no type a man to do none of that. He was quiet, decent and refined — too fine for the company he kept. I always say, "You lay down with dogs, you'll get up with fleas."

Memphis Ma and Pa just grieved they self to death. Both died in they sleep within a week of each other.

Ain' nothing else they could do to help Memphis out of this mess. They done work hard all they life to raise that boy to be a fine man. Uncle Sam took him to Vietnam and send him back all messed up and now this.

Ain't that enough to kill you 'bout your own child? You know the Cooleys loved the ground Memphis walked on. And he was a loving good son to them too. That boy used to come to see his Ma and Pa every Sunday God send. He ain' miss a Sunday since he moved away from here. Now they gone and he in prison, going to the chair for a crime he ain' commit.

You might know his wife, Verona Valle, done turn on him too. Well I ain' gonna turn on him. I held him in my arms when he was a baby. I looked after him while his Ma and Pa worked in they candy store. I'll tell anybody it's a lie. Memphis ain' kill nobody. And he ain' rape nobody either. That boy never touch Verona, his own wife. Now if that's a lie she told it. I believe Verona trying to frame him though, that's why she claiming Memphis confessed to the crime in his sleep. Well, she musta been his accomplice, cause God know that boy can't move off'n that wheel chair less'n you help him.

Now ain' but a few people know this but Memphis is the ghost writer of Romantic Love Novels by Verona Valle. Yea, they real popular. They sell at the check-out counter in the supermarket. They won that national romantic book award for three years. And they be's on the best seller's list all the time. They all about love and way out sex among the jet set. You know? Well, Verona is Memphis Cooley's wife but he is the real author of those novels, not that lying Verona. He just use her name to keep the door open. You know how that is?

It started back when Memphis come home from the Army paralyzed and both arms cut off from the shoulder. Bea and Tom Cooley confided to me that Memphis was through being brave — those medals of honor wadn't no substitute for his body. He didn't want to live just sittin' in a wheel chair sellin' pencils with peoples staring at him likena he's a freak or somethin'. Cause that boy used to be some good-looker before he got blown up in that Vietnam war. Tall dark and handsome, that's what they used to call him, with the biggest prettiest brown eyes you ever see. And now ain' none of his ole girl friends want him. So his Ma and Pa start him writing those love stories.

Ole man Cooley publish those stories himself, they called 'em Exotic Love Novels, and sold 'em in they candy store right here in Harlem. Well sir, the peoples went wild over Memphis' love stories. And soon all kinda peoples come up here asking for the latest Exotic Love Novel. One day this Verona Valle come to the Cooley's store looking for Memphis 'bout his Exotic Love Novels. She had collected all Memphis' novels. She went on and on 'bout what a great writer Memphis was and how she wanted to help him get a Madison Avenue publisher. Tom Cooley turn her away, but one day she met Memphis settin' in front of the candy store in his wheel chair typing his next Exotic Love Novel with a pencil in his teeth. She ask him was he Memphis Cooley and did he write the Exotic Love Novels she had in her hands. Well, she was real pretty and classy dressed. Memphis took a liking to her right off.

So he admitted he was the author of Exotic Love Novels. And Verona commenced to raving about how good the novels were and how she could get him a big time Madison Avenue publisher and make him a lot of money. Well, to make a long story short, she was the Madison Avenue publisher and now she was the author of Memphis' novels and he was the ghost writer.

They changed the name from Exotic Love Novels to Romantic Love Novels and Memphis start to makin' big money from his books. Next thing we know Memphis and this Verona Valle got married. She move him down town away from his Ma and Pa. And now they say he done kill and rape some 19 year ole white girl and threw her dead body in the Harlem River.

They been draggin' that river for one year now and ain' come up with no dead white girl yet — cause ain' none. They claim they got some witnesses saw Memphis throw the girl off the bridge and the other claim he saw the throat slashin' and rape. Well, they sure saw a lie, cause ain' no paralyzed man can rape and ain' no armless man can throw no nineteen year old woman off'n no bridge.

And ain' no reason for Memphis to kill no girl just cause her boyfriend call him Nigger in a bar. Memphis got money and success as a writer with his novels. What he care 'bout some ole trashy white folks calling him Nigger? If it hadn't been for that scheming wife of his, he wouldn't been jetting round in that fancy wheel chair bar-hoppin' till all hours of the night, when the police be out there lookin' for a nigger to pin some dirt on.

The text of this *Flag Story Quilt* is written on an American flag design. I appliquéd the red stripes with tie-dyed fabrics and for the stars I made tiny white profiled heads with sequined eyes appliquéd against a field of blue tie-dyed fabric. The story appears on the flag's white canvas stripes.

Great-great-grandma Susie Shannon, circa 1900

Most of my stories are about women and all of my narrators are female. These narrators are fashioned after the women I heard tell stories as I sat quietly, so as not to be sent off to bed, listening intently to the often tragic details of the lives of family members and friends told in that way that black women had in my childhood of expressing themselves. On occasion I have also made a man the center of a story quilt, but his story can only unfold as I begin to hear a woman telling it. I won't give you the text of this next quilt, but I'll tell you about it. Unlike the *Flag Story Quilt,* which is based on the classic victimization of the black American male, *Street Story Quilt,* which I made in 1985, is about A.J., a tragic-youth-turned-hero — a young black man who, despite adversity, miraculously achieves the American Dream.

The *Street Story Quilt* is composed in three long rectangular sections (*The Accident, The Fire,* and *The Homecoming*). In Part I, A.J., only ten at the time, witnesses the accidental death of his mother and four younger brothers when a drunk driver slams into Big Al's car in front of their Harlem tenement. Big Al (A.J.'s father) was driving the family to Concy Island for corn on the cob. Strangely enough, A.J., who was usually first in the car, decided to stay home that day and play Chinese Checkers with Ma Teedy (his grandma). Although Big Al was at the wheel of his car, he had nothing to do with the accident — but still he could not forgive himself for the death of his wife and four children. I portray A.J. and his grandmother on the stoop as they witness this tragic event while their neighbors peer from their windows in disbelief and horror.

In Part 2, *The Fire,* Big Al had grieved so much over the death of his wife and four sons in the car accident that he takes to drinking all day in the basement of the tenement building. One day while drinking, he falls asleep and drops a lit cigarette on the mattress. It goes up like a tinderbox, burning up most of the building. Big Al dies in the fire but A.J. and Ma Teedy, though they occupy a first-floor apartment, are unharmed. For this

Groovin' High,
1986, Acrylic on canvas; tie-dyed and pieced fabric.
56 x 92 inches.
Collection of Barbara and Ronald Davis Balsar

middle section of the quilt I show the building with charred and burning windows, and people being helped to safety on rescue ladders. Below on the street there are fire trucks, firemen, and frightened tenants. In the rest of the text for this section, I describe A.J.'s teenage years. Despondent over the loss of his family, he becomes a numbers runner, a drug pusher, and a pimp, and ultimately mobsters run him out of Harlem. He hides out in the South Bronx and then enlists to go to Vietnam. Throughout all of this, Ma Teedy's support is unwavering.

In Part 3, *The Homecoming,* A.J. returns from Vietnam to write his life story, having survived Vietnam as well as Harlem and the South Bronx. He becomes a successful writer in Paris and Hollywood and receives a Pulitzer Prize for his story and an Oscar for portraying himself in the leading role of the movie.

A.J. comes back to his Harlem tenement to take Ma Teedy to live with him in Hollywood. The image of this last section of the quilt is of the tenement with its boarded-up, burned-out windows now unoccupied except for Ma Teedy and Aunt Gracie (who is the narrator for this tale). A.J's white-chauffeured limousine waits at the curb.

Writing story quilts has now become a very natural means of expression for me; indeed, it seems almost necessary for texts to accompany the images painted on quilts. Over seven years the process has made me feel more confident about my writing abilities so that in 1991 I was ready to author my first children's book, *Tar Beach.*

I have observed that many people read the stories on the quilts standing up in the gallery. Indeed, some people come back to an exhibition over and over again in order to read all the stories or to reread the same ones. Clearly, a story has to evolve quickly with as few words as possible. For that reason, the story quilts are actually written in the same way that I was to write my children's stories. However, children's stories can be much more imaginative than stories written for an adult audience.

Since 1987 I had tried to get my story quilts published but was constantly told, "Oh, but they are art books and there is no market for them." However, Andrea Cascardi, then the editor of children's books at Crown Books (a subsidiary of Random House), saw a poster of my 1988 story quilt *Tar Beach* (owned by the Guggenheim Museum) and recognized immediately that the story would make a good children's book. I must say I had not realized that I could write children's stories; rather, I was simply trying to recall my childhood experience of going up to "Tar Beach" and writing in a child's voice. (Michele had told me that a good writer has to develop a unique voice, just as an artist has a unique vision.) At any rate, *Tar Beach* launched my new career as a published writer and illustrator of children's books and it has won more than twenty awards including a Caldecott Honor, the Coretta Scott King Award, and the New York Times Award for the best illustrated children's books for 1991.

Tar Beach is a story of an eight-year-old girl named Cassie whose family takes her up to the roof ("Tar Beach") on hot summer nights. Cassie dreams of a steady good job for her father, who is a construction worker but was denied a union card because of racism. Cassie also dreams that her mother could sleep late (just like Mrs. Honey, their next-door neighbor) and not cry all day when her husband goes looking for work and then doesn't come home.

Being on the roof with the stars all around her and the beautiful George Washington Bridge in the distance makes Cassie fantasize that she can fly over buildings and claim them as her own. Accordingly, she flies over the Union Building and gives it to her father. She also flies over the ice cream factory so that she and Be Be, her brother, can have ice cream every night for dessert. At the end of the tale, Cassie tells Be Be: "Anyone can fly, all you have to do is have somewhere to go that you can't get to any other way and the next thing you know you're flying among the stars."

Since composing *Tar Beach* I have written and illustrated *Aunt Harriet's Underground Railroad in the Sky* (Crown Books,1992) and *Dinner at Aunt Connie's House* (Hyperion Books for Young Readers, 1993). In *Aunt Harriet's Underground Railroad in the Sky*, Cassie and Be Be

Atlanta Children, *1981, Mixed media, 30 x 40 x 15 inches, Artist's collection*

meet Harriet Tubman as she is in the middle of calling the runaway slaves to board the train to freedom. Be Be jumps aboard and the train pulls out of the station leaving Cassie behind. She follows Be Be, however, as Tubman's whispering voice guides her through the same underground route from Tubman's slave plantation in Maryland all the way to Canada. Cassie sleeps by day and by night follows the North Star, stopping at farmhouses, funeral parlors, and graveyards and traveling in hearses and concealed compartments. When Cassie finally catches up with Be Be and Aunt Harriet in Canada, she is exhausted but happy. She makes Be Be promise that he will never leave her again. Be Be responds lovingly, but tells Cassie that "being free is more important than just being together."

Dinner at Aunt Connie's House is a rewrite of a 1986 story quilt, *The Dinner Quilt*. In this story Melody meets her newly adopted cousin Lonnie at a family dinner at Aunt Connie's house. The two children have an immediate attraction for one another and set out to find Aunt Connie's surprise paintings, which she intends to present to the family at dinner. In the attic the children discover these twelve portraits of famous African-American women. The paintings tell the children about their heroic lives. The twelve women whom Aunt Connie has painted are Rosa Parks, Fannie Lou Hamer, Mary McLeod Bethune, Augusta Savage, Dorothy Dandridge, Zora Neale Hurston, Maria W. Stewart, Bessie Smith, Harriet Tubman, Sojourner Truth, Marian Anderson, and Madame C. J. Walker. Lonnie is inspired to be an opera singer like Marian Anderson and Melody thinks she'd like to be president of the United States. The children fantasize they will one day marry and share the secret of Aunt Connie's paintings with their children. Lonnie, still somewhat baffled by the experience of talking to paintings, asks Melody what their children will think of Aunt Connie's secret. "Our children will love the secret," responds Melody. "We will have delicious family dinners, and they will be magical just like Aunt Connie's, and our children, Lonnie, will be just like us."

I am currently finishing two more children's books to be published in 1995 and 1996. *Bonjour Lonnie* is about the little boy with red hair and green eyes who, as the adopted son of Aunt Connie and Uncle Bates, has appeared already in *Dinner at Aunt Connie's House.* A love bird flies into Lonnie's window at the orphanage and leads him to Paris where he discovers his roots lie in a mixed parentage, beginning with his grandfather who went to France in 1917 as one of the famed Harlem Hell fighters during World War I and married a French woman. The story ends at Aunt Connie's house (where the dinner quilt begins), with Lonnie finding a home. The other book I am doing has a working title of *Martin's Dream,* about Martin Luther King Jr., the ultimate dreamer.

These children's books seek to explain to children some of the hard facts of slavery and racial prejudice, issues that are difficult but crucial to their education. But my books are even more about children having dreams, and instilling in them a belief that they can change things. When Cassie believes she can fly, it is not because she wants to go to Florida to see her grandma, but rather because she envisions a better life for her family. Already at eight years old she wisely recognizes that all good things start with a dream. So flying is about achieving a seemingly impossible goal with no more guarantee of success than an avowed commitment to do it.

*The Death of Apartheid, 1984,
Mixed media collage, 78 x 78 inches,
Artist's collection*

Being born and raised in Harlem, I have seen and been inspired by many great black leaders, but they were all men — Adam Clayton Powell Sr. and Jr., Malcolm X, Martin Luther King Jr., Supreme Court Justice Thurgood Marshall, W. E. B. Du Bois, and others. The first women I saw as leaders were Dorothy Height and Shirley Chisholm, both of whom have greatly inspired me over the years. But my field was art and that made it difficult to find a role model — male or female, black or otherwise — who could inspire the kind of leadership artists need. So what I have done over the past twenty-five years is not aspire to leadership myself but rather to become an ad hoc activist in order to address some of the problems that confront people of color in the visual arts.

In 1971, realizing how difficult it was to achieve anything alone, I decided to create a black women's art group. Kay Brown and I founded Where We At, which turned out to

Moira Roth in Morocco, 1992

be a nonactivist although socially conscious women's exhibition group. I felt that just having shows was not enough to give black women artists the kind of involvement in the art world that could make a difference. I had negotiated a show of our art with Nigel Jackson, the black director-owner of the Acts of Art Gallery, a black art gallery in Greenwich Village. I proposed that the show would remain "open" so that if any other black women heard about it after the opening they could still be included. But the majority of the women wanted the show closed to such possible latecomers. Later I had to confront Nigel — the other women didn't mind Nigel representing our point of view on women's issues, but I did. I quickly felt the need to be with people who were confronting issues. So, after our initial show in 1971, it was time for me to split. I quit the group, leaving Kay Brown as its group leader. It continued to function throughout the seventies and into the eighties, presiding over community art workshops and holding local exhibitions and other cultural events.

Art Without Walls, another group I founded in 1972, was a volunteer group of about twelve artists (black and white, male and female, including students from Brandeis High School and Wagner College where I was then teaching) who went every Sunday to the Women's House of Detention on Rikers Island to do art and discussion workshops. Mother, Michele, and I had initially conducted discussions with the women about their plans for staying out of jail. However, our participation in Art Without Walls was short-lived; the prison officials preferred workshops like yoga, dance, and face-painting to our discussion groups. Yet we had been doing well with the women, exploring with them the possibilities of halfway houses to give support when they got out. (The women we were talking to had been arrested for nonviolent crimes like prostitution, shoplifting, and possession of drugs.) Our group was eliminated, however, before we could really figure out how they could manage this. The women confided in Mother the details of their arrests. I thought they would be turned off when she questioned their judgment and morals and suggested that they attend church and put God in their lives. Yet I don't think they had known a woman like my Mother: they couldn't get enough of her, and on Sundays when she did not appear it was obvious they missed her presence and advice.

Most of the young women inmates were black and Latina and so I naively thought it important to bring young black male artists to the prison, but these men only came once, never to return. I found out from my young black male students that these black artists were being propositioned and felt threatened by the women's overt sexual aggressiveness toward them. All in all, this was a world as far away from the high-toned art world as you could get. As far as I know, Art Without Walls is now a formal part of the prison program and the artists are paid to conduct supervised programs of art activities. This was a time when the penal system was under rather close scrutiny and when many artists were committed to go in and help out.

From the mid-1970s for the next five years I worked pretty much in isolation, feeling alienated from both the mainstream art world and what was left of the New York feminist art movement. By the early 1980s, however, I renewed my affiliation with the Women's Caucus for Art and in 1987 founded Coast to Coast. This was not only the last organization I was to found, but also easily the most successful. Since 1970, I had dreamed of a network of women artists committed to bringing women of color into the mainstream of American art. I had tried my hand earlier in working with men in the 1960s for change, and in the 1970s with the (mostly white) women artists movement. But a women artists of color network (rather than merely black women) became a more timely and challenging goal.

In 1986, Ofelia Garcia, then national president of the Women's Caucus for Art (WCA), appointed me vice president of minority affairs. I had been active in the caucus since 1982, when Muriel Magenta first invited me to sit on the national board. We were concerned with cultural, social, and political change, and to this day I count many of these women as my friends.

Yet I still had had very little success in networking with women of color, so I proposed a "caucus" of women of color, supported by the WCA. In 1987 this idea began gaining acceptance.

I was living in New York at the time, teaching at the University of California in San Diego, and making frequent trips across the country to do performances and lectures. I realized I could use that mobility to talk to women of color about a collaborative project. This could conceivably bring together a network of artists that would give them much-needed visibility, support, and national attention; perhaps in the words of Martin Luther King Jr., in 1987 this was "an idea whose time had come."

Initially, I traveled to Berkeley, California, and stayed with my friend Moira Roth. Moira and I talked into the night about what would be the right first project for an artists-of-color collaboration. We came up with the idea of an artist book, a way of communicating with women coast to coast. My hope was that women would come together to collaborate and would stay on to network and to build something lasting. Furthermore, through collaboration they would discover a wonderful way to be productive, make friends, and have fun.

I met and talked with several women of color in the Bay Area, suggesting to them the artist book project. I told them that it would be exhibited at the WCA conference to be held the next year in Houston, Texas. They had never heard of the WCA and were confused about the definition of artist books. By the end of this visit, they seemed less than enthusiastic but that was no indication of events to come.

My next trip was to Los Angeles, where Margaret Gallegos, painter, printmaker, and WCA board member, invited thirty-five or more women of color to meet me for lunch at a Chinese restaurant in Santa Monica. We sat together talking excitedly: Latina, African-American, Asian-American, and Native American women artists including Betye Saar, Varnette and Stephanie Honeywood, Anita Holguin, Julia Nee Chu, Diane Gamboa, Alma Lopez, Gloria Longval, and Roslyn Mesquita. Many of the women pledged their commitment to create a book.

Margaret Gallegos became the West Coast coordinator, and when I returned to New York City, I met with Clarissa Sligh, photographer, printmaker, and mixed-media artist, and asked her if she would be the East Coast coordinator. (The recent death of her husband had given her a vacuum of time to fill.) She agreed. Later, I told Gallegos about my meeting with Sligh and our idea to call the project "Coast to Coast, a Women of Color National Artists Book Project." She liked the idea, too, and so Coast to Coast was created.

Returning to California, I met with Gallegos, who had computerized the information we had collected to date. Together we wrote a letter inviting women of color all over the country to participate in our artist book project. The first mailing went out to over two hundred women from over thirty states whose bloodlines included Latina, Native American, Asian-American, African-American, and others of mixed blood. Their responses began pouring in; by December of 1987 the books were ready to be shipped for exhibition.

The first exhibition of Coast to Coast was held during the WCA national meeting in February of 1988 at Diverse Works Gallery in Houston, Texas. The exhibition's hundred and twenty books varied in content, technique, and materials. They were about love, hate, food, family, friendship, childbirth, sex, marriage, motherhood, war, rape, incest, music, AIDS, being black, poor, a woman, Native American, Chicana, or Asian. There were books made of paper and string, fabric and wood, metal and plastic, sewn and printed, painted and stamped. Some of the books contained a written text, while others had only pictures; some had no pictures and no words. And yet, they all seemed to declaim, "I am a woman of color, making a serious statement about my life and work." Among the many well-known women artists in the show were Josely Carvalho, Yong Soon Min, Rosalyn Mesquita, Maren Hassinger, Michi Itami, Emma Amos, Joyce Scott, Pena Bonita, Kumi Korf, Sophie Rivera, Mary Ting, Elizabeth Catlett, Howardena Pindell, Jaune Quick-To-See-Smith, Zarina Hashmi, Adrian Piper, Beverly Buchanan, and Vivian Browne.

Since the WCA meeting was held at the same time as the CAA convention (College Art Association is a national organization for artists, art historians, critics, and museum personnel), artists, art historians, critics, museum professionals, and art professors from all over the country viewed our exhibition of artist books. The opening provided a great exhibition as well as a fun party. Both Lucy Lippard and Moira Roth, well known as white women writers and critics committed to the cause of artists of color, visited our exhibition; neither had ever seen an exhibition of artist books of this caliber. Lippard told me that the show "brings a whole new body of experience into the artist book field. Since I cofounded Printed Matter, an artist's bookstore in New York City, I found there were very few artists of color making books. [Here there is] such an explosion of ideas not at all the kind of uniform white covers with little black lines on the front. The common thread is in maintaining their own culture." Roth commented that "there is a wonderful female presence here and you can see, literally, a sense of women's hands at work."

With the success of our first exhibition in 1988 behind us, Coast to Coast was to become a permanent network. Clarissa Sligh became both the East and West Coast coordinator when Margaret Gallegos dropped out because of prior commitments. The first meeting of the New York Coast to Coast committee brought together women from as far north as Ithaca, New York, and as far south as Virginia. The committee had grown to include Carole Byard, Miriam Hernandez, Marcia McNair, Michele Godwin, Carmen Sanchez, Lisa Yi, Kiosa Summers, Tomie Arai, Lotus Do Brooks, Bisa Washington, Beverly Singer, Sharon Jaddis, and Mary Ting. The Coast to Coast artist book exhibition had a very successful national tour to a number of museums and university galleries. But it didn't end there: Coast to Coast continues to mount exhibitions and tour them nationally.

In order to get one's career as a professional artist started, one needs first to acquire an audience for the work. Exhibitions and accompanying articles and reviews in art

Oprah and me at Harpo, 1988

magazines and art columns in the major newspapers will give the artist exposure to collectors and the art-buying public. Excuses don't count: if you don't have a dealer, you have to do it yourself.

In the summer of 1967 I met Vivian Browne, the painter, who said something that has stuck with me ever since. We were discussing the problems that black artists have in becoming successful: having neither dealers to represent them nor galleries to show their work. Yet Vivian didn't care about that; all she wanted was to have her work in important museums and private collections. I remember thinking that sounded so sophisticated, what some people might call "neat." I wondered how one could make that happen, and a little later in conversation with Lil Picard, I asked her about this. She told me there were over four hundred museums and private collections in the art world whose business it is to acquire the works of important artists and that this is clearly how artists become rich and famous. Artists may not know the names of these museums and collections but they know that art dealers sell to them; accordingly, they are willing to give dealers a thirty to fifty (and sometimes even sixty) percent commission. For that percentage of the sale, the dealer agrees to exhibit, sell, and generally promote the artist's work to the art world (in some cases buy the work and occasionally even give a stipend so that the artist can continue to make art when not selling). This puts the dealer in a close and unique position with the artist. Many artists with no dealers, however, have independently to find a way to get to the "four hundred collectors" on their own. Obviously, that's tough to figure out.

Black artists have an additional problem. There are relatively few black people, even if they have the resources, who want to spend their hard-earned money on original works of art. I must tell you that three important exceptions are Oprah Winfrey and Bill and Camille Cosby. I don't mean to minimize the risk factor involved with collecting art. One must develop an "eye" to select artists whose work portrays that unique vision that renders it worthy of being collected. Collecting art is not a skill that comes easily, and people who want to collect have to learn to see — which means looking not just at the work of black artists but at all art and forms of art. Only then will their eyes be sufficiently trained to comprehend and appreciate art. Appreciating visual art is not a finger-popping thing; you don't feel the vibrations of it. Unlike the case with dance music, you can't do something else while you are appreciating it. It is a lot to ask people to stop what they are doing to stare at a work of art. But that is what all we artists are asking of our viewers. The dealer, on the other hand, may just be asking the viewer to buy.

One of the first things I did when I decided to become an artist was to keep a record of all the work I had done in color slides, transparencies, and black-and-white photographs. When Malcolm Varon, my photographer at that time, became so famous I could no longer afford him, I bought a camera and he instructed me how to take pictures on my own. I also kept, arranged year by year, all my letters, reviews, articles, brochures, and catalogues in portfolios. Today my archive has grown from just a few portfolios on a shelf in my bookcase in the 1960s to an entire office of portfolios on shelves in the 1990s. So representing myself as an artist has never been a problem to me. When I started in the 1960s, I didn't think about the market so much as I did amassing a body of work to be exhibited and reviewed, as well as making public appearances and acquiring a broad and appreciative audience for my art.

From 1986 to August of 1992 I was represented by the Bernice Steinbaum Gallery in SoHo. This was for the most part a highly productive and financially rewarding period for me. It was Bernice who discovered my market and introduced me to the "four hundred collectors," and I worked very hard to make sure it paid off. Out of this association we became good friends but unfortunately, with the expansion of my career as a children's book writer and illustrator, we had conflicting notions about how my business vis-à-vis the gallery was to be handled. When the time came to leave I felt very confident it was the right thing to do. I always like to feel that I have the vision to see my future, so that I can live for today but with an eye for tomorrow. I have examined long and hard the fact that black women in art have traditionally had a tragic history. Many of them — although talented, committed, and productive artists — failed to live out the American dream. Witness the fact that Augusta Savage took a pickax to her sculptures and destroyed all of them.

The awful truth that plagues people of color in this country is that we are not in the traditional mainstream of American life; therefore, we don't know what is going on there. Instead of following the standard of being an artist in the tradition of white artists (something most of us can never know anything about), why not cut a new pattern and make up some new rules for success?

Maybe find a new path to the "four hundred collectors" or even a new "four hundred." In 1993 I accelerated the business operations in my studio to include being my own dealer. At this time I hired an assistant whose duty would be to keep up with requests for exhibitions, sales, commissions, licensing copyrights, artist-in-residencies, lectures, book signings, and other public appearances. Our office is well run thanks to Vanessa Williams, my assistant. I also rely heavily on Marie Brown, my literary agent, Barbara Hoffman, my lawyer, and Marjorie Durden, my accountant. We collectively take care of a lot of business these days.

I would not discount having a dealer to handle my affairs in the future, but that person would have to be someone who understands that my art includes writing as well as painting — and may in the future include other means of expression as well. An artist needs a dealer who is not only interested in the commission but understands the goals of the artist, and who has the necessary resources to take the artist where she/he cannot go alone. I must remind you that a dealer is a business woman or man — be they black or white. Let us not romanticize the role. Instead let us also learn to represent ourselves — after all we can give our "four hundred collectors" that thirty to fifty percent dealer's commission as a bonus for doing business directly with us, the artists.

Along with courses in painting and sculpture, an artist should take a course in business. It can prove a very expensive mistake to ignore the many ways in which artists can make money from their art. The most obvious and the most crucial to the success of any artist is the sale of his or her work, hopefully in his or her lifetime. However, the sale of the art has nothing to do with the issue of copyright unless you sell that, too. No artist who understands the business will ever part with the copyright, however, or allow others to use it without her knowledge and approval — and in most cases a fee. When they buy your work, they buy the object but the image of that object is still "owned" by your copyright, and thus still belongs to you.

For me, the licensing of rights to use reproductions of images runs a close second to the actual sale of the art object, especially in the case of posters and other commercial uses made of my story quilts. In the 1960s and 1970s I sold only a few works of art; however, I licensed many images to be reproduced, including *The Flag is Bleeding, U.S. Postage Stamp Commemorating the Advent of Black Power,* and *Flag for the Moon: Die Nigger.* All of these works are in my permanent collection, yet the licensing of these 1960s images — some critics have spoken of them as contemporary icons — continues to bring in revenue. (Incidentally, over the last few years the fee for licensing them has increased tenfold.)

We go to the cinema to see films, to the theater to see plays, to the concert hall to hear music, and to the museum to see art. If your work is to survive for the next generation, hearing about it by word of mouth is not good enough. It simply has to be seen, and the museum is the place for that. Rather than ignoring the power of museums, the informed public should make them accountable. You should go to museums and ask to see bought and exhibited the art you admire. No one group of people, no matter how rich or learned, can dictate the standards for quality in art. Only time and a cross section of informed viewers can ultimately determine the value and significance of the art of an era.

Along with many other artists of color and women, I now have the sweet good fortune of an audience of children who will grow up knowing that an artist does not have to be white or male. This alone will change the art world in the next decade. These young people will be our next artists, museum directors, curators, collectors, art critics, and teachers of art. They will be inspired by, collect, exhibit, and write about the art that they have learned as children to see as beautiful.

I have a story to tell you that is both a museum story and the best children's story I know — God bless them every one. Children all over the country tell me that when their parents bring them to New York they demand to be taken to the Guggenheim to see *Tar Beach*. How can I explain to children that museums often acquire works of art from collectors and yet never show them? (*Tar Beach* was bought by Judith Lieber, the pocketbook mogul, who then donated it to the Guggenheim in 1989.) So I said nothing and the children continued to go to the Guggenheim in search of *Tar Beach*. Understandably, the personnel at the Guggenheim had never heard of *Tar Beach;* how could they possibly know the thousands of works of art in their permanent collection? But as the children continued to request to see *Tar Beach,* the personnel became annoyed with their persistence, and asked me why the kids thought it would be on view. I replied frankly that "I guess it is because they know *Tar Beach* is in your collection and they would like to see it on exhibition there." Finally, I received a letter from a museum administrator in which he wrote: "If you are not already aware, you should know that *Tar Beach* is currently one of, if not the most requested objects from our collection for loan to other institutions." But still, between you and me, I don't know what it would take to have this totally Eurocentric male-dominated Guggenheim Museum exhibit a painted story quilt by an African-American woman. So I don't hold my breath, but it was the innocence of children that initially broached the subject. And if *Tar Beach* ever hangs on the walls of the Guggenheim, it will be due to the children.

When I received my doctorate of Fine Arts in 1991 at City College of New York

The issue of racism and sexism in the art world is a continuing problem that most people know very little about. Citizens don't demand equal rights for artists of color and women in museums and public funding agencies. Most people think if you're good enough, you'll make it to the top and so they don't urge their appointed officials to canvass the museums and other cultural institutions to see if they are spending public money to represent the best art done by artists regardless of race and sex.

Ninety-nine and nine-tenths percent of the significant art production of men and women of color is ignored by the major art institutions in this country and only token representation is given to the rest. I'd like to see that end — and it will. But right now the art world continues to have a field day and for the most part the only team players are white men.

Despite all of these obstacles, it has never occurred to me to stop, give up, and go away — even though I know that is what oppression is designed to make me do. I continue to look for alternative routes to get where I want to be. That is why I have worked in so many different media: the posters, tankas, soft sculpture, and dolls in the 1970s; the performances and story quilts in the 1980s; and so far in the 1990s the writing and illustration of children's books, the rewriting of history in The French Collection, and this autobiography. These things have given me a constantly expanding audience and the flexibility I need to continue working in the face of adversity.

I don't want the story of my life to be about racism, though it has played a major role. I want my story to be about attainment, love of family, art, helping others, courage, values, dreams coming true. Although my struggle to overcome may seem like a hard life, it is not as hard as it seems — in fact, struggle is as natural to me as walking. I embrace it, but I could also learn to live without it.

In 1992 Birdie and I bought a ranch house in Englewood, New Jersey. Originally I got the idea to go there because I wanted to have a studio in the country. Englewood is just over the George Washington Bridge, fifteen minutes from downtown New York City and just a stone's throw away from my beloved birthplace — I'd never want to live too far from Harlem. I had been looking for one of those beautiful brownstones there but found them all too small to accommodate the large-scale works I was now doing. But when Birdie and I moved, we didn't go to New Jersey to be the only black family on Jones Road in Englewood. Sarah Vaughan, Dizzy Gillespie, and Wilson Pickett lived in Englewood years ago and

Artists at the Studio Museum in 1995 in front of The Gift *by Emma Amos; some of the forty-eight watercolor portraits in the background*

now Whitney Houston, Carol Martin, and Eddie Murphy also live in Englewood. So, when it became necessary to move I thought it would be a good idea to join Carol and Dizzy and Eddie in Englewood — just a cool eight minutes from Harlem but in another world and one so beautiful. But I soon had a rude awakening — certain people in Englewood were very ugly.

Soon after we moved, I filed an application with the town's board of adjustments in order to build an art studio on top of our two-bedroom ranch house. This was interpreted by my white neighbors as an attempt to create a two-family house in a one-family zone. Much to my surprise, the neighbors hired a lawyer to cross-examine me in an attempt to prove their case and therefore deny me the right to build a studio onto my house. I refused to be cross-examined by their attorney since mine was not present. In anger, one of the neighbors spoke up, declaring that "I did not pay much attention to what was going on until I received a letter stating that there would be an addition. . . . We do like to have residents in the neighborhood. However, I am hearing work, visitors, studios, paintings, books. . . . It gives me an uneasy feeling about exactly what is going to happen in that house. We've always lived in this neighborhood and it's what you call Triple A, residential. . . . There should be no work whatsoever," she announced, and concluded with the asinine analysis that "if it looks like it, smells like it . . ." I felt totally violated. I had to keep reminding myself that this woman really was referring to me and in the most hateful spirit imaginable. I realized I was dealing with something I was not prepared to fully comprehend — an all-but-raging fear that whites sometimes have when a black family moves into their neighborhood. If I had had any idea I would be confronted with this form of intolerance on the East Hill of Englewood, I would have never moved there.

Since the zoning ordinance does permit homeowners to have an artist's studio, what I was encountering was clear and simple racism. Well, as it turned out I was able to pass the board of adjustments, but it cost me a great deal of time and aggravation, not to mention the added expense of hiring an attorney to look out for my rights. A crowning irony was that one day one of the neighbors approached me in my yard. He told me that he had done his homework and that he wanted to see some of my art and wished me luck with my construction. So now he knows who I am, but I still don't know who he is.

A white face is no résumé. It is frightening to see how difficult it still is to live free in America.

A disheartening update: In 1994 I had bilateral total knee replacement surgery. My doctor advised me to build my studio on the ground floor. The neighbors once more opposed me and this time they won. So the struggle to build my studio in Englewood continues now in court.

Despite these painfully demeaning episodes, this is still the best time of my life: from June to January living in the country just over my favorite bridge from New York; and for the rest of the year teaching at the University of California in San Diego in La Jolla. Birdie is retired now after thirty-five years at General Motors. He spends his days feeding the birds, raking the leaves, and sweeping off the snow. The rest of the time he listens to his jazz collection, plays drums, and just raps with his lifelong friend Donald Lipscomb and the rest of the boys in their Racoons Club, an all-men's retirement group which meets weekly at our house in Englewood. So, dear reader, I'd like to report my family and I are well. The art and writing are productive and I am going on with my life.

When asked how he was doing, my father, Andrew Louis Jones Sr., used to respond with one of his famous sayings: "I'm kicking but not high." Well, this book is dedicated to my father, who took me up to Tar Beach — from which we could see the George Washington Bridge — and made me think I was unique. But in retrospect I never did very much for him. Even when he would ask me, "Who is the greatest man in the world?" I don't think I ever told him: "You are, Daddy." But, being a father, he must have known he was the greatest man in my life and he would be proud to know that now we have flown over the bridge. It is exhilarating and surprising in my later life to be, like my daddy, kicking but not high — but who cares how high you can kick when you can fly?

APPENDIX: MATISSE'S CHAPEL

Dear Aunt Melissa,

I had a dream last night that the dead members of our family had gathered in Henri Matisse's Chapel in Vence. All dressed in black and white, they made a striking contrast to Matisse's blue, green and white patterns. The old folks sat up front: Grandma and Grandpa on either side of Great-Grandma Betsy and Great-Great-Grandma Susie.

Behind them on their left sat my sister, Barbara and baby brother Ralph, like *l'enfant Jésus* in Mama's lap, and Daddy next to her, and brother Andrew, looking handsome-as-a-Greek-God next to Daddy. All my uncles and aunts and cousins were seated in the back of the chapel with Daddy's Mama and Papa standing off to themselves.

As I arrived at the Chapel Grandma Betsy was telling a story. Her voice filled the chapel like music bouncing off the windows and walls to our ears. "There was a story my Mama Susie told us young-uns 'bout slavery. I never will forget. She ain' never talk much 'bout slavery, so when this white man ask her how she feel 'bout being descendant from slaves? She come back at him.

"How you feel descendant from SLAVERS?" He turn beet red, tell her this story: "My grandma and grandpa was on a ocean liner come from Europe. They was slavers in South Carolina. A slave ship was having trouble and signal they vessel to help. As the ship approach they could smell the stink and see the shackled bodies of men, women and children packed together on the deck of the slave ship."

"The prissy white ladies on the ocean liner, with they white clothes and faces and they little children all scrubbed clean and perfect, stood on the deck glaring at the human cargo from Africa." Well, there is a God somewhere. "A sudden strong wind swept all that stink from the slave ship spraying the ocean liner like a madame sprays perfume, only the scent was pure shit."

"Them white folks was throwing up all over they fine clothes and stampeding each other to get away from the stench, and the sight of all them stinking slaves shackled together. And the slaves was waving and smiling, some of them was even singing and laughing."

"The ocean liner caught fire below and the trapped smoke and the stench was unbearable in the low parts of the ship and was even worse on the aft side. The only breath of air bearable was on the deck, facing the stinking, waving niggers bound for America to be free labor on white folks' plantations."

"Even the ocean liner's food was seasoned with the stench of human excrement." The white man was near tears telling this story. "I can actually see and smell those bodies just from the story my grandfather told me, and even now as I talk to you," the white man said, "I smell myself stinking."

"Whenever I think about the slave ship my grandfather saw, I start to see shit on my own hands and all over my body too. And I have to go change my clothes and wash myself. But I just never come clean. No matter how much I bathe, I still smell. That is what being the descendant of slave owners did to me."

"Well Mister," Mama Susie said, "My Ma and Pa was on that slave ship your grandpa told you that story 'bout. They survive that hellish voyage to work on your grandpa's plantation and to raise me up to hear that story 'bout your funky hands. I hopes you get them clean real soon. You is right. They do smell bad. And ain't just you smells them either."

Mama Susie knew just what she thought about everything and everybody. But what he expect her to say 'bout that story? No, they can't wash away the shit smell of slavery. They can scrub 'til they is raw cause it's they own shit they smell from they own stinkin' ass. Some folks thinks they can spread they shit so thin it don't stink or put it off on somebody else and say it's their shit.

"God don't love ugly. That white man got to live his own story and we got to live ours." Everyone applauded Grandma Betsy's story, and Great-grandma Susie, looking strong at 110, just sat there being real proud of Grandma Betsy, her storyteller daughter and her granddaughter Ida, and her great-granddaughter Willia which is me.

FAITH RINGGOLD CHRONOLOGY

1930 Born October 8 at Harlem Hospital in New York City to Andrew Louis Jones Sr. and Willi Posey Jones. She has two older siblings, Andrew and Barbara. Frequently sick with asthma as a small child; art becomes a major pastime.

1942 Her family moves from the "Valley" to Sugar Hill in Harlem.

1950 Marries Robert Earl Wallace, a classical and jazz pianist, while majoring in art at the City College of New York. Obtains first studio space for independent oil painting projects.

1952 Has two children: Michele Faith Wallace, January 4; Barbara Faith Wallace, December 15.

1954 Permanent separation and divorce proceedings begin, completed in 1956. Flo Kennedy acts as attorney.

1955 Graduates from City College with B.S. in Fine Art. Begins teaching art in the New York City public schools (1955–1973). Faith first hears of James Baldwin through his baby sister, Paula, who is a student of hers at J.H.S. 136.

1957 Spends the first of many summers in Provincetown, Massachusetts, doing oil paintings of houses, landscapes, fishing boats, ocean.

1959 Completes M.A. in Art at City College.

1961 First trip to Europe (with mother and daughters) aboard the S.S. *Liberté*. Tours the museums of Paris, Nice, Florence, and Rome. Brother dies while they are in Rome, causing them to return to the U.S. abruptly. Faith's dining area in her home becomes studio space.

1962 Marries Burdette (Birdie) Ringgold, May 19.

1963 During a summer at Oak Bluffs on Martha's Vineyard, develops first mature painting style.

Influenced by writings of James Baldwin and Amiri Baraka (then Leroi Jones). This work she calls "super realism." Results in the American People Series of oil paintings (1963–1967).

1964 Begins search for a New York gallery. Writes letters to Romare Bearden and Hale Woodruff in an attempt to join Spiral, the black artists' group, and to exhibit in the first Black Arts Festival in Senegal. Unsuccessful on both counts.

1965 Meets Leroi Jones at his Black Arts Theater and School in Harlem.

1966 Participates in the first black exhibition in Harlem since the 1930s. Meets Romare Bearden, Ernie Crichlow, Norman Lewis, Charles Alston, Hale Woodruff, Betty Blayton; first real contact with black artists. Joins Spectrum Gallery on 57th Street, Robert Newman, director.

1967 Paints first murals — *The Flag is Bleeding, U.S. Postage Stamp Commemorating the Advent of Black Power,* and *Die* — while daughters are in Europe for the summer. First one-person show at Spectrum Gallery. Meets art historian James Porter of Howard University, who buys *Bride of Martha's Vineyard* from the American People Series. Begins development of "Black Light" using palette of darkened colors, in pursuit of a more affirmative black aesthetic.

1968 Participates in benefit exhibition for Martin Luther King Jr. at the Museum of Modern Art. Meets Jacob Lawrence, Henri Ghent, and Ed Taylor. Initiates first demonstration of black artists at the Whitney Museum. Joins Art Workers' Coalition. Meets Lucy Lippard, Yvonne Rainier, and Lil Picard. Demonstrates with Tom Lloyd, light sculptor, against MOMA to demand a black artist wing for Martin Luther King Jr. Instead, their efforts result in two blacks on the board of trustees of the museum and a major exhibition for Romare Bearden and Richard Hunt in 1971.

275

1969 Paints *Flag for the Moon: Die Nigger* as a response to first U.S. moon landing. Begins series of political posters. Daughters in Mexico for the summer. Father dies.

1970 Has second one-person show: "America Black," featuring Black Light Series, at Spectrum Gallery. Begins teaching at Pratt Institute, Bank Street Graduate School for Teachers, and Wagner College. Cofounds WSABAL (Women Students and Artists for Black Art Liberation) with daughter Michele, and does first feminist art action. Confronts Robert Morris and Poppy Johnson of Art Strike with demands for fifty percent women and blacks to be included in Liberated Venice Biennale. Participates in demonstrations of Ad Hoc Women's Art Group at the Whitney Museum. Her recommendations result in the inclusion of Betye Saar and Barbara Chase-Riboud in the Biennial, making them the first black women ever to exhibit at the Whitney.

1971 Cofounds Where We At, black women artists' group, with Kay Brown and Dinga McCannon. Guest curator of Where We At exhibition at Acts of Art Gallery. Does *United States of Attica* poster. Wins CAPS Grant to do mural for the Women's House of Detention. While doing a television show called *On Free Time* (PBS), hosted by Julius Lester, meets Louise Nevelson, Alice Neel, and Pat Mainardi.

1972 *For the Women's House* is permanently installed at the Women's House of Detention on Rikers Island. This painting uses all-female imagery for the first time. As a result of this, Art without walls (an artists's group to bring art to prison inmates) is formed. Develops tankas (soft cloth frames) after seeing an exhibition of Tibetan art at the Rijks Museum in Amsterdam. Puts political posters and feminist papers in Documenta in Kassel, Germany. Participates in first American Women Artists Show in Hamburg. Begins lecture tours and traveling exhibitions to colleges and universities around the country.

1973 Ten-year retrospective at Voorhees Gallery at Rutgers University. Resigns from teaching position in New York City Public Schools to continue touring and to make art full-time. Does first dolls, Family of Woman Masks, and Slave Rape Series of paintings. Collaborates with Willi Posey (her mother, who was a fashion designer) on costumes for masks and tankas for paintings.

1974 Develops hanging soft sculptures: Wilt and Couple Series; both series feature painted coconut heads. Does Windows of the Wedding Series, abstract paintings based on African Kuba design, and uses them as environment for soft sculptures. Michele graduates from City College and Barbara completes her senior year of college at the University of London.

1975 Curates "Eleven" in New York, black women's show at Women's Interarts Center. Begins to do art performances with masks and costumes. Does first stuffed figures *Zora and Fish* (bag man and woman), first portrait masks of Harlem Series, which includes Adam Clayton Powell Jr. and Martin Luther King Jr. Develops appliqué soft masks for workshop at University of Wisconsin. Barbara graduates with a B.A. in linguistics at the University of London, stays on to do graduate work.

1976 Artist in residence at Wilson College, where she develops *The Wake and Resurrection of the Bicentennial Negro,* a multimedia masked performance piece. With Monica Freeman, Margo Jefferson, Pat Jones, and Michele, codirects the Sojourner Truth Festival of the Arts, which is held at the Women's Interarts Center, and includes exhibition of *Dear Joanna Letters,* a documentation piece. Goes to Africa for the first time. Tours Ghana and Nigeria to see art and people.

1977 Participates in Festac 77 in Lagos, Nigeria. Does first freestanding soft sculptures, Woman on a Pedestal Series. Begins writing autobiography "Being My Own Woman." Barbara receives graduate diploma from the University of London, returns to U.S. to do Ph.D. in African linguistics at City University Graduate Center. Mother remarries.

1978 Receives National Endowment for the Arts Award for sculpture. Develops Ringgold Doll and creates Harlem '78, a series of soft sculptures and a public participation graffiti mural.

1979 Develops International Dolls Collection and Ringgold Doll Kits (Sew Real). Michele publishes first book, *Black Macho and the Myth of the Superwoman.* Appears on the cover of *Ms. Magazine* with picture of family inside.

1980 Faith and her mother begin work on their final collaborative project, Faith's first quilt, *Echoes of*

Harlem, for "The Artist and the Quilt" show. Completes first draft of autobiography. Appears in first masked performance piece, which acts as an oral "publication" of this unpublished manuscript titled "Being My Own Woman." Michele begins Ph.D. in American Studies at Yale University. Barbara marries and receives master of philosophy at City University of New York (CUNY). Faith meets Moira Roth.

1981 Faith and her mother work on packaging of Ringgold Doll Kits. Does Atlanta Series in memory of the twenty-seven black children murdered in Atlanta. Mother dies. Barbara divorces. Michele leaves Yale and returns home.

1982 Curates the Wild Art Show at P.S. 1 for the Women's Caucus for Art. First grandchild, Baby Faith, born. Begins painting again at MacDowell Colony: Emanon Series and Baby Faith and Willi Series. Michele and Faith perform *No Name Performance #1: A Masked Performance Piece* at Kenkelaba House. Does painted dolls. Sister dies.

1983 Begins Dah Series of paintings. First excerpt from autobiography published in *Confirmation: An Anthology of African American Women*, edited by Amiri Baraka and Amina Baraka. Does *Mother's Quilt* and first story quilt, *Who's Afraid of Aunt Jemima?* Wins Wonder Woman Award from Warner Communications. Performs *No Name Performance #2* in which audience dances, speaks out, and, in a finale, takes over the stage.

1984 Receives twenty-year retrospective at Studio Museum in Harlem. Michele edits the accompanying catalogue. Becomes a visiting associate professor at the University of California in San Diego. Michele also holds a temporary teaching position at UCSD. Continues painting Dah Series (California Dah) to be used as a backdrop for *No Name #2*. Does series of aquatints called *The Death of Apartheid* and participates in exhibitions organized by Artists Against Apartheid. Begins printmaking as Visiting Artist at Bob Blackburn's Printmaking Workshop in New York. Does etching on canvas to be used to make story quilts. In the fall, Michele begins teaching at University of Oklahoma in Norman.

1985 Continues story quilts, and develops a new storytelling performance, *The Bitter Nest.* Is appointed to a permanent position as full professor at UCSD and is now bicoastal. Sets up bicoastal living pattern of half the year in San Diego and the other half in New York. Exhibits Flag Series of paintings from 1960s in group exhibition; *Tradition & Conflict: Images of a Turbulent Decade 1963–1973,* at the Studio Museum in Harlem. Barbara marries again and has second child, Theodora.

1986 Receives honorary doctorate of Fine Art from Moore College of Art. Joins the Bernice Steinbaum Gallery and prepares for solo show of story quilts in January of 1987. Loses weight (over one hundred pounds), documenting this in a videotape, quilt, and performance entitled *Change.* Receives Candace award with Ella Baker, Judge Constance Baker Motley, and Rosa Parks from One Hundred Black Women.

1987 Receives solo show and catalogue at Bernice Steinbaum Gallery, *Change: Faith Ringgold's Over 100 Pounds Weight Loss Performance Story Quilt.* Major articles in *Arts, Art in America,* and other periodicals. Meets Eleanor Flomenhaft. Receives Fellowship from John Solomon Guggenheim Memorial Foundation, also Public Art Fund Award from the Port Authority of New York and New Jersey. Is awarded honorary doctorate of Fine Art at College of Wooster, Wooster, Ohio. Curates Home Show at Goddard Riverside Community Center. Travels to Tokyo, Japan, with Lois Mailou Jones, William T. Williams, and David Driskel for cultural exchange exhibit. Founds Coast to Coast: A Women of Color Artist Book Project. Their first project is a traveling artist book exhibition.

1988 Has a second solo exhibition at Bernice Steinbaum Gallery. Receives New York Foundation for the Arts Award. Is included in Leslie Sills, *Inspirations: Stories of Women Artists for Children* along with Georgia O'Keeffe, Alice Neel, and Frida Kahlo. Barbara has third child, Martha.

1989 Receives NEA Arts Award for painting; the la Napoule Award, artist-in-residency in France; and the Mid-Atlantic Arts Foundation Award. Michele marries actor Eugene Nesmith.

1990 Major exhibition, "Faith Ringgold: A Twenty-Five-Year Survey" curated by Eleanor Flomenhaft at the Fine Arts Museum of Long Island, starts a thirteen-museum tour, which includes the High Museum of Art at Georgia Pacific and the Arizona State Art

Museum at Tempe, Arizona. Completes first children's book, *Tar Beach*, and a silk screen edition of twenty-four quilts titled *Tar Beach 2* printed at the Fabric Workshop in Philadelphia. During a stay of four months in Paris and la Napoule in the south of France. She begins to paint The French Collection Series. Travels to Milan, Barcelona, Madrid, and Granada.

1991 Tour of "Faith Ringgold: A Twenty-Five-Year Survey" at Miami University Art Museum, Oxford, Ohio; Albright Knox Art Museum, Buffalo, New York. Returns to Paris and takes an apartment at the Hôtel Ferrandi on rue de Cher Che Midi while making sketches for part 2 of The French Collection. Completes *Change 3*, a nude representation of herself during forty years of weight loss and gain. Moves to a studio in the garment district in New York to work on large-scale mural for Percent for Art commission for Public School 22 in Crown Heights, Brooklyn. *Tar Beach*, first children's book, is published by Crown Publishers in January. Receives an honorary doctorate from alma mater, the City College of New York.

1992 Tour continues of "Twenty-Five-Year Survey": Museum of Art Davenport, Iowa; University of Michigan Museum of Art, Ann Arbor, Michigan; Women's Center Gallery, University of California, Santa Barbara, California; Mills College Art Gallery, Oakland, California; ends at Tacoma Museum, Tacoma, Washington, in February of 1993. Receives a Caldecott Honor and a Coretta Scott King Award for *Tar Beach* as best African-American illustrated book for 1991. The second children's book, *Aunt Harriet's Underground Railroad in the Sky*, is published by Crown Publishers. "The French Collection" exhibition opens at the Bernice Steinbaum Gallery in New York City. Moira Roth and Faith receive a National Endowment of the Arts travel award to go to Tangier, Morocco, and Paris to collaborate on a forthcoming book on The French Collection Series. Meets with Michel Fabre at the Sorbonne and talks about the African American in Paris to research *Bonjour Lonnie*, a children's book to be published in 1996. Severs relations with the Bernice Steinbaum Gallery and resumes self-representation of her art. Buys a ranch house in Englewood, New Jersey, with plans to build a studio in the country. Receives a commission from the Metropolitan Transit Authority to create two thirty-foot mosaic murals for the 125th Street IRT subway station platform.

1993 Publishes third children's book, *Dinner at Aunt Connie's House*, at Hyperion Books for Young Readers. Receives an honorary doctorate at the California College of Arts and Crafts, where she meets Marlon Riggs, the filmmaker. Creates *The Black Family Dinner Quilt*, and donates it to the Museum of the National Association of Negro Women in tribute to Mary McLeod Bethune and Dr. Dorothy Height. The Children's Museum of Manhattan mounts an ongoing interactive exhibition of *Tar Beach*. Receives commission to create a nine-by-seventeen-foot painted mural based on the life of Eugenio Maria de Hostos for de Hostos Community College; it is permanently installed in 1994.

1994 Receives contract from Little, Brown to publish autobiography, renamed *We Flew over the Bridge*. Begins rewrite with Moira Roth as editor. Their first editing session begins in Paris in January during a conference in Paris titled "A Visual Arts Encounter, African Americans in Europe" at the Luxembourg Gardens. Howardina Pindell, Lorna Simpson, Betye Saar, Sam Gilliam attend the conference, which is organized by Maica Sancone and Raymond Saunders. Book to be published in September of 1995. Moves studio back to Harlem in preparation for building a new studio in Englewood, New Jersey. Goes to Madrid, Spain, to participate in an exhibition curated by Dan Cameron at the Reina Sofia Museum in Madrid. Participates in Cairo Biennial organized by Debbie Cullen of the Printmaking Workshop. Goes to Egypt with Bob Blackburn, Mel Edwards, Kay Walkingstick, and Juan Sanchez. Completes a painted story quilt in memoriam to Marlon Riggs, who died in 1994 of AIDS. Begins work on fifth children's book, *Martin's Dream*, to be published by Crown in 1995. Faith receives her seventh honorary doctorate in Fine Arts at the Rhode Island School of Design. Birdie and Faith are invited to attend a black-tie dinner at the White House. Shares table with Hillary Clinton.

PUBLIC AND PRIVATE COLLECTIONS

American Association of Retired Persons,
Washington, DC

American Craft Museum, New York City

ARCO Chemical, Philadelphia

Brooklyn Children's Museum,
Brooklyn, New York

Chase Manhattan Bank Collection,
New York City

Clark Museum, Williamstown, Massachusetts

Coca-Cola, Atlanta, Georgia

Fort Wayne Museum of Art,
Fort Wayne, Indiana

Solomon R. Guggenheim Museum of Art,
New York City

High Museum of Art, Atlanta, Georgia

Eugenio Maria de Hostos Community College,
Bronx, New York

Metropolitan Museum of Art, New York City

Metropolitan Transit Authority, New York City

Museum of Fine Art, Boston

Museum of Modern Art, New York City

Newark Museum, Newark, New Jersey

Philadelphia Muscum of Art, Philadelphia

Philip Morris Collection, New York City

Public School 22, Crown Heights,
Brooklyn, New York

Saint Louis Museum of Art,
Saint Louis, Missouri

Spenser Museum, Lawrence, Kansas

The Studio Museum in Harlem, New York City

Harold Washington Library, Chicago

Women's House of Detention,
Rikers Island, New York

Maya Angelou, Winston Salem, North Carolina

Ronald and Barbara Balsar, Atlanta, Georgia

Lucinda Bunnen, Atlanta, Georgia

Fred Collins Esq., Brooklyn, New York

Bill and Camille Cosby, New York City

Eric Dobkin, Pound Ridge, New York

Roy Eaton, Roosevelt Island, New York

Eleanor and Leonard Flomenhaft,
Hewlett Harbor, New York

Ardis B. James, Chappaqua, New York

Marilyn Lanfear, San Antonio, Texas

Judith Lieber, New York City

Dorothy and James Porter, Washington, DC

Moira Roth, Berkeley, California

Joanne and John Spohler, New Jersey

Si and Sandi Tamny, Canton, Ohio

Oprah Winfrey, Chicago

Florence and Cyrus Wolf,
North Woodmere, New York

INDEX